BELT and BRA

The term 'Belt and Braces' refers to caution.

Belts and braces are meant to hold one's trousers up. Going 'belt and braces' is a double insurance against having them fall down. Applied to business this means to always have a backup plan.

Douglas J. Clark

BELT AND BRACES

THE OFFICIAL BIOGRAPHY OF DOUGLAS J. CLARK

BY EUAN ROSE

Matador
9 Priory Business Park
Kibworth Beauchamp
Leicestershire LE8 0RX, UK
Tel: (+44) 116 279 2299
Fax: (+44) 116 279 2277
Email: books@troubador.co.uk
Web: www.troubador.co.uk/matador

ISBN 978 1780883 571

British Library Cataloguing in Publication Data.
A catalogue record for this book is available from the British Library.

Cover Art Illustration by Michael Hatcher
Typography by Andy Findon Graphics

Matador is an imprint of Troubador Publishing Ltd

Dedication
To my dear and loved grandson, Thomas George Duggan.

Table of Contents

PART FOUR 1980–1990

PART FIVE 1990–2000

PART SIX 2000–2010

Epilogue

Index

Acknowledgments

A lot of people contributed their time in sharing memories and recollections with my writer Euan Rose in his research for this biography. The memory clouds with age and without their help the chronology would have been a few years and in some cases decades out of place. So I would like to express my gratitude and appreciation to the following people:

Malcolm Clark *who provided much valuable detail and helped me compile the photographs.*

Yvonne Evans *who has played such an important part in my life and 'Clarks'; she patiently read the first draft out loud to me. It turned into a three day marathon, almost losing her voice in the process!*

Euan Rose *who has captured my life, almost as if he had lived it with me. He is an extremely talented writer whom I describe as being, as deep as the ocean and as bright as the sun.*

Acknowledgments continued:

Slade Arthur

Alan Blundell

Tony Bird

Michael Chapman

Noel Clark

Richard Dodd

David Dryhurst

Johannah Dyer

Royston Evans

Andy Findon

John Fisher

Dave Fletcher

Dennis Greaves

Mike Hatcher

Robin Hunter

Paul Johnson

Glynn Jones

David Partington

Melanie Radford

Eleanor Rigby

Michael Rowley

David Sills

Mr. Paul Spiteri BA (Hons) ENG.

Jim Stanley

Leigh Toogood

Mike Warley

Preface:

First Impressions

The phone call was from my cousin David Sills, who I hadn't seen in many years. It came as a surprise therefore when I checked the answer-phone messages and heard this blast from the past asking me to contact him regarding ghosting an autobiography. It came as an even bigger surprise when we actually spoke and I discovered the person in question was none other than Doug Clark, a local legend.

Although I can never actually recall meeting Doug in person, I was to discover that our paths had indeed crossed back in the hazy, crazy days of the 60's when we were both playing in bands. As you did! Over the years I had heard many tales about Doug and his brother Malcolm. Their meteoric rise to financial fame, Doug's daredevil exploits, his knack of deal making and a phrase that still occurs today when you mention his name – "He's ruthless!"

David gave my number to Doug, who was in Canada. A few days later we talked on the phone. He was due back in England for a few days; his time was limited and although retired, his diary full of meetings. However, he was keen to meet me and discuss whether or not this was a book I could write and if he was comfortable with me doing it. I did what I always do when I'm going to interview someone for the first time; I drew an imaginary picture of him in my head. This done and taking on board the "ruthless" comments , I pictured some suited and booted stereotypical ex-CEO who wore his wealth on his back, lest you didn't know who he was when he walked into the room. Probably a pinstripe suit, hand-made shirt and shoes, maybe even garish red city braces. His hands would be perfectly manicured, (a trait often seen in businessmen that start off having to work with them manually before they substituted hands for brains) and thinning, carefully groomed hair. Oh! And let's not forget the eyes; they would be cold and un-giving, making him very difficult to read - poker eyes.

What I got was a revelation and a man I warmed to from the first handshake. No city suit, nor slicked back or receding hairline, no arrogance and certainly no manicured hands. He was softly spoken, dressed like a country and western singer and had what I thought was a whale's tooth on a chain around his neck. I made a mental note to find out the significance of that. His eyes twinkled as if ready to share a joke with you. His English holiday home is an idyllic cottage set in glorious natural countryside. Inside, it is an Aladdin's cave of eccentricity and memorabilia. Obviously, every stick of furniture and ornament holds a story. From the Gibson guitars proudly displayed on stands to the choice of coffee mugs we drank from, nothing was usual. Here was someone who loved and cared for things, not a collector of possessions but a collector of memories. This was a house where everything had its place. Here was order and purpose, just as the owner had lived his life, I was to discover.

We talked for over four hours. I made copious notes and soon realised here indeed was a story worth sharing. A story of hardship and challenge, one with its share of successes but not without its failures! Above all, it is a story to inspire others. A story of a man who lives his life by his own set of rules and values. A man who doesn't and didn't suffer fools gladly yet has the compassion to understand the frailty of others who, unlike him, do not possess that unique ability to revel in adversity and, in his own words, to make sure that every deal done, every step taken, is signed, sealed and delivered "Belt and Braces".

The journey in writing his autobiography is not going to be a short one. As I am writing this foreword I glance at the small mountain of press cuttings that will be my next task to date and use for chronological reference.

I have a small list of people to interview who have either played their part in the story or have observed it from the sidelines. As Doug is somewhat nomadic these days, with holiday homes in the USA and Canada in addition to the cottage and a main domicile home in Malta, getting prime time with him will probably be the most difficult part of the job. Nevertheless, without that time this story will remain untold and that would be such a pity. Doug Clark is a legend and his life deserves to be recorded and celebrated, not relegated to folklore. When, as I will, I complete this book, however long that takes, I will write an epilogue in addition to this preface, which should make an interesting comparison.

Euan Rose

Part One 1942 – 1960

1 – It's Only Rock 'n' Roll

Music was my first love

And it will be my last!

Music - John Miles

I

Our Bedford CA van careered from side to side, narrowly avoiding the red wall of the arctic that had strayed into the outside lane just as Malc, my brother and our roadie, had his pedal to the metal, zooming past it. This was a rude awakening from the dream of stardom I was enjoying, which had The Suedes on Top of the Pops. Tony Blackburn had just announced us to the baying crowd. Trouble was, I had, for some reason known only to myself, ripped off all my clothes and now I couldn't find them anywhere. I was understandably panicking. "Put the straps down so the guitar covers the naughty bits," I told myself. However, the rest of the band was having none of it. "Sabotage" was the gentlest of the comments that pounded my ears as our passion wagon narrowly missed piling into the central reservation.

"Bloody 'ell Malcolm," I shouted.

"Not my fault Doug, tell the twat in the cattle truck," came the reply.

"Well slow down anyway, there's no mad panic," I replied.

"Yeah, loads of time," Terry joined in.

I ignored Terry's smile and feigned sleep again. The truth was I was feeling guilty about my dream. Today was the biggest day of our lives, the chance of a two-year overseas tour, starting in Germany where The Beatles were taking Hamburg by storm. Maybe a recording contract with EMI? I knew the rest of the guys had already turned professional in their heads. They could see a number one record on the horizon; a national tour with girls in every town and city in the country. Oh yeah, I shared the dream but not the agenda. I had other plans. Still, why wreck the big day? If they didn't sign us up nothing would be lost. If they did then I'm sure lead guitarists would be queuing up.

The 2 I's Coffee Bar in Old Compton Street, Soho, was a tiny unassuming place from the outside. Unless you knew what you were looking for you'd miss it completely. Just a plain old plate glass window and a glass door with a chrome handle. There was a 'Seven-Up' sign pasted to the door, I think just to let you know it was there and you didn't walk straight through it. Over the top was the painted 2 I's sign and then below it, in smaller letters, 'Home of the Stars' with the star being a Pepsi Cola bottle top. Hard to believe that this was Mecca to the likes of Adam Faith, Cliff Richard, The Shadows and the man who started it all - Tommy Steele. Who would be in today? Mickey Most? Larry Parnes? Roy Tempest? Don Arden? Brian Epstein? This is where all the big agents came to book groups for tours and the record company scouts came star spotting. Yes, here, on this hallowed ground, where the greatest names in Rock'n'Roll had sung, strummed, blown and banged their way to stardom we, little Suedes from the back end of nowhere, were following in their illustrious footsteps. Humbling, exhilarating and definitely awesome.

We parked up and went in to see where to unload the gear. There was a large American Wurlitzer jukebox with garish neon tubes surrounding it just inside the door, then a serving counter with its famous espresso coffee machine and an orange juice dispenser. A couple of girls in mini-skirts were drinking coffee from miniscule coffee cups. They looked up. "Who are you?" a brunette with stacked up hair asked.

"The Suedes," Joe replied.

"Never 'eard of ya mate," she said disdainfully and her blonde friend collapsed with laughter.

"Ah, but you will, sweetheart," I told her.

Then, to save the day, up the stairs from the basement, which was, we were to discover, where the bands played, came the legendary Brylcreemed, Tom Littlewood, manager and owner of the 2 I's. "Boys; boys," he said. "Welcome to the 2 I's; get your gear in, you're on in half an hour."

That was the last time we saw him until he paid us later on - five quid minus ten bob, his commission.

It was quite a game lugging the equipment down the narrow and steep staircase. Today, it wouldn't pass health and safety but in the sixties no one worried about such things. Downstairs was crammed with wall to wall Rock'n'Roll people. The clothes, the hair, were all so much more sophisticated to our simple eyes than what we were used to. The room would, I suppose, hold about sixty at a push and it was nearly to capacity. A stepladder was shoved up against a delivery hatch, which was open to let out some of the smoke and the heat. The heat, that's what hit you, even the walls were sweating. It was cramped, the ceiling was so low you felt it was going to come down on your head but this was indeed a very special place and boy, did we play well. A few bars into 'Johnny B Goode' and the blokes from the smoke and the Soho sophisticates had forgotten and forgiven that we were the boys from beyond Watford, where all life ceased to exist. That would be, of course, pre-Liverpool and what followed there.

"Good set lads; well done," the agent, whose name I can't remember, said, warmly shaking our hands. "I'll be in touch."

"Are you going to sign us?" Terry asked, stating what we all were thinking.

"I said I'll be in touch," he said, disappearing into the haze of Marlborough cigarette smoke. Another band was already setting up.

Suddenly I wanted this, not because I was going to do it, because I wasn't. But I wanted the choice to be mine. Lesson one – be master of your own destiny!

It was May 1963 - a very good year for destiny.

II

They got their contract and duly went off to attempt to conquer Europe, or at least have a bloody good time along the way. I don't know whether or not they succeeded because we lost touch after I told them I wasn't going. I have no regrets over that, the decision had been mine and I knew that it wasn't the end of rock and roll for me, it's something I would return to, and I have.

2 – Early Lessons

I

I was born in 1942, 24th February to be precise, on the same day Paul Jones, the lead singer with the fabulous Manfred Mann, was born in Portsmouth. The 24th was a Wednesday; as the old poem goes, 'Wednesday's child is full of woe'. Think I was born on the wrong day. Never been one to have regrets or doubts, only to make decisions.

From an early age, and something I still do today, I'd write down any ideas that come to me in the night then, in the morning, review them. Not a revolutionary modus operandi I know, but that little note pad by the side of my bed has certainly served me well. I review the list over a cup of tea and then expand on the notions and think how to make them come about. It's not all about buying a property, launching a brand new venture or re branding an item that isn't working or selling. It can be something as simple as thanking someone who has been of service with a small gift or sending a card for no special reason - those are often the best. Mostly, it's a trigger to adding value to what I'm already doing. So, I like to think I was born on the cusp with Thursday, where the child has far to go.

The Second World War was still going strong in 1942 and we weren't doing terribly well. The Japanese seemed unstoppable in the Far East. Singapore and Kuala Lumpur fell and, in the desert, we weren't scoring too many goals against the Germans. An inspiration to us all was Malta (where in later years

I spent many happy times) where the Maltese nation was awarded the George Cross for bravery in holding out against permanent bombardment, starvation and seemingly impossible odds. Thankfully, towards the end of the year, the tide started to turn when Monty and his 8th Army gave Rommel, the Desert Fox, a bloody nose at El Alamein. Dad, (Douglas Noel Clark) was away serving as a ground crew mechanic with the 218 Bomber Command Squadron, based in East Anglia, when I came kicking and screaming into the world at the family home in Mustow Green. That's about three miles as the crow flies from another little sleepy village, Chaddesley Corbett, itself a few miles west of Bromsgrove in Worcestershire. I still have a holiday home in Chaddesley Corbett, so you could say I haven't travelled very far; then again, you could say I've been on one incredible journey and come back to the beginning again, full circle.

In order to know where we're going, vis-à-vis this chronicle of my life, it's important to know where I came from. I will attempt to provide a simple family tree prior to my arrival point in the Clark heritage. Let's start with Grandad Fred and Grandma Nellie Morris. Grandad and Grandma Morris lived at the bottom end of Chaddesley Village, in a house attached to the Fox Inn (nowadays it's the dining room of the pub). It had a walled garden and a yard to the side plus a small workshop which we called 'The Little Garage'. Grandad started out as a carpenter then trained as a wheelwright, so he could turn his hand to most things. Actually, during his carpentry apprenticeship he also learnt how to make coffins so, when first he set up a carpentry workshop in The Little Garage, he doubled it up as an undertakers. As he was also good at repairing anything mechanical, he developed his one–man business into fixing anything that folk brought him to fix, from bikes to farm machinery as well as the odd car that was very much the privilege of the rich in the 1920's. He bought the property across the road, which was actually no more than a large shed. This went on to become Chaddesley Garage and his first car doubled as a hearse when need arose.

At the top end of the village there was to be another garage. This was run by Grandad (Gramps) on my Dad's side. He was Ernest Jesse Clark, born in 1878 in Aston, Birmingham. He served his apprenticeship making bicycles, including penny-farthings. In 1909, with the advent of the car business, he joined Herbert Austin (later Lord Austin) as a wheelwright and is rumoured to have fitted the wheels on the very first Austin Seven car ever produced. In the early days, Austin's mainstay of business was actually tractors. Now, my great grandad on Dad's side was another Jesse Clark; he was in the Royal Hussars, fought in the Crimean War and died from tetanus, which he got from a rusty horseshoe nail. That's really all I know about him but I'm quite proud of the military connection.

Gramps moved to the Lickeys (The Lickey Hills) when he married my Grandma Amelia. There is a shroud of mystery here. Grandma Amelia was Scottish and the product of an illicit liaison between Great Granny and a laird. Yes, a real life Monarch of the Glen, in whose great house, set in a massive estate in the Highlands, she worked as a junior housekeeper. Such was the shame and uproar in the higher echelons of the clan when it was found that the laird had been sharing what he had under his kilt with Great Granny, making her 'with bairn', that it was decreed that Granny should be bought off and banished from the Highlands. A caveat dictated that she would never breathe a word to a living soul as to the true parentage of her unborn child. I have tried to trace the trail and have a pretty solid idea as to whom the laird actually was, but a pact of silence has been handed down through the generations, so who am I to break the tradition now? As my story evolves, you will discover it is somewhat of an understatement to say my life has been a trifle colourful. There will be many an instance when I will share with you the facts but not the names. I have been and done many things from the exotic to the outrageous, but I have always lived by my own code, which includes trying not to do a blatant wrong to someone else. So, as it would be unfair to name the laird in this book, you'll just have to guess.

Great Granny moved to Worcestershire and set up home on the proceeds of the Scottish payoff. Granny Amelia was born a few months later in 1887. I don't even have Great Grandma's full name and don't know exactly what happened to her. Who raised Grandma remains somewhat cloudy. She had the surname Guest and was one of seven sisters.

The next real solid detail is that she married Gramps (Ernest Clark) and they had four children: Ernest, Ivy, Reginald and my Dad, Douglas. In 1912 Gramps bought a lovely cottage in the Lickeys, which they called 'Pinehurst'. It is still there, more or less as it was then, opposite the pub which everyone knows as The Chalet. The Chalet has changed hands and names many times since it first started life as The Chalet Tea Rooms, at the gateway to the Lickey Hills at the turn of the century. Named 'Chalet' because it looks just like a Swiss Chalet and when it snows in the Lickeys you could be forgiven for thinking you were in Gstaad, not Birmingham. The Lickeys were to play the most important part in my life, but that is for later on. For now, if you don't mind, we'll stick with the early history. In May 1920, Gramps sold up Pinehurst and moved to Chaddesley where he bought Bluntington Cottage along with seven acres of land at the top of the village. There, he opened Bluntington Garage, where Grandma Amelia gave birth to my Dad (Douglas Noel Clark). The name Noel seemed a natural choice as he was born on Christmas Day in 1920.

It was ironic that Noel from Bluntington Garage would go on to marry Dorothy from Chaddesley Garage; one at the top, one at the bottom. 'A marriage made in metal', you could say. Sadly, it was not to be.

II

Mom was a cracker to look at, auburn haired, sparkling eyes and five foot six inches of sultry beauty dressed in a fox fur. A Rita Hayworth look-alike to give you a vision; she was also just seventeen when she had me. I turned out to be the eldest of eight brothers and sisters. They sprang forth almost on an annual basis. Not all by Dad. It's a bit of a grey area really. In chronological order: there was me in 1942, Valerie (1943), Pam (1944), Carol (1946), Malcolm (1947), Richard (1949), Tony (1951) and finally Susan (1952) who was disabled and died before reaching her eighth birthday.

On reflection, there were really three people in the marriage: my Mom, my Dad and then Harvey Rutter, whom Mom later married when she was divorced from Dad. With the Clark clan it's all a bit of a who's whose and unspoken thoughts. But let's not jump the gun; I'll come onto all that in due course.

III

"Sit down or you'll get Saint Vitus's dance," Mom used to say to me. I was always on the go from the moment I could walk. Why walk when you could run? Why sit when there is so much to do? To this day I still go up and down stairs three at a time. Gramps (Ernest Jessie Clark) was always incredibly fit so that's probably where I get it from. He used to astound me with his athletic prowess. He would stand behind an armchair and just jump over it from that stationary position, without a run up or anything. Always on the go, from first light in the morning till the sun went down at night and in robust health, "Fit as a fiddle," Gramps would say, "that's me."

Bluntington Garage was in business for eighty years and never advertised once. Not that he made lots of money out of it; like Grandad Morris, he wasn't really a businessman, nor my Dad either. They just enjoyed what they did with pecuniary rewards always an afterthought. As long as there was enough money for a beer and a gamble, to which objectives like feeding the family became secondary.

Gramps also had another skill which used to have me gasping in amazement. He would make big hot-air balloons out of wire and tissue paper, ignite them with a meths burner and then set them off, glowing like beautiful extraterrestrials into the sky. My Dad learnt to make those too. They were good, very good, but not as good as Gramp's.

IV

Village life could be wonderful; everybody knew each other and spoke to you. You could buy day-old chicks off Miss Perrins (from the very same Perrins family as the Lea & Perrins Sauce Company) and handmade pies and suet puddings from Samuel Jukes the village baker, even a knitted woolly jumper from Mrs. Turbott. Although they were austere times during and just after the war, there didn't seem to be much you couldn't get if you tried hard enough. There was always someone who knew someone with a little something. I have vague recollections of the celebrations in the village when the war ended; red, white and blue bunting, tables in the High Street and lots of homemade beer and lemonade floating around and a massive cake.

It was near to my fifth birthday when Mom told me she and Dad were separating. She was pregnant as usual, which made it even worse. Dad went back to live with Gramps and Grandma at the top end of the village and we had to leave Mustow Green and move to Chaddesley Corbett too, into a rented dwelling even smaller than the tiny cottage of Grandad and Grandma (Nan) Morris.

Dad was a popular man who could charm the birds down out of the trees. That is a literal, he would put bread and biscuit crumbs in the palm of his hand and sometimes on his head and the birds would come down and feed off him. He always had a smile and a story to tell. His eyes would twinkle with mischief that could be quite intoxicating, but there was another side to him; his nickname was 'Killer'. I think that was short for lady killer as he was one handsome man and was never short of female company, but when he left Mom, he didn't leave her with a penny for even a loaf of bread. Later on, when he did give her the odd handout, it was only after a knock on the door from us kids. My mother was a proud woman and she just stopped asking. There was no child support agency or anyone to turn to legally in those days. That's why divorce was rare; women were, by and large, frightened of being left to bring up the kids with no financial help whatsoever. In our case, Grandad took care of us as best he could. He drummed into us the difference between right and wrong and I'll always be grateful to him for that. True what they say about formative years and role models moulding you into what you become in later life. Grandad, however, was no businessman, so, whilst he taught me the moral codes and the skills of an engineer, the business acumen must have been somewhere inside waiting to come out. He did jobs for nothing half the time, times became very hard indeed and I experienced poverty, real poverty, for the first time in my young life.

V

Yes, my little world was shattered. I saw Dad only rarely. Mom gave birth to my brother Malcolm and so her hands were more than full with four kids to look after. I saw much more of Gramps than I did Dad and Grandad Morris all but took Dad's place in my heart and mind. I found myself being left on my own more and more and I didn't have too many friends. I don't think the parents of other children in the village actually approved of us too much and so, when invitations to birthday parties and the like went round, I rarely got an invite.

One of Mom's expressions and words of warning were: "Behave or I'll put you in Jolie's Pit." This was an old quarry full of dark, dank water at the back of the house and to me, a very real threat, which gave me the odd nightmare. So, whilst other kids would be at birthday parties, I would take myself off on imaginary safaris in the countryside, keeping out of Mom's way lest I should meet a watery grave.

VI

It was on one particularly hot summer's day that I found myself bored and looking at the gravestones in Saint Cassian's churchyard in the village. Apparently, there are only two Saint Cassian churches in the world. Old Cassian was a court recorder at the trial of St. Marcellus the Centurion. Aurelius Arcola, Deputy Prefect in the Roman province in North Africa, conducted the trial. When the death penalty was imposed on St. Marcellus, Cassian threw down his pen and declared that he was a Christian. He was arrested immediately and put to death. Cassian is patron of modern stenographers, now there's a bit of trivia for you. Anyway, the church bells started ringing and, fascinated, I went inside the church to investigate how they worked. It was there I met two people that were to influence my early days for the better. The first was the ringer of the bells, Pooch Jones. He seemed as old as the church itself; he had a hunched back and, for a moment, I thought I'd encountered the legendary Quasimodo from Notre Dame in Paris. He was a lovely man and with a smile he invited me to view the bells. He was in fact the master of the bells at Saint Cassian's and he enrolled me on the team there and then. It was a few weeks though before he let me ring my first public note. That was on a hand bell and I was allowed just that one note, the 'Peel' in 'D'ye ken John Peel'. Come Christmas, I was allowed to become one of his chosen hand bell ringers that accompanied the church choir around the village. That was on Christmas Eve and it gave me an insight into real wealth when the whole choir and we bell ringers were invited into the huge lounge of Colonel Woods of Typhoo Tea's house, 'Yestlecote', to perform for the family. We were rewarded with mulled wine and mince pies. Pooch frowned and smiled at me at the same time when he observed I had a pie in each hand. He never seemed to age and also seemed to live forever, remaining 'The Master' right up to the time I left Chaddesley. I returned for his funeral a year later and, believe me, you couldn't have got another person in the church with a shoe horn, such was his popularity.

The second person I met that day was the vicar, Vicar Vincent he was called and he seemed as old as Pooch Jones. Very staid - but he also helped me find solace away from the nightmare of Mom's ever-increasing tempers, the new man on the block, (Harvey Rutter) and the total lack of space and privacy at home. Besides bell ringing, I used to do odd jobs in the church and, as soon as I was old enough, I joined the choir. I had the highest soprano voice of all and got to sing most of the solos which I loved. Church was my sanctuary and I remain to this day a committed Christian.

Dear old Vicar Vincent almost died in the pulpit in the middle of a sermon. He was making some particularly impassioned oration about sinners being struck down and, next minute, he clutched his chest, disappeared from view and came a full roly-poly down the stone steps, landing arse over tip by the choir. We choir boys were trying hard not to chuckle and a church warden, Mr. Meredith, took over whilst Vicar Vincent was taken off to hospital - never to return. He was replaced by what you would now call a happy-clappy new-age vibrant vicar named the Rev. Thursfield. He descended on our sleepy little village like Jesus entering the house of the money lenders. Well, roared in more like on his Royal Enfield 350 motorbike, more of him later.

VII

When I was seven, the separation turned into a divorce. I didn't really know the difference at that point. Just remember catching Mom crying and, seeing me, she held out her arms and pulled me in close to her and sobbed and sobbed. I remember the wetness and warmth of those tears running down her face and almost soaking the back of my head. No words were spoken. I wanted to say that I would look after her, but I didn't. The moment was broken by Grandad coming in and softly telling me to go and wash my hands. I listened at the door, but there were only muffled voices. I do remember my name being spoken though, and with kindness. It was the only time I ever saw her cry. She was as hard as nails normally, but then we all have a trigger somewhere that will turn on the waterworks - just that most of us, me included, are too proud to admit it.

From that point on, Grandad took me under his wing more and more. It was as though up to this point he had kept a little distance in the hope that Dad would come back. The divorce put paid to any chance of that. I would watch Grandad at work in the garage, meticulously taking apart a lawn mower or something similar, soaking the parts in oil, tightening screws, reassembling it and polishing 'til it shone. This made me jump to the conclusion that, if something wouldn't work, all you had to do was take it apart and put it back together again and, hey presto, good as new. It came as quite a rude awakening to learn that there was more to it than that. I think it was the Rev. Thursfield's pride and joy Royal Enfield that was my learning curve. It was rattling and spluttering and I proudly told him I knew all about motor bike engines and would fix it for him. Well, I wheeled it home and took it to pieces, cleaned it down, oiled it and tried to put it back together. After numerous attempts, I more or less had everything back in the right order. Well, maybe not quite everything and, after one last frustrating attempt, I decided that, rather than admit defeat, it was best that it should disappear. So I took it apart again and scattered the pieces far and wide and made ready a story that, having got it pristine again, some thief in the night had roared off with it. Luckily I never had to tell the lie as he never referred to it again. To this day I can't work out why.

Meanwhile, I was on a learning curve with Grandad Morris. He would take me out with him to the farms in the surrounding countryside where he serviced manual and petrol-powered farm machinery. Those were wonderful days, like scenes from 'The Darling Buds of May'. We would be given 'doorstopper' cheese and pickle sandwiches and apples. He would get a beer for his troubles from the farmer's wife and I would get a glass of milk, straight from the cow.

VIII

Of all my brothers and sisters, Malcolm was the one I was, and remain to this day, really close to. Joined at the hip you might say. He is a fair bit smaller than me and maybe not quite as manic, but getting on that way. So great was our bond that, from a very early age, Malc actually believed I was his Dad and not his brother. I used to walk him in his posh Silver Cross pram along with my sister Valerie. His earliest memory is of gazing up at me from a ditch when we had pushed the pram a little too hard forward causing it to tip over and out of sight. Feisty little tyke that he was, all he did was grin from ear to ear. One of his favourite games was to play giants, where I would pick him up with one hand and fly him in the air like an aeroplane, much to his delight. It was a bit like discovering there is no Father Christmas when the truth finally dawned on him that I was actually only his brother. In later years, Malc would say our relationship was something out of James Herriot, 'Do as I say, not as I do'. In business we became known as the Jack Russell and the Rottweiler. Yes, I was the big one with the jaws of steel, but Malc was the one who would nip your ankles and wouldn't let go.

This seems a good point to explain a little more about how tenacious Malc can be; that's why we worked so well together in business. I would insist that everything we did was sewn up tight, 'belt and braces' I call it. Well, Malc usually got to do the tightening, whilst I was off starting the next venture. About a mile from where we lived in Chaddesley and not far from our favourite playground, the local tip, there lived another family with similar ages to us. They were 'The Manns' and were our sworn enemies. Over the years, we had many full-on scraps and would carry out carefully planned sabotage of their peddle bikes and anything else we could get our hands on. The two oldest brothers in the Mann family were Michael and Adrian; Michael was the same age as me and Adrian a couple of years younger. I think I was about fifteen when Michael committed the ultimate sin of getting my sister, Pamela, pregnant at a very tender age. This had no 'West Side Story' ending though; the baby boy was adopted and our venom taken out in a scrap to end all scraps. Many years later, Pamela was reunited with her son who had searched for his Mom. The law being what it was then, Pamela wasn't allowed to search for him.

On the day that Malc started at the Grange School in Stourbridge, he had to travel on the bus with Adrian Mann. Adrian told him in no uncertain terms that, whilst he was at the school, he would do exactly as the Mann's told him and that his life was going to be pretty unpleasant. Well, once off the bus Adrian started belting Malc, to give him a taste of what his school days were going to be like. Malcolm was two years younger than him and much smaller, so he took evasive action by biting a chunk out of his persecutor's leg. Unfortunately, this flesh gouging occurred at the same time as the most ferocious teacher in the school, Jessie James, happened to be passing. Adrian was crying and screaming; Malc was labelled a delinquent hooligan and excluded on the day he started. Back home, the poor kid faced another beating from Mom. The only thing for me was to sort out Michael Mann once more, which I did, big time. After that, Malc was left relatively in peace at the school and the feud which was ongoing throughout our teenage years was kept outside of the classroom. Adrian Mann was sadly killed in a motor accident at Blakedown just a couple of years after he left school. He shot over the parapet of the bridge there and was literally broken into pieces along with his car. I'm not sure he and Malc would ever have made friends, but neither would Malc have wished that fate upon him.

IX

Nan rarely came into our house. I don't think she could cope with see-ing how we lived and, as there was precious little she could do about it, turned a blind eye. In reality, we barely had enough to eat. Personal hygiene was very important to us though, even if that meant sharing washing water and the luxury of a tin bath once in a while. Our clothes were often given to us and anything new would be handmade. They would be mostly second-hand when they came to me and when I grew out of them, they were passed on down to my broth-ers and sisters till they couldn't be mended any more. Even then, the recycling hadn't finished as they ended up getting used for cleaning rags, either at home or in Grandad's workshop.

Next door to us lived this eccentric old gentleman called Bill Turbott. He was a World War One veteran and would always dress in a three-piece suit and flat hat, no matter what the weather. He had a damson tree in his garden too, which was a magnet to kids who couldn't afford sweets and so we would scrump. Bill knew what was going on and would shout to us: "Do you want me to shake the bloody tree for you?" This was our cue to make a sharp exit, only to come back later for a rematch. We would feign innocence to Mom, but she would belt us anyway, just in case.

An episode which still brings a smile to my face was when I acquired a 410 shotgun from somewhere. I think I swapped it for a bike I'd made. Anyway, we had some fun with that gun. I know you couldn't do that today, but shotguns in those days were all part of the country culture, not the criminal culture; most people in the village had one for shooting rabbits. I can't say I was a crack shot or that the old gun was particularly accurate, but one day I was out in the fields with young Malc and a friend of his, Podgy Davis, and they both had catapults. From out of nowhere, a duck came flying overhead and as they let loose with their slingshots I fired at it. I think the odds on my shooting it must have been a hundred to one, but by some remote chance, I actually got it full on and it dropped dead about fifty yards from us. We scampered over and then realised that this wasn't a wild bird, but someone's pet. Podgy started to get all righteous, saying that he was going home to tell his mother that Dougie Clark had shot a duck. "She'll tell your Mom and then you'll cop it!" A bit of quick thinking was called for and with Malcolm's help I convinced him that he had actually killed it with his catapult and best keep quiet about it. Terrified at the thought of what he'd done, he vacated the scene in floods of tears and remorse.

Meanwhile, we took the duck back to Grandad's who took one look at it and said, "You silly buggers, that's Farmer John Green's pet duck." Well, even though he chastised us, there was a twinkle in his eye and the duck ended up in the cooking pot. Christmas Day was always spent at Nan and Grandads. The presents were always the same: a new pair of Wellington boots for each and every one of us, lined up inside the door. This was a joy not a disappointment and would serve us nearly every day and for every adventure until the next Christmas came round. We would have the biggest turkey you could imagine. Grandad was always given this by one of the farmers. Well, I say given, it was in fact actually traded for a repair or a service to a farm vehicle. The turkey was always much too big to go in the oven and so I would go with Grandad early on Christmas morning up to Samuel Jukes, the baker, who would roast it to perfection in his giant bread oven. In return for this, Grandad would give the baker's van a service. What a lovely way to do business. At two o'clock sharp, Grandad and I would be back up at Sam Jukes's to collect it, carry it proudly down the high street and into the cottage amidst screams of excitement from all assembled. Not just Mom and we kids, there would be other relatives and friends as well. Grandma made massive piles of roast potatoes and a whole host of vegetables, sausages wrapped in bacon and homemade stuffing. After that, it was Christmas pudding ignited to a glorious blaze with a spoonful of brandy. Real homemade custard and a big jug of cream accompanied it. Next came the big hunt to determine who was lucky enough to find a silver sixpence in their portion. There wasn't just one in our pudding; Grandad would make sure there was a veritable handful. Hence, there was nary a currant or sultana left. As you can imagine, we didn't get a lot in the way of toys except for hand-me-downs from rich folk in some of the big houses nearby, who took pity on us.

Our benefactors included a Mrs. Griffin who lived in The Holloway, the poshest part of Chaddesley and was one of the owners of Beatties, the famous and fabulous department store in Wolverhampton. It's still there today, but under the House of Fraser name. The last Mr. Beattie sold it to them in 2003 and then committed suicide not long after. Perhaps he couldn't cope with seeing the unique family business turn into just another store. Getting back to Mrs. Griffin; she was a sister as she didn't have the Beattie family surname. Anyway, she was always kind to Mom when she was pregnant (which was more often than not). Mrs. Griffin was also instrumental in helping with the adoption when Pam got pregnant by Michael Mann. She would give us groceries, clothes and the odd assortment of secondhand toys. Once, this included a wonderful box of Meccano compiled from various incomplete sets. I spent hours, days and weeks building a giant crane which I was so proud of. I showed it to Grandad when it was nearly finished and I couldn't get the pulley to work as I had several key pieces missing. Not my fault, like poor old Rev. Thursfield's motor bike: they were never in the box in the first place. "There's no such word as can't", Grandad told me, that being one of his favourite expressions. So, inspired, I managed to make the missing bits from some of the other pieces and a bit of a tin can. This took a great deal of mechanical ingenuity for a young lad, but I got there and had a grand 'crane launch' for my brothers and sisters - complete with a bottle of homemade pop. My handiwork was short lived though; having upset Mom over something trivial and leaping out of the way of her flaying hand, she took revenge on the nearest thing available and the dearest to my heart. My crane was thrown with all the force she could muster out of the bedroom window to shatter into non-repairable pieces on the concrete beneath. My verbal remonstrations were rewarded with a cuff round the ear that left me dizzy and my being locked in the bedroom for twenty-four hours without even a glass of water.

The bedroom lock-in was a favourite punishment of Mom's. Sometimes we would all be locked in. Often, we took our frustration out on the plaster on the walls, chipping it off and gouging it out. It began to look like a war zone, which in hindsight it was.

X

I found myself being left more and more in charge of the rest of the family whilst Mom, when she wasn't seeing Harvey, seemed to have no shortage of suitors. Sometimes, she brought them back and you can imagine us all pressed up against the wall, even tiptoeing across the landing, to hear the sexual noises coming from her room. The visitors rarely came into the house though, but would just flash their lights and she would disappear, off out into the night, with the threat of what would happen to us, particularly me, if we misbehaved. Of course we always did, kids being kids, even in the sure and certain knowledge that the slightest misdemeanour would be met with a strong arm brandishing the nearest implement that came to her hand. I would station one of us on sentry duty to watch out for the eventuality of an early return, whilst the rest of us got down to fun and games. This included smoking and at a very early age. One particular night we had the Woodbines on the go, when the shout went up that Mom was back. It turned out to be a false alarm, but in the panic all the fags were thrown into a chest of drawers. One of them couldn't have been put out properly as, within five minutes, we had a major blaze going on. It was put out with cups of water, but the damage was done, the chest was ruined and black smoke stains covered the walls. We padded ourselves up and waited for Mom's return. Everyone copped it that night and she belted us with everything from a wooden coat hanger to a poker. We were black and blue.

Another night when Mom was out there was a big accident on the notoriously dangerous bend opposite our house. An Austin Healey going flat out hadn't realised there was a sudden bend until it was too late; it hit the bank and spun several times with all the noise of a herd of elephants on the rampage. There were police cars, ambulances and some very excited kids who thought this a glorious adventure.

Mom became an even more ferocious woman, her eyes would blaze with madness and her violence increased as she grew older. The day came when I was big enough not to run, but faced her out. I took the walking stick off her and broke it in half. She looked at me with respect and treated me differently from the others after that. I was allowed the tiny back bedroom on my own, whilst my brothers and sisters still slept head to toe in the front bedroom, all in the same bed, regardless of gender. My room was barely big enough to take a single bed, but to me it was a five-star hotel.

For all her faults though, I have to admit that Mom was a remarkable woman. She was in fact one of the few women to be driving at the time. Not that she had her own car, but she would do chauffeuring work for Grandad's customers, whether that was conveying a dead body or a business trip. She even got to drive the ex-Prime Minister, Neville Chamberlain, when he was going to Kidderminster to open a new carpet factory a few years after the war.

I remember she used to sit with Nan in a car on the garage forecourt, drinking a jug of tea and knitting, just getting out to serve the petrol. This was from where I was to get the idea of attended service later on. It was also where I learnt another salutary lesson. One day I offered to make the tea for them, so I went across to Nan's and into the kitchen. Rather than getting something to stand on to reach into the top shelf of the cupboard, where the jugs were kept, I fumbled around knocking one of her best pieces of china onto the floor, where it shattered into a dozen or more pieces. I scooped up the evidence and buried it behind the wall in The Little Garage, then made the tea and returned smiling. "Did you break something, Doug?" Nan asked knowingly.

"What? No Nan," I replied, turning redder by the second.

"Could have sworn I heard a tinkle," she tutted. I couldn't think of a smart reply so said nothing, just stood there cringing in embarrassment. I learnt then and there if you screw up, admit it; lies will be sure to find you out. Many a time something has gone wrong with a car and I could have lied, but I remembered that look on Nan's face and came clean, it worked every time. Trust of the people who are dealing with you is more important than saving face. Best thing is to admit the truth for the right reasons in order to be forgiven or understood. I'm no paragon. Of course, there have been white lies, but ones where to tell the truth would help no one. Usually to do with having my trousers down round my ankles in the wrong place at the wrong time.

XI

Need was the mother of invention as far as obtaining money was concerned. Mom had no pocket money for us and so I would do everything possible to make a penny. I must admit the one and sixpence from the choir was a good start, but I also did a paper round, cleaned cars and knocked doors for odd jobs. 'Penny for the Guy' and carol singing excursions were carefully planned, to extract every possible sum, to bolster the coffers. If someone wasn't at home, we'd go back again and again until we caught them in and would guard our territory from rival callers, particularly the Manns.

I made a trolley for my bike with some bits and pieces from the tip and would take Malc with me on the paper rounds from when he was about three years old. He used to crawl out of the trolley, run and shove the papers through the doors as fast as his little legs would carry him. It must have looked hilarious. I would also hand-wash the cars at the big houses 'til they gleamed. I still show people today how to use a chamois leather correctly, it really is a skill. One in particular became a regular, Mr. Butler of the brewery family, Mitchells and Butlers. He lived in Brockencote Hall, now a four-star hotel and restaurant. Who would have thought then, that later on in life I would be offered Brockencote Hall to buy as a home? Certainly not me when I was washing the cars. In fact, in later years, I brokered many a deal over lunch in that fine dining room and hosted some major business briefings there too.

Seasonal income came from pea and potato picking, which was back-breaking work and brought calluses out on your hands, that often became infected and blistered. Another good money-making venture was the local point-to-point race meeting. In those days, bicycles were a popular form of transport and so we would turn the yard at Grandad's into a bike park. We charged a few pennies to park a bike and would stack them up to the sky; caused a few problems when people came to retrieve them though, as you can imagine. I also remember spending the whole half-a-crown, which was my share of the spoils, on a bag of Mars bars. I literally ate them till I was sick.

Whilst Mom nabbed most of the money, one treat I used to get was going to ABC Minors Cinema on a Saturday morning in Kidderminster. There, I got lost in the exploits of Flash Gordon and his battle to stop Ming the Merciless from global domination. I used to love the gadgets and would make imitation laser guns from stuff I got from the tip.

XII

At the top of the village, Gramps died. I was eleven and, as I understand it, he was chasing one of his inflatable lanterns down the lawn when he had a heart seizure and collapsed. It was instant and perhaps a lovely way to go. It meant Dad was now the owner of the garage after buying out Jess and Ernie, his two brothers. Not that this made any difference to me. I wasn't invited to go to the funeral, neither was Mom. I visited his grave not long after though (he is buried in St. Cassian's), staying for quite a while and reflecting on the good times.

When I was fourteen, Grandad died and everything changed once again. His wasn't a peaceful passing like Gramps'; he had suffered from back pain for many years and his way of dealing with it was to swallow aspirin by the handful. In the end, I think he just destroyed his liver. I went to his funeral and a sad affair it was too. One of the few times in my life I'm not ashamed to admit to shedding a tear or two; maybe, if I'm honest, enough to fill a rain bucket.

I went to try and do Grandad's work at the garage, but it was all too much for a school kid. So, Nan Morris sold the garage and business to Esso, for how much I don't know, but a fair old sum, I guess. Later, she also sold her old house to the brewery. They had been after it for some time, apparently to extend The Fox pub that it was attached to. It was turned into, and remains today, a dining room.

From the proceeds, Nan had this beautiful house built on the three to four acres she owned next to the garage. Grandad left Mom something too, but she spent the lot on a big flashy Ford Zodiac. Lord knows why, when we had barely enough to eat and clothe ourselves. The registration 646 DNP is imprinted on my brain.

Esso put a manager into the garage, gave it a face-lift, and it seemed to prosper. However, it was turned into a 'petrol sales only' station to the delight of Dad and Bluntington Garage up at the top end of the village. It took away the competition, but did he capitalise on it? Not really. The new manager dissuaded us kids from going anywhere near it, so this turned into a mini vendetta especially with Malc, young tearaway that he was. He would cycle as close as he could and give him 'V' signs and verbal abuse.

XIII

Two years before Grandad died, he had taught me to drive. I learnt in his Austin A35 van which he called 'The Nipper'. A nipper it was too, it smelt beautiful inside, not real leather, but this sweet PVC. I loved the chrome switch at the side of the steering column, which turned on the headlights and the indicator switch from on the top of the dashboard, which flashed red rays like something from 'War of the Worlds'. "The Martians are coming," I used to say to Grandad as he slept in the passenger seat. I remember that registration too, TWP 987. My lessons were always at night. Grandad would drive down to the Park Gate Inn about two miles away on the Kidderminster to Bromsgrove road. He would have a few pints and I would drive him back. It was a memorable and unique experience learning to drive like that. At first, I would swing the steering wheel from side to side, like I'd seen James Cagney do in the movies, then I realised you only actually have to move the wheel if you want to turn, otherwise just let it be. We had embarked on a wonderful project, which was to build me a Ford Falcon special. This was a modified Ford 8 and a real prize. It was to have a side-valve engine and, when finished, would look a bit like the early D-Type Jaguar. I removed it from the garage (before it was taken over) and, over a period of time, finished it off myself with a little help from Malc over in 'The Little Garage' at Nan's old house. When it was finally road worthy I had the finishing touch added, a huge Donald Duck painted on the bonnet by a biker friend, 'Titchy' Payne. I was so proud of that machine, WWP 781.

I was sixteen when I finally finished it and, on one of my first outings, I was stopped by the police in Bromsgrove. As you have no doubt guessed, I didn't have a driving licence. My test was due the following week on my seventeenth birthday, which I passed. I took the necessary paperwork to the police station. The duty sergeant couldn't help but notice that I didn't have a licence when I was stopped and sent it all off to the Chief Constable for a ruling. I decided to write a letter myself to the Chief Constable 'begging forgiveness', so desperate was I not to lose my newly acquired license. A few weeks later, I heard back saying they would be lenient on this occasion and would take no action. I've still got the letter; I can't help but think everyone was a little more human in those days.

XIV

With the sale of the garage came the inevitable loss of Mom's job. Money was even scarcer; she even did the unthinkable and would send Malcolm and the youngsters up to knock on Dad's door at the top of the village. He would give them the odd ten bob, which didn't go far. There was really only one thing for it. I had to leave school and get a job. As I was only fourteen, that needed special permission, which was granted due to the family circumstances.

By this time Mom had married Harvey Rutter, for a bit of financial security I suppose. Not that it made much difference to the household funds as most of his money went on his passion for grass track motor bike racing; also, he already had another family to keep. I quite liked him but to have him in our house on a permanent basis I considered a gross intrusion. However, his passion for grass tracking rubbed off on me, I have to admit he was pretty hot at it and a good teacher to boot. He even took me to the 'Grass Track Event Awards Dinner' where I got up and made my first public appearance singing 'You are my Sunshine' with the band. At the top end of the village, Dad took up grass tracking too and the competition between him and Harvey Rutter continued. Sadly, it was to be a short-lived contest, as Harvey met an early and pretty awful fate when he fell through the asbestos roof of the barn which he was repairing at Yardley's farm in Cakebole lane. He went straight through and dropped into the grass dryer. He died forty-eight hours later in hospital from multiple fractures including his spine. It was a horrible way to go and he was still a young man in his prime.

Mom, once again, was on her own, but not for long. She was soon courted by husband number three, Gordon Owen. I didn't really have a lot to do with him and I'd moved out by the time they were married. I know he used to try and order us about a lot, which we took scant notice of. Still, he did do the house up very well, which was much needed as everything was on the verge of collapse. Gordon had two youngsters of his own and so it was a bit like Mother Hubbard, living in the proverbial shoe. His children had a rude awakening too. Meeting the roughest kids in Chaddesley, the Clark's! Best education for life they could have had, I reckon.

XV

So I got my very first job, with Stanley Goodwin, a Jaguar Dealership in Kidderminster (nowadays it's Sealine Marine, major international boat builders). I worked in the stores, cleaned the cars and did every odd job that no one else wanted to do. I was paid the princely sum of one pound, nineteen shillings and two pence a week, of which my mother took the pound. That didn't matter; I was independent, grown up and on my way. I used to cycle to Kidderminster and back every day, five miles each way, which certainly kept me fit.

After a few months, I saved up enough money for my first motorbike, a Triumph Tiger Cub; boy, was I proud of that. I also sent off for a guitar from a newspaper ad and taught myself a few chords. Money brought independence, which was a wonderful thing.

Along with the motorbike came a new set of friends, the 'Chaddesley Sparrow Gang'. I had the leather jacket with an eagle painted on the back; I grew my hair a bit and felt every inch a Jack-the-lad. We would race, run in a pack and visit the local biker coffee bars like Smokey Joe's in Northfield and the Silver Grill in Bromsgrove. All this ended one fateful night when I overshot a bend out at Battlefield Dip. I had an almighty crash; the bike, my pride and joy, was totalled and I was lucky to escape alive with just a few broken bones and bruised from head to toe. So, it was back to the pushbike as far as work was concerned. I went on to have lots of other bikes and raced them, which I'll come on to later, but I never actually took a motorbike test until I was 52, in 1994, and then just to prove to myself I could do it.

I used to love talking to the customers and they seemed to enjoy talking to me. So much so, that one day, when I had been particularly verbose on a variety of subjects including the fact that I had a full driving licence having passed my test on my seventeenth birthday, opportunity knocked. Ron Tomlinson, the manager of the Bromsgrove branch of Tansers Tyres, who had just lost his own driving license, offered me a job working for him, selling tyres on a round. The big carrot was that I got to drive a van, a Ford 100E, which I could use in my own time, after dropping him home at night. I didn't hesitate to say yes. It was then I found that I had a natural ability for sales and selling techniques. Firstly, I mastered the art of selling tyres through the hands-on friendly approach. Oh yes, Doug Clark was everybody's mate, but more importantly you could rely on him to deliver on time. Then I came up with a winning concept. I would fit the tyres myself or get them fitted. No job was too big or too small. Well, the tyre sales for our branch went through the roof and I earned more in bonuses than I did in salary, good tips too. And as for the van, I drove that like a formula one racing car and tuned it up like one.

My biggest sale ever was to Eric Pillon who owned the Chateau Impney at that time. I fitted a whole set of the most expensive tyres that money could buy onto his shining silver Rolls Royce. For anyone that doesn't know the Chateau, it is a complete full-size replica of a French chateau, set in wonderful landscaped gardens with streams, bridges and even a water garden. It was built by salt mine millionaire John Corbett in the 1920's for his young French wife who pined for home. Didn't do him a lot of good though as she left him anyway. Eric Pillon turned it into a nightclub, complete with casino. It enjoyed a reputation as the best den of iniquity in the region. Nowadays, it is a hotel, but still looks impressively out of place standing back from the road on the approach to Droitwich. You would be excused for thinking you were in the Loire Valley not the middle of England. I suppose I would have carried on selling tyres and, who knows? Maybe even set up my own tyre-fitting company if fate hadn't interfered once more. I received a message that Dad wanted to see me. It would prove to be a meeting that would change my life forever.

3 – Learning The Trade

I

It was in the summer of 1959 that I called at Uncle Jess's garage half-way up the Lickeys, 'E. J. Clark Rednal Garage' as it was then. I had never met him in my life before. Not having had too much to do with Dad, I was even less likely to have had any reason to know his brother. Uncle Jess was a bit of a family legend though in that he only had one leg, having lost the other in a motor cycle accident in his early 20's. He had a false one which was filled with miniature ball bearings.

Incidentally, Dad had now remarried Kathleen (of whom I became very fond in later years) and had a son named Noel after himself. He'd have been about ten then and I hadn't met him either, even though we lived just a few hundred yards apart. The garage was a tip, totally disorganised, and when I said I was from Tansers Tyres he wasn't overly impressed. Nor was he when I told him I was his nephew; it was obvious that there was to be no nepotism here. What did impress him though was my willingness to fit the tyres. Anything that would save Uncle Jess doing the hard graft was right up his street, I was to discover later. "Let me see you do it," he said, "go and fit that tyre on that Wolseley over there, the one with the wheel off". So I did, and a greasy, sweaty job it was too, but he was impressed. "I'll think about it," he said. It wasn't one of our tyres I had fitted and no money changed hands, but I didn't mind that, I'd made the contact and I would hound him from now on till he bought all his tyres from me.

Turned out that wasn't needed. A meeting was arranged with Dad so that he could put a proposition to me. It was then that I met my half brother Noel for the first time. I couldn't help thinking how better dressed he was than I had been at his age and on his feet gleamed new shoes.

Dad told me that Uncle Jess had been to see him; he was apparently quite taken with me and would like me to go and work for him. An incentive was that if I took the job with Uncle Jess then Dad would loan me one of his cars to get there, a Fiat Topolino - if you don't remember it was tiny and shaped like a Noddy car. It wasn't the car that made my mind up though; it was the number of opportunities missed that had been raging through my mind. I had said to Malcolm, "If only I had that place, I would turn it into a gold mine." Well, opportunity knocked and I grasped it with both hands.

I went home and told young Malc all about it; we stayed up half the night whispering away. "I'll have you there with me soon enough," I told him.

"When?" He asked.

"Give me a chance, I haven't started yet, but happen it will, Malc, I promise you."

II

In 1959 an event took place which was to change the motoring world forever and I cannot over-emphasise the impact this would have on my future. It was the launch of the Mini. This was the single greatest advance since the first car was produced, in my humble opinion. It revolutionized motoring and made it accessible to a whole new entry level of would-be drivers. The Mini was trendy, cute and affordable. "Get yourself a Mini, mate" was the topic in every pub. When it became immortalised in film as the real star of 'The Italian Job' it just went from strength to strength. It was followed by the souped-up Mini Cooper, the Cooper 'S' and the Mini Moke. The Moke didn't catch on, but look at golf courses around the world today and it's found its niche all right. The Mini was a family car, a boy racer and a girl's car. They came in wonderful pastel colours; people added stripes, graphics of feet entwined in love making and bullet mark transfers on the wind screen, Disney characters, suede roofs and some were actually covered in turf. The Mini was the car of the swinging sixties and broke down class, age and gender barriers.

I gave my notice in at Tansers. They were really sorry to see me go, but wished me well. I promised to give them as much business as possible, which I indeed did.

Uncle Jess gave me a wage of £7.00 a week. Far less than I had been earning at Tansers, but in my mind this was just the beginning. Also, I was now playing a few gigs in the evenings with my first band, 'The Deadbeats' - skiffle music - so this helped make up the shortfall. Down the road at the Austin works, I could have got a job on the track at four times what I was earning but it never even crossed my mind.

I was put to graft manning the pumps, sweeping up and delivering paraffin in the old Wolseley. Uncle Jess was very pleasantly surprised when he found I could actually do work on the cars. He had a mechanic called Billy Tristan. Billy only did what he had to; he was unmotivated and had scant respect for Uncle Jess. So, as Jess found a willing work horse in me, it wasn't long before he let Billy go and put me in charge of servicing as well as deliveries, serving petrol and taxi driving. Talk about his pound of flesh.

The servicing consisted mostly of decoking and re-bores, replacing kingpins and bushes and clutches. The kingpin was the swivel for the hub on the steering, later to be replaced with ball joints. Today these last forever; back in the early sixties, it was anybody's guess. This was still the era of the agricultural mechanics; the state-of-the-art revolution from Germany and Japan was a decade away yet. Also, petrol at that time was so heavily leaded that cars were in constant need of decoking or they would simply seize up. That's why we sold 'Redex Shots' alongside the petrol to mix it up a little but, in reality, that was just a gimmick from the oil companies.

With Billy gone it presented the ideal opportunity to bring little Malc over. Uncle Jess nearly bit my hand off - slave labour. Malc was twelve now and started to come across at weekends, doing the sweeping up, serving petrol and watching me take the cars apart - learning all the time, as I had from Grandad. He also got to drive the Austin 16 up the road and turn it round. That was the highlight of his weekends.

III

Now, I think it would be helpful if I actually described the garage here. It was tiny and stood on the concrete and shingle outside an old pub called The Barracks, which had closed many years earlier. The store room for the garage was the old cellar of the pub; the workshop was a shed with just about enough room inside it to get around a single car. There was no pit or anything like that, so the cars just had to be jacked up and you lay on the stone-cold floor to work on them. The petrol pumps were not concreted in, just bolted down, and pretty shaky they were too. Behind the pub was a massive steep bank, which was an overgrown garden for The Barracks. This stretched right up to the foot of the woods at the base of the Lickey Hills Park itself. To the left of the garage, looking across the road from the tram station, stood a couple of small joined-together cottages and then came another two cottages, facing up the bank. The first of these was an antique shop of sorts. The owner was Mr. Ward, a loopy but lovable eccentric. His best customer was my Auntie Ivy. Then came two more cottages, steeply terraced. You'll see why this detail is important as the story progresses. Next in line was a brick-built hot dog stand, behind which was a large house belonging to George Smart's sister, then a ladies hairdresser and finally, Smart's Amusement Arcade. The road continued down the hill to Grandad's original house, 'Pinehurst'. A short time after I started, Uncle Jess bought the cottages next door and the antique shop to add to his empire. He didn't live in any of them, preferring to be in Hagley.

To the right, was another cottage owned by Mrs. Webb who ran a part-time tea shop from there. She did a thriving business on weekends when it seemed all the people from Birmingham would flock to the Lickeys for a day out. The cottages continued up the hill until you reached an old fashioned open-all-hours hardware store and then 'Pickens', another old-fashioned shop - this time, a grocery-store-cum-newsagents. I remember Mr. Picken always dressed in a spotless white doctor's coat and had a pencil behind his ear which he would use to tot up the bill on the back of a brown paper bag. Then there was a really steep unmade road up to some more houses, one of which my good friend, David Sills, lived in. More about him in a little while.

Across the other side of that road was Jack Hines' place; he was a black-smith, welder and farrier. This was known affectionately as The Old Smithy. Then, a cut-throat barber who would shave and give 'basin' trims to elderly gentlemen outside, weather permitting; no doubt offering 'something for the weekend' as well. Next, cobblers – no, I've got that wrong. The cobbler, Mr. Haslam, who was Middle Eastern, was behind Pickens the grocer. I think you can establish in your mind a picture of our little community. Oh, there was a brass business behind the welders (that's important) and a post office and a tea room to the front and finally, another amusement arcade. Fletcher's Penny Arcade, I think it was called at the time. It had some wonderful things like 'What the Butler Saw' where, for the princely sum of one old penny, you could turn the handle and watch a twenties flapper girl strip down to her panties and blow you a kiss. There was also a laughing policeman, a fortune-telling machine and a haunted graveyard. All wonderful pieces of mechanical engineering without any of the flashing lights and out-of-space sounds you get today. The hot dogs were wonderful if dicey on the tummy and if you were really hard up, you could have a roll dipped in fat for tuppence.

IV

Upstairs in the old pub lived Uncle Jess's sister, Aunty Ivy, a bizarre looking woman who would frighten you to death if you didn't know her. She was short and fat, weighing in at over eighteen stone and she had this weird hairstyle, parted down the middle then tied at the sides in two huge bunches, which made her look like she was permanently wearing ear-phones. She lived there with her Welsh husband, Glynn Hughes, and their son, David. They certainly weren't the tidiest or cleanest of people and Auntie Ivy seemed to spend her life collecting junk - from bundles of old newspapers to eccentric bric-a-brac, things that were neither of value nor of use. She did have this amazing peddle piano though, which you put a roll of music inside, peddled like mad and it turned and moved the keys on its own whilst churning out 'Tin Soldiers', over and over again.

Glynn Hughes used to be in partnership in the garage with Uncle Jess, which was long before I worked there. They had a falling-out over something or other and Glynn had left to start his own garage in Alvechurch, a few miles away. He and Jess rarely spoke and I had little to do with Glynn myself, disaffected loyalty I suppose.

I never really got on with David either, even though he was around the same age as me. He didn't have a lot of drive and, like every other local lad of his age, went to work at the Austin - in his case, in the accounts department. He did one thing of service to me though. It was through him that I met David Sills. I was always attracted by, not exactly eccentrics, but people with a little spark of devilment and David Sills had that all right, in spades. He was a friend of David Hughes; don't ask why because they were poles apart. I suppose it was just because they lived close to each other and both attended the Bluecoat School in Edgbaston. The memorable day I met big David (he was six foot four) was when the Hughes were off to a wedding and young David really did not want to go. He was standing outside moaning his lot, all dressed up in a new three piece suit.

"Well don't bloody go then," Dave Sills told him loudly.

"That's easy for you to say," young David told him. "Think you're so bright; tell me how to get out of it."

"Hang on a minute," Sills told him and with that walked over to the workshop where I was greasing an Austin 10. "Can I borrow this?" He asked, pointing to a bucket of not-too-clean water.

"Be my guest," I told him, and followed, intrigued to see what would happen next. Well, Sills, as cool as a cucumber, walked back to young David and just threw the whole bucket-full over him, leaving a dirty drowned wreck with his mouth open.

"See, easy-peasy." Sills told him. "Now you ain't going nowhere." With that, he retreated back up the hill to avoid the raised Welsh voices that were to follow. David didn't go to the wedding and I made a point of making a mate out of David Sills.

V

This was at the point in my life when I had not long got my first guitar - from a newspaper advert, complete with instructions on how to learn in seven days. Well, I was getting nowhere; so, finding out that Dave Sills was quite a musician (in fact an extremely accomplished classical and jazz pianist as well as a commander of most instruments), I asked him to help. He taught me my first chord of D; I remember it well. Then, every spare moment I got, I was up at his house learning more. Dave Sills also had a band, 'The Deadbeats'. This was during the age of Skiffle, Lonnie Donegan's 'Rock Island Line' and all that. I went to see them play at the Ewe and Lamb pub out at Bromsgrove on a Sunday night and was really impressed; so much so that I wanted to join them. Well, six months after learning that first chord I did, as lead guitar, and I loved it. The line-up was Pat Saunders on drums, his sister Anne on vocals and washboard, Tony Jones on rhythm guitar, Roger (Sticky) Glue on banjo, Ant Davis on tea chest bass and Dave Sills, band leader, on piano.

I was the youngest member of the group at seventeen. Not old enough to drink in the pubs we played at, but no-one seemed to mind. Those were such great days and the band was a magnet for the girls. What I had dabbled with before, in terms of the opposite sex, I now set about turning into a notch on the bedpost list and on many an occasion an art form in itself. Motors, music and muff - the magic threesome; life was wonderful.

I wasn't too impressed, though, at how much we got paid at the Ewe and Lamb - barely enough to cover the beer. So, as the audiences built up to the point where Roy the landlord wanted us twice a week, I seized the opportunity to get Dave Sills to ask for a massive hike in our fees or a percentage of the door. He did it with me hovering in the background and the landlord reluctantly agreed. Suddenly, I was earning as much, if not more, playing with the 'Deadbeats' than I was at the garage. I could start saving for cars and guitars again. I also wrote my first song, a sort of Country and Western number called 'Old Bill'. It was kind of my version of 'Frankie and Johnny'; anyway, the band thought it good enough to include in the set.

We started getting other gigs and bigger venues like The Winter Gardens in Droitwich and the Imperial Hotel in Birmingham town centre, bigger fees too - and more girls. Got to the point where there was a different one in my car every time we played. Trouble was, I had nowhere really to take them back to and was getting a little bored with car seat sex, particularly in my Austin Healey Sprite, which was my pride and joy, but not conducive to gyrating the loins. It was time to put phase two of my plan into operation.

VI

Malcolm was now coming up to fifteen and was itching to leave school and join me at the garage full time, so he just didn't go back after the Easter term at school. No-one chased him; today it would be different, like so many other things. I persuaded Uncle Jess to let us convert the old billiard room, in the pub where aunty Ivy lived, into a flat.

"Won't cost you a penny," I told him. "Me and Malc will do all the work ourselves and pay for everything; put a lot of value on your property, Uncle Jess, and it means we'll be able to start earlier and work later". Well, that did it; he was sold on the idea and I was going to create someplace I could bring the girls back to.

Now, bear in mind that, when Malcolm joined full-time, Uncle Jess paid him the princely sum of thirty bob a week - that's just one pound fifty pence in today's money. I was on seven quid a week, but you could add another ten pounds a week to that for what I was earning in the band. Malcolm wanted to pay his way in getting the materials together for the flat so he took an evening job at the brass works up the road. We would often start work on the flat when I got back from playing and he'd finished at the brass works, sometimes right through till it was time to start at the garage. There was, as yet, nowhere to sleep so we would grab a few winks in a sleeping-bag on the floor.

Although I had never really done any building work before, I didn't think it would be a great deal different to reassembling a car. I drew out a plan of how our flat was going to look on a piece of paper. This was something that I have continued doing through later years as we developed, refurbished and launched new showrooms. I always sketched out how my concepts would look. My drawings may not have been artistic masterpieces, but architects learned the hard way that I wouldn't deviate from my own vision.

VII

The vision of the flat was of an open-plan party palace with easy access from the living area to the bedroom - no need to bother with doors. The kitchen was really just a cooker and a sink with a small cupboard. The living area had a couple of settees and a big fireplace, which we painted red, surmounted by a stag's head from Aunty Ivy's pile of jumble. The bedroom had two beds partitioned off from the lounge with a bit of studding, but still open plan. Between the beds was a radiogram from which Elvis and Gene Vincent would be permanently entertaining us. On top of the radiogram was a Grundig tape recorder, which we would use to make the most bizarre recordings of fake fights and other absolute nonsense - but it had us and our entourage in fits.

Pretty well everything came from the scrap yard. We even connected the water up from Aunty Ivy's by way of taped-together radiator hoses and tubes. Bad mistake! We flooded everything when the tubes expanded with the hot water. Oh, and for heating, we had a paraffin heater as well as the fireplace. How we didn't actually burn the place down was a minor miracle; we got close on many an occasion, including one night when the stag's head went up in flames. It looked like a visit from Lucifer with his horns ablaze.

This was my first real home and phase two was accomplished. Life always has a little sting in the tail though, doesn't it? Just when you're on your way, something happens to make you take a reality check. Gordon Owen, Mom's third husband, came to see us and told us that Mom was dying - terminal cancer - she was just 43. She died inside the month and the funeral was a sad affair, one of the only times when all of the brothers and sisters were together. Each of us had our own memories of her who was, despite her violence, one remarkable woman. Maybe she was not a mother in the usual maternal sense of the word, but certainly an inspiration. Gordon Owen lived on in the house for a while after she died; it was rented, so there was no monetary value. When the rent was due he just moved his own kids out and I never heard hide nor hair of him again. The rest of my clan were old enough to move on too and so the house ceased to be connected with the Clark's and an era came to a close.

Part Two 1960 – 1970

4 – All Work And Still Time To Play

I

So there I was, living above the shop, literally, with not enough hours in the day to do everything I wanted.

Things were going well, but not well enough. I wanted to improve the business; after all, I was determined that it would be mine in the not too distant future. I wasn't too sure how to achieve that and in the absence of anything better, by way of a master plan, I just saved what I could from the band, the tips I got from a bit of taxiing, encouraged my kid brother to do the same and waited for the day when Uncle Jess was ready to hang up his clogs.

The day would start almost at first light with cornflakes and coffee - together. Yes, together; I determined that if we poured the coffee over the cornflakes then that saved valuable working time and got us kick-started for the day. I've always wondered why Kellogg's hadn't discovered this and marketed it as the ultimate morning adrenalin booster; but then I suppose it is an acquired taste. After breakfast it was down the steps to the garage three at a time and start on the servicing. Customers would leave their cars overnight. If the forecourt was full then they would use the tram terminus over the road and put the keys through the office door. We would sort them into order and by the time Uncle Jess rolled in there was already half a day's work done, much to his delight. He would then disrupt the day by sending me off on paraffin deliveries and the like, which meant I had to leave a car jacked up and half finished. Malcolm wasn't supposed to touch them, but he did and I'd come back and have to sort out the pieces. I didn't discourage him though: it was how I'd learnt from Grandad Fred and that now seemed a lifetime ago.

Uncle Jess never said no to us taking on anything to fix, including lawn mowers and all kinds of horticultural machinery. Who else was lucky enough to have two willing workhorses like me and Malc? As the day progressed, we avoided eating the lunch that Aunty Ivy brought down to us ('walking botulism' we called it) and it ended its sad life in the bin - we never let on, just thanked her.

"Bit noisy last night, boys," was her usual comment.

"Sorry Auntie, had a few friends round." I'd give the same old response.

Indeed, we had too. After work, Malc would go off to the brass works and I'd go out either playing, rehearsing or having some nookie. Then back to the flat with whoever wanted to come. On would go the music and the party would start all over again. That was our life, seven days a week.

II

It was freezing cold in the workshop and, after complaining to Uncle Jess for the umpteenth time, he bought a little infrared heater out of the News of the World newspaper, for the princely sum of one pound nineteen shillings and sixpence. Well, it was the most useless heater you could imagine. You could get warmer by striking a match so we decided to take matters into our own hands and bought ourselves a Salamander heater from an agricultural sale. This was a monster, which ran on paraffin and gave out such heat that it turned our cold dungeon into the Caribbean, all winter long. Trouble was, it was also incredibly dangerous. It had to be lit by means of an oil soaked rag, which was lit and offered up to the heater, suspended from the rafters by two strong chains. One fateful day though, when the lighting process was under way, I noticed that it wasn't lighting properly, but vaporizing. Sensing what was about to happen I yelled to Malcolm to run! Run we did, to be followed seconds later by a huge explosion which rocked the whole building and set off a huge mushroom cloud. Luckily, Uncle Jess was out and we'd managed to repair much of the damage by the time he got back, but it was the end of warmth and as spring was just around the corner we just went back to working in Arctic conditions. In reality, it was a narrow escape; we could have been blinded, maimed or killed, but we didn't think about that till many years later.

III

"I'm fed up with scraping my back on that floor in the workshop," I announced one morning to Malc just before we leapt out of bed. We had twin beds side by side with the record player in the middle. "And we're going to do something about it."

"Like what, Doug? Uncle Jess won't pay to have the floor redone, tight bastard," Malc responded.

"Don't need to. When he goes off for the bank holiday weekend, we're going to dig a pit and have it finished when he gets in on Wednesday morning. It'll mean we can be far more productive and, hopefully, I'll avoid early lumbago."

Now, I don't know how much digging you've ever done, but let me tell you that digging out a pit - deep enough to stand in and wide enough to walk about under a car - is a bit like digging your own swimming pool. We are not talking a bean trench here but a World War One job. However, in my mind it wasn't a daunting task and we set-to on Friday night with pickaxes and spades and worked until the early hours when we were absolutely knackered. We grabbed a couple of hours sleep and woke up aching in every joint, but carried on again. During the Saturday a few friends came along to lend a hand, but in truth they were more hindrance than help. Our pit was becoming the talk of Rednal - with George Smart and Jimmy Fletcher, who owned the amusement arcades, coming along amongst others, laughing themselves silly. Come Sunday night we boarded up the sides with old planks of wood we had got from the local tip and then made up a concrete mix and poured it in. It was held in place with rusty old angle irons. Monday morning, we concreted the floor and sides, then early Tuesday, we removed the boards and, hey presto, we had our pit - eight foot long, three foot wide and five foot-six inches deep. The construction would not have won any engineering awards; in fact, we would probably be locked up for it today. Nevertheless, it was a massive milestone for us. I shook Malc's hand and said "Here's to us, kid, the Fabulous Clark Brothers - there's nothing we can't do".

Uncle Jess was bewildered, but impressed, so much so that he had my Dad over to look at it and, despite the chuckles, it was perhaps the most positive move we could have made. The Isle of Man TT race was coming up and Dad and Uncle Jess invited me to go along with them. I was absolutely over the moon and felt like I had been moved up the ladder a few rungs in their estimation. The trip was not without incident. I can't remember how it happened, but Uncle Jess's leg came off. Well, not 'came off' exactly, but split open, sending hundreds of ball bearings cascading down the street with me and Dad chasing after them like kids at an Easter egg race. Passers-by saw the dilemma and joined in the hunt. Soon there were dozens of tourists all coming back with hands and pockets full of ball bearings, which we poured back into his leg. We tied it all up together with sticky plasters and string until we could get him back home and a proper repair job done. It was very funny and even Uncle Jess saw the humorous side.

IV

When we got back I discovered that the pit leaked. I hadn't even taken that into consideration. Every day, before we started work, we had to bail out over a foot of water and as the day went on the bailout bucket was in semi-constant use. In the end, we got fed up with fighting it and just lived in harmony with our pit-come-swimming-pool and waded about in wellies.

Two things happened in fairly quick succession. Firstly, I was invited to join a newly-formed rock and roll group, The Citizens. The second was I met my wife-to-be, Jeanette, but let me come back to that. First - The Citizens. I was bored with playing skiffle; it was dying and my mate and mentor, Dave Sills, was ready to move on to traditional jazz anyway. So, it was rock and roll and The Citizens for me. It's amazing how bands were formed in the early sixties. The Citizens came out of a chance meeting at the infamous Smokey Joe's coffee bar in Northfield. This was the seediest den of iniquity in the Midlands; basically, it was a transport cafe with a huge mirror behind the bar onto which was etched the figure of a reclining nude, smoking. That was one of the most sensuous works of art I have ever seen. It also became world famous. I don't know what happened to it when 'Smokes' (as it was affectionately known) was demolished to make way for a shopping centre in the seventies. Rumour has it that it found its way to California and into a bar there; more likely, it ended up in a skip. What a tragedy! Smokey Joe's was owned by a great character and businessman, Les Dews. I don't know how much he got for the sale of the cafe when it was demolished, bearing in mind they built a whole shopping complex on much of it, but the fact that he very nearly bought the Chateau Impney from the proceeds is an indication. He invested in all sorts of projects, including two nice hotels in Malta. Not so successful with those because, when dear villainous Mintoff came to power, he repossessed them for the government - along with so many other businesses. In later years, Les's son, John, became and remains a great mate. Not only did he follow in his father's footsteps as a fine businessman, he now owns the boat marina in Stratford upon Avon and is also a very talented artist. I am proud to have, hanging on my wall at the cottage in Chaddesley, what's best described as a 'dreamscape' which he entitled 'Doug's

Freedom'. Anyway, Smokes was the venue where many a villainous plot was hatched by the criminal fraternity, where clandestine business meetings took place away from the prying eyes of the rest of the board and where designs for new cars were furtively shown. It was also an extra-marital meeting ground and a haven for tramps who would scratch each other's eyes out for a nub-end and where winos spent the time in between pubs' opening hours, topping up a never-ending coffee from a brown paper bag with a bottle of cheap spirits inside it. It was also where Dennis Greaves had a chance meeting with Pete Snipe. They hadn't seen each other since being mates whilst at school, Handsworth Technical College to be precise. Pete was a very accomplished keyboard player and Dennis a lead guitarist. They decided then and there to form a group and the name, The Citizens, came to be over a mug of frothy coffee. Joining them in the weeks that followed were: Twink on rhythm guitar, Neal Walsh on drums and John Hughes as lead vocals. In those days, there was always a singer fronting the band - before The Beatles changed everything. They were gigging within a month of forming and as they were playing a lot of Jerry Lee Lewis, Eddie Cochran and the like, were really ripping a storm wherever they went.

I come into the story at another coffee bar meeting, this time at the Silver Grill, a biker's haunt in Bromsgrove. Twink was a biker and I had got to know him quite well. He told me that, good as the band was, things were not working out with John Hughes fronting on vocals. The others had asked Twink to take over and have a parting of the ways with John.

"Means I can't play guitar as well, though," he told me.

"How about me?" I asked him.

"What about The Deadbeats?" he replied.

"Just about dead!" I told him. "I'm ready to rock, man" (we all called each other 'man' in those early sixties' days), "Skiffle is yesterday's music and I want to be part of today's."

So, I was auditioned at The Black Cross in Bromsgrove. I remember, when I walked into the room, the band was rehearsing the Cliff Richard number 'Do you wanna dance?' I immediately felt at home and became a Citizen there and then. So began my halcyon rock days. More and better gigs and more money. I changed the MGTC for an Austin Healey Sprite, into which my Selmer amp fitted neatly in the boot when you pulled the passenger seat forward to gain access. Only trouble with this was there was no room left for nookie.

We entered the equivalent competition to 'Battle of the Bands', winning our heat and coming second in the all-Midlands finals at the Mecca-owned Locarno Ballroom. The band that won it was Mike Sheridan and the Night Riders who also got a recording contract. But coming second was enough to up the ante yet again as far as money and gigs were concerned. We started to be offered society do's and factory parties like Archdale's, the famous (and now lamented like so much of our manufacturing industry) machine tool company - now, they were big payers. We used the money from our first Archdale's gig to buy band suits. They were the business: chocolate brown, high button jobs, right up to the neck, just like The Beatles' and hand-made by John Hughes the tailor at Longbridge who was getting all the top Birmingham group business (not the same John Hughes who used to sing with us).

One particular booking will be forever etched in my memory: Droitwich Girls School. It was there that we experienced Beatle Mania. The 'Fab Four' were taking the country by storm and screaming fans had become a phenomenon. Well, those Droitwich girls screamed their heads off at us - to the point where it didn't matter what we played, we couldn't even hear ourselves. They stormed the stage and rocked the cars as we left. We felt like gods. As The Citizens started, so it began to end. Dennis had a lust to wander and gave us notice that he was leaving to live in Cornwall for a bit; I think he fancied the romance of a beatnik life style by the sea. It was an amicable split and I took over playing lead and changed the musical direction to a more 'Beatles' style. We got on the Young Farmers Club circuit and did many a hunt ball. Pete Snipe was in demand for session work and even played on the Moody Blues classic 'Go Now'. He was offered a share of the royalties or fifty seven quid; he took the money, which wasn't the wisest decision he would ever make in his life. He became highly sought after as a tour musician too, doing the circuit with some of the greats, including the legendary Chuck Berry.

Twink had had enough and he was looking to settle down and raise a family. Keith Mustow was becoming more and more obsessive about his wife, to the point where his jealousy caused him to smash up his bass guitar in the middle of a set when he didn't like her dancing with some guy. Could never for the life of me see why he was so jealous. Not surprisingly, after the guitar smashing incident, Keith left. He was replaced by Tony Garry, a good bass player, but he worked a fortnight-about on nights at the Austin, so it restricted us taking bookings. I actually took Tony on his honeymoon in a harvest-gold Austin 1100. I drove them down into Spain and when we got to Tarragona there was a fiesta in full swing. I got Tony so pissed he was banned from the matrimonial bed on the first night of his marriage and he ended up sleeping on our floor. Yes, crazy days. So, we didn't really make a conscious decision to finish, just drifted apart. I had the opportunity to join an even bigger band, The Suedes, which is where this book started and my rock and roll career ended.

During that two-year 'Citizen' period I also met some other characters that would influence my musical life: Dave Mason and Jim Capaldi who we played at gigs together with; they were then called The Hellions. They went on to form Traffic with Steve Winwood.

Then there was Mick Banner. He headed up a group called The Playboys, which was a very apt name for him, as he was the ultimate party animal. It was Mick who introduced me to weed and many a night in the flat you could cut the smoke of the rope with a knife. It wasn't that I really liked it, but The Beatles did it and we lesser rock and roll mortals just emulated the lifestyle. But it wasn't just drugs that I learnt about from Mick Banner, he taught me guitar tricks and how to stand on stage like Eddie Cochran. One thing I couldn't copy though was his Cossack act. He would sit on an upside down waste paper bin and move his legs like he was animated; it was an act that had us in fits of laughter and gasps of adulation, especially after a few tokes.

Yes, I had some wild times with Mick Banner and there's more of him to come. We lost touch somewhere down the line; I moved on, he preferred to remain a permanent student. Last I heard, he was trying his hand as an art dealer in Wales. Wherever he is, I wish him well and will always remember him with a smile.

Not long after joining The Citizens, as I said, I met my wife-to-be. It was one night at Bromsgrove Jazz Club, held at the Perry Hall Hotel in Bromsgrove. Dave Sills had dragged me along to watch some band he thought was wonderful and was so unmemorable to me that I can't even remember their name. Anyway, I saw this stunning girl, dressed in the tightest mini skirt and top, with gorgeous brunette hair almost down to her waist. Within seconds I was introducing myself, buying her a drink, dancing and falling in love. Her name was Jeanette Walters and she had twinkling eyes and a wicked sense of humour, matching mine. She was a hairdresser at Victors in Droitwich; later, she was to move to the famed Edward's Coiffeur in Bromsgrove, which was the top ladies salon around. I can't say we became inseparable as there were so many other diversions going on in my life, but we certainly spent a great deal of time together and married a few years later. Malcolm was best man. We had a big church wedding on Passion Sunday at Hanbury Church and a massive reception at The Chalet. One hundred and eighty guests including all my brothers and sisters and their partners and kids were there, along with Dad and Kathleen, Uncle Jess and Margaret, even Auntie Ivy and countless cousins. This was the only time I can recall that the Clark's were together in such numbers. Certainly outnumbered the in-laws by about ten to one. It was when I bought my first real suit, a navy blue three-piece in which I truly felt like the dog's bollocks. Jan had a long-trailed traditional white dress, which she designed herself and had made locally. She looked like a princess and I felt like the king of the castle on that day. It was one hell of a knees-up; so good in fact that I was actually loath to leave the revellers and go off on honeymoon. Malcolm lent me his beloved E-type Jaguar for that journey (down to Fowey in Cornwall) and stood guard to make sure no-one tied tin cans to the bumpers.

V

Jan and I stayed together for twenty nine years, during which time she put up with a lot. Let's say she stayed and I strayed which is why I thought it was fair enough when she divorced me for unreasonable behaviour. The wonder is that she lasted the course for so long. I admit that living with me in those early days was enough to test anyone's sanity and stability. I expect she thought things might calm down, but they never did. Still, she was a hairdresser when I met her and a very wealthy lady when we parted - hair to high society. Jan was the most supportive and understanding of women. Too nice really; on reflection, we were incompatible in most things except the love we still share for a beautiful daughter and grandson.

VI

"Doug'll fix it" became Uncle Jess's catchphrase to customers - and I did indeed 'fix it', sometimes at really silly prices. Uncle Jess liked to be seen as everyone's pal and would charge his friends far less than the going rate, which was really annoying. He would buy new suits, things for his home and even new shoes for my half-brother Noel - that really riled me. When he wasn't taxiing the more important clients, the big tippers, he would sit in the office with his feet up, reading the paper and drinking tea, whilst Malc and I worked our fingers to the bone. The rankle turned into frustration, which might well have boiled over into something as dramatic as moving on - when opportunity knocked.

I used to chat to Harry Brown, the representative from Shell who we bought our petrol from, whenever he came in.

"This really is a dump you know Doug," he said on one occasion.

"Tell me about it," I replied, "but what can I do? Uncle Jess won't spend any money on it."

"How do you think he would take to Shell buying it and doing it up?" Harry asked.

My lips started to twitch with excitement; this was the chance I had been waiting for. "How would Shell feel about me taking it over if Uncle Jess sold to you?"

"I think we could come to some arrangement over that," he said with a smile. So, game on! From that moment my mission was to persuade Uncle Jess it was time to cash in and retire in luxury to his beloved Hagley.

VII

I should explain that by now we had a board of directors, with Uncle Jess in the chair and his wife, Margaret, a director. She was a lovely lady who always tried to be fair to us, much more so than Uncle Jess. She would go for days without speaking to him; some of those fallouts were over his treatment of us. Malcolm and I were made directors too, this was a bit of a meaningless ploy by Uncle Jess to make sure his gift horses didn't go away with his golden apple. He certainly didn't think of increasing our wages or anything like that.

"One day you'll be running things," he used to say.

We were, and had been for a long time. We were now called Clark's Motor Services (Rednal) Limited which was, at least, recognition.

"I think it's time me and Malc had some shares," I announced at the next board meeting.

"You don't need anything fancy like that," said Uncle Jess.

"I can see where they're coming from, Jess," Margaret intervened.

I seized the opportunity and spoke out quite forcefully. "It's not before time, Jess (I dropped the uncle); we're not asking for a share of the profits, just a share of the say in the future. We want to move forward; otherwise, what's the point?"

That clinched it; realising that he would still be keeping the lion's share of the money, he agreed. We had the share issue drawn up and a shareholders' agreement put in place, giving Uncle Jess and Margaret 51% and me and Malc 49%. That night we were too excited to sleep and chatted away till the early hours. My plan was in place; now I could really talk to Shell. I was using my brain in ways I hadn't comprehended before. That might sound strange, but it was like it was actually evolving - brain power I suppose. When sleep eventually came, I dreamt of clean garages, attendants in pristine uniforms, a beautiful girl in a pencil skirt doing the accounts, a staff canteen, other garages. But it was then just a dream.

VIII

It was about this time that I caught our first thief. I was on my own in The Little Garage and no one was on the pumps. We rarely left the kiosk unattended, but Jess had been called away next door and Malc wasn't working. Anyway, I had to go up to The Barracks for a packet of fags and en route I noticed this figure standing by the till. On closer inspection I saw he was stuffing his pockets full of money. I quickly tried to shut the door and lock him in, but he realised what was happening and charged me. He was a big chap and I went flying. He leapt onto his BSA Bantam, which he had obviously brought in to fill up and, seeing the place unattended, had commenced his opportunistic thievery. As he tried to get on board the bike with me now on my feet and advancing, he caught his trouser leg on a saddle spring and ripped his cavalry twills from top to bottom. He zoomed off with the material flapping in the wind like a flag.

I jumped into the Queen Mary, an Austin 16, and commenced a 'cops and robbers' chase, which went on for a few miles. Eventually, I forced him over onto the central reservation outside the Kalamazoo factory where he tumbled over the handlebars and fell off. He staggered up dazed and dishevelled and tried to run. By now there were lots of onlookers who I called to "stop thief!" He was pounced on and I made my one and only citizen's arrest.

IX

Since Malc was working on the pumps, the petrol business had increased quite dramatically. This meant that we would run out of petrol, as like as not, before delivery date; so, I had an idea to rectify that position. As I told you earlier, Jess had bought up the two cottages and another two that the antique shop was housed in. Whilst the antique place was still occupied, there came a time when the first two cottages were unoccupied. Jess was all set to rent them out, but I managed to persuade him that they would be worth much more to him demolished.

"How do you work that out Douglas?" He asked me quizzically at a board meeting (which were now held weekly - not in working hours).

"Well," I started, "with them out of the way we can put in a much bigger storage tank, three times the size, I reckon. Means we wouldn't run out, sales would go up as people would find us more reliable. Means we'd get more regulars."

"What about my rents?" He asked.

"You'll get more return from petrol. Look, I've done some figures," I replied, prepared for the question.

He looked at them for a minute then handed them to Margaret.

"Impressive, Douglas," she beamed at me.

Jess scowled, he didn't like any idea that he hadn't thought of. Good job he didn't realise what was going on in my mind: that it would make a nice space for the workshops I wanted Shell to build for us. "No, no, no! It'll cost a small fortune to get them demolished. I'm sorry, Douglas, but you haven't thought this through," he said, as wisely and smugly as he could muster.

"I'll do it," I told him. "All it will cost you is a sledgehammer and a crowbar, and I've already got them - bought them just in case - here's the receipt. Let me do it this weekend and I'll have them razed to the ground by Monday morning," I said determinedly and stared him straight in the eye.

"You know nothing about demolition boy, be serious," he stared back.

"I couldn't build them, but it's not rocket science to bring them down; trust me Uncle." I softened my tone.

"Then there's the tank, that's got to be fitted," he added.

"I'll do that too. I'll fit the tank and get Shell to connect it up. We built the pit, remember - me and Malc." It was in the balance now, I knew he could jump either way.

"Well, I suppose you could give it a crack; don't want to hold back progress now, do we? Never call me a Luddite," he conceded after a pause. "give him the ten bob out of petty cash for the hammer, Margaret."

X

So it came to pass that Douglas Clark, sledgehammer in hand and crowbar through belt, demolished the cottages. I smashed in the roof first then worked down, which seemed logical to me. At the end of the weekend the only thing that remained was a smouldering bonfire as Malc and I burnt anything that was combustible. The bricks we broke into hardcore to form a base for the new yard, which was to be concreted over later. I was black and blue, with biceps like Mr. Universe, knackered but proud at what I had achieved.

Malc brought me a beer by the fire. "Fabulous Clark Brothers strike again," he said.

"One day, Malc;" I said, "one day soon, you're going to see a phoenix rising from the ashes here. It's going to be the most state-of-the-art garage in the midlands, if not the world."

"You know what, Doug?" He said.

"What?" I asked.

"I believe you."

And he did.

XI

We put a three-thousand gallon tank on that site, not without it falling over into a big trench we'd dug though. Well, I think I'd done pretty well to get that far without mishap. Took half a day to rectify it; much to the amusement of George Smart and a few other neighbours.

Over the next twelve months I had many a clandestine meeting with the people from Shell until the point where I had a gentleman's agreement that, if I could persuade Uncle Jess to sell the garage to them, then they would gut it and renovate it, keep the contract for petrol, but sell the business to me and Malcolm. We would keep all the servicing profits and they would build us a little forecourt shop. They had no idea why I wanted that as part of the deal, but then they didn't know what was going on inside my head.

XII

I broached the subject of Shell at the next board meeting.

"I was talking to Harry Brown the other day," I told Uncle Jess innocently. "He told me that Shell have a policy of buying up small garages at the moment and turning them into Shell garages."

"They wouldn't be interested in this one," Jess responded.

"No, probably not, but I could ask the question if you like." I sowed the seed.

"No. No, we're all right as we are and, besides, what would you boys do? I want to be fair."

"You're not getting any younger Uncle, and they might let us stay on and run it. If not, then we could take our share and go and get a job somewhere else," I replied.

"Your share?" He raised his eyebrows.

"Yes, their share," Margaret smiled; "They have forty-nine percent, remember."

"Yes, and we have fifty one, which means that we make the decisions," he said, resuming his composure.

"Tell you what Uncle: you talk to them, but only if you want, then come back and tell us what you think we should do, if anything," I beamed and the lower lip started to twitch. He was hooked.

XIII

I was straight on the phone to Harry. We arranged that he should drop by casually and let Jess make the approach. A few days later, he did just that. Jess called him into the office and sent Malc for a jug of tea from the cafe next door. They were in there a long time. When he had gone I couldn't restrain myself from asking how it went. "Like I said, they're not really interested in little garages like ours," he lied.

The man from Shell rang me that night; Jess was ready to sell, it was just a question of how much. Obviously, I wanted them to get it for as little as possible as we were going to buy it back at the same price.

The cloak and dagger stuff went on 'til a sale was finally agreed. Uncle Jess sombrely told us of his decision at the only extraordinary board meeting we ever held.

"I think they'll be willing to give you a crack at running it, lads, but you won't have me there to guide you. Could you cope? After all, you're mechanics; running a business is very different," he lectured us. Jess was on a roll and enjoying it.

"We'll try not to let you down, Uncle Jess, if they give us the chance. We just want to see you and Margaret enjoying retirement in a little luxury. Me and Malc have got all our lives ahead of us."

"That's very nice of you, Douglas," Margaret beamed.

"Just one thing, Uncle Jess; if we are going to be involved in the future in some small way, would you mind if I talked to them about the development plans?" I asked.

"Don't see a problem with that. Frankly I'm not interested, but they haven't agreed to you running it yet so don't jump your guns," he told me.

"Of course not," I said, putting on my best poker face. In true Doug Clark style, I had already drawn out how I'd like the garage too look in freehand and had shown it to them.

XIV

In games of poker it's no use counting your money whilst sitting at the table. What I learnt then was another salutary lesson. Always read and re-read the small print and, when you've done that, get it checked over by a legal eagle. Oh yes, me and Malc had 49% all right; voting shares only though, not equity. Uncle Jess was set to get the lot. I rang my man from Shell and said we wouldn't be in a position to buy it right away so would they rent it to us in the meantime?

I might have felt a prat, but I certainly didn't sound like one and they agreed. So, Uncle Jess signed the business over to Shell. I didn't sleep too well that night. What if Shell did us over? There was no legal obligation to rent it to us for now and sell it to us later. Furthermore, even if they kept their word on that issue, would they keep their word on the price? "Small point, Doug," Malc said from his bed. "Where's the money coming from to buy it?"

"We'll have to sell our cars and bikes; in fact, sell everything we can, and what we can't raise we'll borrow," I told him, "and we'll work - round the clock if necessary."

"I suppose we could go to Dad," he ventured.

"That's a definite no! Even if he would help, which I doubt, we'd have another Uncle Jess on our hands. No thanks, it's me and you Malc."

"The Fabulous Clark Brothers," Malc responded.

"You've got it," I told him and with that, finally went to sleep.

XV

This was 1963. The year of the big epic movies: 'Cleopatra' and 'Lawrence of Arabia'; the year 'Doctor Who' was first broadcast on BBC television; the year of Beatlemania, with 'Love Me Do', 'Please, Please Me' and 'I Want To Hold Your Hand' all making number one; the year Buddy Holly sang 'Bo Diddly' and Lesley Gore told us 'It's My Party'; the year film director Quentin Tarantino was born; the year the great country singer Patsy Cline was killed in a plane crash; the year the infamous Alcatraz prison was closed; the year Dr. Beeching axed a huge chunk of the railway network; the year of the great train robbery; the year of the big freeze and the year President John F. Kennedy was assassinated. But for us, it was the year that we started in business.

5 – Growing Pains And Pleasures

I

As soon as Jess got his money he was off. The only time we saw him was when he came in for free repairs. He seemed to think that was his right. He'd park his black Austin 16 right in the centre of the forecourt, put his hands on his braces and call out.

"Ah boys, one of you take a look at this for me please, bit of a rattle coming from somewhere. Not busy are you?"

I don't think he thought the development would actually happen; but then it didn't really bother him, he'd got his money and could spend all his time on permanent holiday. I know he bought young Noel yet another pair of new shoes out of the proceeds, as he proudly showed them to me once when he was filling up, but I don't know what else; I'm sure he was well catered for though. All we got was to toast his departure in a jug of tea. But you know what? That was Dom Perignon to me and Malc.

II

Shell was as good as their word; they rented the garage back to us and we started to make some serious money from day one. We continued to work whilst planning permission was obtained, which took nigh on a year. Now all the profits were ours. Boy, did we work; every car serviced was a bit more of the business we were, one day, going to buy and there was more than enough to treat ourselves to some goodies - like grass track bikes and, guess what?

There came another Clark brother into the Fabulous Clark Brothers: Noel of 'new shoes' fame. Not in the business, but in racing. I had to go and see Dad to get something signed, which gave me the opportunity to really talk to Noel for the first time. He showed me the bikes he had built in his workshop and told me about his racing. All the bitterness towards the golden child drained away and I saw him for the thoroughly nice chap he is. When we later raced as the 'Fabulous Clark Brothers', there were three of us. The bikes, incidentally, ran on methanol, a wood alcohol so clear you can't see the flame once ignited. It's an extremely high-performance fuel and is being heralded today as one of the leading environmental possibilities.

Besides the bikes, I also bought a speedboat, which I think I used once. I even changed my brand of cigarette to Dunhill International and bought them in packs of two hundred. When we went clubbing, it was always with a big wad of notes in the back pocket. Our champagne fountains at the Cedar Club were legendary. In those days champagne glasses had the wide 'Babycham' type bowls and could be stacked like a pyramid. We would do this on the counter and pour Moet into the top and let it flow. Then we would be hosts to all the totty and friends - and the hangers on. There was an advert on TV for a brand of cigarettes called Strand; it featured this guy in a raincoat and had the message: "You're never alone with a Strand". Well, we adopted this to our own saying: "You're never alone with a grand."

I don't regret those days; when you come from nothing and then have money coming out of your ears, I think you're entitled to a mad period. This new-found wealth made me realise just how much Jess had been taking out of the business and, believe me, removed any last remaining conscience I may have had about dealing behind his back.

III

The M5 motorway opened and we started getting lots of calls to taxi people away from the many breakdowns happening on it. We didn't go for any repair works though because we weren't geared up to do that, but the ferrying was highly lucrative - and to all parts of the country, even as far as Scotland.

We also had some regular private taxi work. One customer we inherited from Jess was the Wilson family of the chemical company, Albright and Wilson. The house was just outside Hereford and, most of the time, I just had to sit in the servants' quarters and wait until, and if, the bell rang and a family member needed taking to, or fetching from, somewhere. Paid all day just to sit, drink coffee and read the paper. Little wonder Jess kept that one to himself.

IV

So busy were we, in fact, that we took on staff. Firstly, there was Arthur Webb, a nice old pensioner who would open up early, serve the petrol and leave us free to concentrate on the servicing. He took a little time to learn the ropes as he didn't drive himself. One day, not long after he had started, Arthur mistakenly filled someone's oil sump rather than the radiator with water from a can. It was a long job to drain, clean and refill it with oil. Was I angry with him? Not really; it was a genuine mistake and even the customer had a good laugh at the naivety of it. I can always forgive failure, but I can't forgive not trying and Arthur certainly tried all right.

Another amusing incident was when Arthur came to me, when I was under a car, saying "Sorry to trouble you boss, but there's a bloke out on the forecourt that keeps buying quarts of oil; he's on his sixth now."

"Best take a look then," I said and, wiping down my own oily hands on my already filthy overalls, I went across to investigate. What greeted me, you would not believe. This well dressed, middle aged man, who had obviously never looked under the bonnet of a car in his life, was attempting to top the oil level up – through the dipstick hole. Ninety five percent of every bottle was going straight onto the forecourt. Peoples' naivety when it comes to the simple things in motoring never ceases to amaze me.

V

Next came Clive Godbolt; he was about eighteen and the son of a good customer. Clive was always hanging around and helping out, so I thought let's take him on full time. What a star he turned out to be as well. He enjoyed the same work ethic as me and Malc and the fact that he had a wicked sense of humour and was a thoroughly nice chap made it all the more of a special relationship. All three of us started attending the grass track events together at the weekends. Me and Malc raced and Clive was the pit man. We were like the three musketeers, inseparable. Clive was like another brother to us both. If events had not taken the course they did later that year, I believe he would have become an equal partner with us.

We nicknamed Clive 'The Guardian of the Pit'. That was because he stopped lots of customers from falling into it. Not all of them though. When our Guardian wasn't there, having gone off to make the tea or something, we got used to the occasional cry of anguish emitting from the depths and would run over to see the inevitable pair of feet pointing skywards. Today, the ambulance chasers would have a field day, but then it was just treated as a joke with no-one hurt - except for pride and a few scratches.

The pit, which was full of water with oil floating on it, would catch fire quite regularly too, usually through a customer flicking a lighted nub end into it. Most times it would be a quick flambé and then go out, but on a couple of occasions it was not so. Once, a customer, Mr. Edgely, a local pig farmer, was chatting to Clive and sharing a joke and a fag - he was belly laughing one minute and then disappearing backwards the next, fag in hand. A blast of flame came up before he did. We rescued him, but what a bedraggled, filthy and scorched individual he was. He was so dazed I think he thought for one minute he was in Hades; then recollection struck and he started to laugh and laugh and laugh.

Another 'tale from the pit' involved a customer called Mr. Barrett; he lived in Leach Green Lane, Rednal, and rode an old Panther motor cycle, which we looked after for him. Well, he sold the bike and bought a three wheel Reliant Robin. Now, if ever there was a dangerous car built, that was it. As it only had three wheels you could drive it on a motor bike licence with no need for a driving test. That made it an ideal vehicle for single pensioners who had ridden bikes till their arthritis kicked in. Unfortunately, it attracted the worst kind of drivers and the number of accidents involving Reliant Robins was legendary. Anyway, on the day Mr. Barrett became the proud owner of a three wheeler, he came in to fill up his new pride and joy with his very young granddaughter in the passenger seat. He was making for the pumps when his foot slipped from brake to accelerator and he charged full pelt towards and into the pit. We rushed over and quickly pulled the little girl out, whilst Mr. Barrett, still in a total state of shock, was unable to remove his foot from the accelerator as it had got jammed. The car was like something from a science fiction movie, with a mind of its own, trying to scale the pit. We eventually managed to turn off the engine and free him from his watery prison.

Would you believe that on the same day, indeed, not an hour after we had manhandled the Reliant Robin out of the pit, it claimed another victim? This was Don the Rep from J. R. Riley; he sold oil filters and always dressed in a nice suit. We used to chant: "Don from Riley's, they speak of so highly," to herald his arrival. Well, this time there was no welcoming committee so he came to find me and, with hand extended to shake mine, walked towards me with a broad smile. In true salesman-like manner he held my gaze as he advanced; unfortunately, I was on the other side of the pit and he walked straight into it, slipped on the bottom and disappeared totally under the water. I took him up to The Barracks to dry his clothes out on the paraffin heater. He sat there in my dressing gown nursing a mug of tea. "Clive," I called, "for Christ's sake, put a car over that pit so nothing else goes in it today."

The worst pit incident though was when I was cleaning off some brake shoes. This involved soaking them with petrol then burning off the deposits with a blowtorch. Well, something happened to make one of those fast moving trails of fire like you see when someone has lit a dynamite fuse in a cowboy movie. Only my trail was heading straight for the petrol can. In one movement the fire trail reached the can and quick-thinking Clive kicked the can into the pit where the can exploded in the oil filled water. The car being serviced above it lifted into the air and bounced down again surrounded by flames and Clive was blown out of the workshop like Superman, with timbers from the roof following him. Meanwhile, a customer that was filling up at the pumps, thinking his number was up, leapt into his car and took off with the hose still locked into his petrol tank. This pulled the whole petrol pump out of its very shaky base, which attempted to follow him until the hose stretched so far that it broke off and boomeranged back, whacking the car, then bounced like a yo-yo along the road beside him. At the same time this was happening, a petrol tanker was about to off-load a bit of contraband into our freestanding tank. Fortune smiled as he was not yet connected and, seeing the danger, reversed swiftly out into the road, straight into and bringing down the pedestrian crossing pelican lights. All this occurred in the space of seconds - just like a scene from a Bruce Willis Die Hard movie.

The only real victim was the car over the pit, it was one huge mess. The number plates had melted to the point that the registration looked as if it had been written in Arabic. The customer wasn't due back until the end of the day and so Clive, Malc and me worked at a pace like they do on a makeover show. We changed bits, cleaned bits, polished and polished and polished - inside and out until it gleamed. The only things missing from the car when he returned were the number plates. I made up some cock-and-bull story that they were cracked and barely legal. The new ones arrived about thirty minutes later and we waved him on his merry way in what truly was his phoenix raised from the ashes.

VI

Now, besides all the amusing anecdotes, it is important that I paint a picture of how we operated during that year. You must remember that I had been raised in an environment of organized chaos so far as garages were concerned. Both Gramp's and Grandad's were untidy workplaces. Bits of machinery were strewn everywhere and, to the onlooker, they must have appeared more of a scrap yard than anything resembling a garage. In fact, when Dad took over from Gramps he did just that - turned the land at the side of Bluntington into a breaker's yard for scrap cars. The neighbours loved that as you can imagine. Clark's Motor Services was, if anything, worse. It was dirty and reeked of oil; Clark's shanty town more like. But I really knew no better. To my mind, the important thing was the quality of the work and that was first rate, which was why it boomed. There were no dissatisfied customers and everyone accepted us for what we were. Well, not everyone; a chance remark from a man in a very smart tweed jacket, who had come to collect his car, set me thinking.

"Douglas Clark?" He asked.

"Yes," I held out an oily hand which he declined.

"Dennis Overton," he announced. "I run an antiques business in Northfield. I came to you because I was recommended and I'm sure you've done a grand job. Are you up for a bit of advice though, young man?"

"Always willing to learn, Mr. Overton," I grinned amiably.

"Call me Dennis," he told me.

"Right then, I'm Doug," I replied. "Sorry about the greasy hands, just changing an oil sump."

"Not a problem," he started. "As I said, Doug, I'm in the antiques business; now, what sets me apart from a junk shop is purely cosmetic. Are you with me?"

"Not really, Mr. Overton," I confessed, confused by what his antique business had to do with me. Best send him up to aunty Ivy I thought.

"Every day my shop is cleaned; once a week all the brass-ware is polished, likewise the silver every fortnight, the glass, every other day. Everything is displayed to attract the customer and I move an item or two every day to entice them in. I spray my shop with musk; in short, I create an atmosphere which is akin to my trade. What sort of atmosphere do you think you create?"

"Oh, one of a garage where we know what we are doing," I told him, pleased at the intelligence of my reply.

"Douglas... Doug," he corrected himself. "I believe you have a unique gift. I have watched you innovate as I drive to work; the tank over there and the hole in the ground."

"The pit," I told him.

"Quite! You have vision and you will, without doubt in my opinion, one day become a millionaire," he said, very matter-of-factly.

"You think?" I smiled.

"I know," he responded, "but the advice I would give you is to treat your workplace as you would your home. In fact, build your business as you would a house, with thought and care and pride in showing people your abode."

"Well, we're just waiting for planning permission and all this is going to change: proper workshops, new pumps and forecourt," I started.

"And will you keep it clean and tidy?" He asked meaningfully.

"I'll take on board what you've said," I humoured him. "It makes sense, but I do run a garage, not a shop."

"It makes no difference. You run a business that is fed by the public coming through your door. What they see is not what they get; they are pleasantly surprised by the quality of the work. How much better if they were not surprised because the quality of the work was a reflection of the surroundings. And, and this is a big 'and', they would be prepared to pay more."

With that, Dennis Overton left the building, but not my life. Over the years, we became good friends and he taught me much about antiques. At that particular stage his words sank in - but not too far. We were making money, big money; maybe if we got a cleaner? "Wait till the development happens," I told myself. Then, lighting up a Dunhill, I remembered my dream about people in pristine uniforms and secretaries in miniskirts.

As I daydreamed I looked up, beyond the garage to the hundred feet of wasteland that rose like a dinosaur to the foot of the woodland behind it, and another idea came to me. "Why hadn't I thought of that before?" I asked myself. Dennis said I had vision; well, I had vision now all right. That land was like landing on Mayfair when playing Monopoly and I was going to buy Mayfair. And I did just that, three months later, from Shell for five grand. They considered it unusable, I thought otherwise. Game on!

VII

Talking of games, the one I most enjoyed was speed. We were grass-tracking most weekends now and starting to win, though brother Noel still beat us most of the time on his state-of-the-art machine. That's to take nothing away from his skills; he was an ace in every racing sense. I suppose my edge was that, when on the machine, I was fearless.

I don't know how much you know about grass tracking but it's fast and furious and a great spectator sport to boot. But it's not just about being fearless; it's a combination of that and science. Quick thinking and action, combining together in lightning reactions.

The bikes differ from speedway bikes in that the suspension is at the rear. The races take place on 600 to 800 yard oval race tracks. There are four laps to a heat and six for the final. We used to attract big crowds at the meetings throughout Wales and the Midlands including Carmarthen, Prestatyn, the Shrewsbury Flower Show and at the famous Three Counties Show, The Fabulous Clark Brothers were the finale of the event and everyone flocked to see our expertise and exploits.

I still have lots of silverware from those days, including the SS Great Britain trophy, The 500, The Unlimited and Fastest Rider of the Day at the same meeting in Bristol. Dad actually took me down to collect the trophies at the gala dinner. Noel was there too, but it was my day and it made it all the more so to see the pride in my Dad's eyes as I went up to the stage.

I was privileged to race against the best, including world champions Peter Collins and Ivan Major (world champion four times and, yes, he beat me, but only just). I even rode in one race with a broken foot. That was at Shrewsbury; I was taking a turn and my foot slipped off the rest and was pulled backwards, snapping it. I ignored the pain and went on to win. Afterwards, I couldn't even stand on it, but managed to drive to a hospital where it was set in plaster and I was out of bike racing for a few months.

Undeterred by accidents and broken bones, Noel, Malc and I went on to race speedway bikes at the Wolverhampton stadium. However, it wasn't enough.

VIII

The ultimate in car stunts is to do something illegal, something to get the blood racing and something to be talked about. What we did was to create a late-night race track and parade ground just outside Barnt Green. Word of mouth would get around when it was going to take place and there was always a good crowd turning out to watch, such became its notoriety. We gave it this wonderful title of 'lapping'. "Is there any lapping going on tonight, Doug?" people would ask me in hushed whispers. There were all sorts of cars: E-types and Lotus, you name it. We would start off by just promenading up and down like gladiators, seeking the adoration of the crowd before the games begun. Then we would race, spin and perform stunts that would grace any James Bond film; in fact, that's where we got a few ideas from.

One night etched in the memory of all those illegal racers was when we were doing a particularly dangerous stunt involving 'banking' the cars without flipping them over. I was driving a highly-charged Cooper 'S', Malc his beloved

E-type and Dick Eggington, who was the son of the Secretary of Delson and Co (the high-end non-ferrous fittings company), a motor bike sprinter and a real Jack-the-lad in a brand new beast of a machine, a Lotus Cortina. I'd supplied us all with false plates. Malc went first in the E type and did some very impressive wheelies and 180° turns with much screeching of brakes. I had Mick Banner with me and we had opted to go last, topping the bill. Dick followed Malc and well, it proved one stunt too many for him. We were starting some way back and gave it a reasonable time before gunning it into the straight where we saw a firework display up ahead. I thought, at first, Dick's Cortina had caught fire, however in reality, he had flipped the beast onto its side and careered down the road sparking like a firework display. That is before it broke up into pieces leaving him sitting in middle of the road on the driver's seat clutching the wheel, which was all that was left of the car. There was glass and debris everywhere which I narrowly avoided, but in doing so, spun so hard that Mick Banner flew out of the passenger seat and landed head first in the ditch. I got out of there double-quick and concealed my car in the woods, creeping back down again to find Mick, muddy, high as a kite and chuckling away, perusing the crime scene from an excellent vantage point behind a hedge. The police, lead by 'Jock', our local copper, were swarming over the area trying to make sense of it. Mick Banner couldn't contain himself and shouted "Evening all," followed by "Hoots mon, there's a moose loose aboot this hoose." A taunt often reserved for Jock.

"I'll 'ave ye buggers," Jock cried out. "Clark, is that you?"

There was nothing for it, but to leg it into the woods with Jock and his crew in hot pursuit, torches blazing like searchlights. It was a close call, but we made it back to the Barracks and were drinking tea innocently when they arrived.

"I canne prove it, but I noo ye wus a-racin' Douglas Clark," Jock scolded. "Och, give us a brew then get your breakdown wagon down there and pick up the pieces."

I think, in a way, there was admiration in his voice, but also a warning and I knew it was time to call a halt to that period of excitement. Local papers were full of it and Dick's wife gave him hell. Jan, bless her heart, laughed it off.

It was Clive's idea to perform our biggest and most outrageous stunt, though. This was to stage a hold-up and a shooting in Wychbold. This involved blasting away at each other with starting pistols and culminated by bundling Clive into the boot of a Jenson A40 - the one with the hood and looking every inch a mob car. It was a carefully arranged sequence of events and would have made a great movie sequence. That romp went on to become folklore.

Another time we concealed a five-gallon water tank in the back of a Mini and, with high pressure sprays, proceeded to wage watery havoc on the shoppers in Bromsgrove High Street. Tears of laughter ran down our faces as they looked to the heavens for the source of the drenching.

Yes, they were mad, halcyon days; life was a blast with no time to sleep, just work and play to the maximum. The Rum Runner, The Cedar Club and The Opposite Lock became our nocturnal playgrounds; four hours sleep and back to business.

IX

It was after a particularly successful day for Noel at the Builth Wells Agricultural Show, where he had won everything, when tragedy struck. We travelled in convoy with the bikes strapped to the back of the cars. I was leading the convoy when I realised there was no-one behind me. I turned back at Hay-on-Wye. Clive was driving the middle car with Kevin Clark (Ernie's son) in the passenger seat. Drawing up the rear was Malcolm and helper, Brian Merrick. I found the road cordoned off and I was told by the police that there had been a terrible accident.

No-one really knows what happened. Clive had just hit a bank head on. He died on impact. Kevin was thrown clear but suffered severe neck and back injuries. Later, he recalled Clive just passing out at the wheel before the crash; maybe a blood clot on the brain or a heart attack. Malcolm tried vainly to give him the kiss of life when he got there and, when that failed, just cradled him in his arms till the ambulance men arrived. We'll never really know the cause, but a young life was tragically taken and a wonderful friend went from my life forever.

The next week I received news that planning permission had at last been granted and work could commence. A new era, the most exciting era, was about to begin and, sadly, Clive, who had dreamed along with us of this moment, wasn't there to enjoy it. Life can be wonderful, but also a bitch.

6 – Steptoe And Bro

I

In the year we waited to get the planning permission we continued to live and party in our 'palace' above The Barracks, right up to the day the demolition squad moved in. By that point, I'd saved enough to buy a house. Well, not quite enough. I sold most of my trappings of early success: the speedboat I'd bought, but rarely had time to use, my Austin Healy sprite, my Selmer amp and yes, my beloved Gibson 335, the last bastion of a rock and roll career I'd had the reluctant courage to turn my back on after the '2 I's'. I had bought that Gibson for a hundred and twenty guineas from Jones and Crossland, the foremost music shop in Birmingham and sold it for quite a bit less - needs must. Today, it would be worth over eighteen grand.

Still, the way I look at it: everything is relative. Who in their wildest dreams could have forecast the phenomenal upward spiral of the price of property? It had, after all, been fairly stable for two decades. House ownership became the affordable dream of the new generation, the sixties children whose aspirations far exceeded those of their parents. We pushed back the barriers in everything from music to business and wanted to have something to show for it: our own homes complete with cocktail bars and barbeque patios. The demand for houses soon outstripped supply. On new developments people often queued all night for the sales office to open and paid cash deposits as they picked out their precious plot of land and style of property. House prices were already starting to rise. It's like climbing a mountain and what you will pay for a glass of water on the way up. That mountain of house ownership was covered in climbers from the middle sixties onwards. Despite plenty of economic forecasters predicting a burst to the bubble, with the exception of a few market corrections due to reverse-equity situations, the number of mountaineers has just continued to grow. After all, living on a small island with an expanding population means that demand will always outstrip supply. The developers got rich and the house owners were delighted with their investments.

I bought a superb detached house, number two, Barnt Green Road and paid just under four and half grand for it. Today, it would be worth at least 400k.

Malcolm moved with me and Jan. Ah yes, I should mention that we got married just before the big move.

I'm not sure what happened to Aunty Ivy and co. I'm sure Jess didn't do them any favours, but go they did with a removal van crammed full of Auntie's worthless antiques.

II

So, on Monday the 5th of June 1965, at first light, in came the bulldozers and the men in hard hats. A little different from me in my torn jeans with sledgehammer accessory when I demolished the cottages. The Barracks was first on the demolition list. It creaked and crumbled, then sighed a sad farewell as it was attacked with a giant swinging steel ball, which gouged holes in its side like a medieval battle scene. I suppose I could never be described as sentimental when it came to demolishing a building, my vision was always focused on what was going to replace it. However, I must admit to a flood of memories as I watched it come down. A lot of them horny; I had pounded a lot of flesh there, but it was here Malc had become a man at a fairly tender age and where all the planning and plotting had gone on; which was at last no longer a dream, but reality.

With reality comes responsibility. Along with the destruction of the Barracks came the end of our workshop.

"We can't close up shop for months," I told Malc and he agreed. "After all, if our customers go elsewhere for their servicing in the meantime, there's a good chance they wouldn't come back." So, in typical Doug Clark 'there are no problems only solutions' mode, I found salvation in army surplus. I bought these two steel-framed and camouflaged canopies that fit on top of army trucks. We erected them on oil drums filled with stones on the open site where the two cottages used to stand. Finding we needed still more space to meet demand, we cheekily also used the tram shelter at the terminus across the road. Under that magnificent Victorian cantilevered glass roof, people queued in amazement for their buses whilst we worked on the motors. The drivers even shared a mug of tea with us and asked for tips on how to do things like change a gasket. Thankfully, the customers still came in their droves and with the added novelty value of having their car serviced by the 'Steptoe and Brother' of the motor trade.

III

One of the biggest sources of revenues was sub-frame replacement. This was a major fault with the Mini's and the Morris and Austin 1100s, but we didn't complain.

However, such was our zeal to change sub-frames that, one day, we took a perfectly innocent Mini to pieces by mistake. Some poor commuter had parked his perfectly okay Mini by the tram station for the day, whilst he went off to work in Birmingham city centre. On his return, I found him scratching his head in disbelief to find his pride and joy disassembled and jacked up on bricks. Luckily, he had a very good sense of humour and, once I had grovelled, saw the funny side. Our innocent motorist was given a free service the very next week and went on to become a regular customer, so there was a silver lining to this sorry tale.

A gorgeous lady, Leigh Toogood, who played a big part in my later life adventures, once said "Put a lump of coal up Doug Clark's arse and it'll turn into a diamond within a week." On reflection, I can't deny there were times when I did indeed enjoy a Midas touch, but prefer to think of them as the rewards of taking risks and seizing opportunities. This cock-up, despite being funny, had cost us four hours labour and it made me take time out to implement an improved system of checking the work sheets to prevent a recurrence.

As always with us, 'The Case of the Wrong Mini' was not the only hilarious incident in that period. One that still makes me chuckle today is 'Colonel Terry and the Mower'. We were still servicing anything that anyone brought to us in 1965 and that included the odd lawn mower.

Colonel Terry lived in a mansion down Mearse Lane, which was locally known as 'Millionaire's Row'. It had extensive grounds with many lawns and an old eccentric gardener named Potter to tend them. The colonel had purchased this enormous, one-off industrial mower at some agricultural show - I think it was probably a prototype. It was huge and had a roller on the back that was more appropriate for working a cricket pitch than a domestic lawn. Anyway, it was a bit of a rogue elephant and was back and forth to us on a regular basis with breakdowns and complaints of being sluggish. So, in frustration and in one moment of madness, I took the engine governor off whilst working on it and 'forgot' to put it back. Well, effectively this turned this sedate contraption into an almighty racing machine.

Normally, I would wait and see that it was working satisfactorily when I dropped it off. However, I'd left the engine out of a Cooper 'S' back at the tram station and I had to get it back in before it got dark, so I didn't hang around, but left the gardener with the immortal words: "It'll go like a rocket now."

Well, when old Potter turned the key, revved it up and put his pedal to the metal, he embarked on a trail of destruction throughout the grounds, leaving havoc and devastation in his wake. As he hung on to the wheel for grim death, foot glued to the accelerator, he tore up flower beds, flattened fruit and vegetable patches with the roller thumping along behind him like a medieval instrument of war. Finally, he turned it over in a successful, last-minute manoeuvre to narrowly avoid landing in a pool.

I got a distress call from the great house and shot up there quickly, reconnecting the governor before the colonel realised what had happened and decided to sue our arses to high heaven. Old Potter was a bit bruised and battered but I think quite enjoyed the experience as he couldn't stop chuckling, "Oh my Lord," over and over again.

Many years later I bumped into some of Colonel Terry's family at the Barnt Green Inn. Over a drink I confessed the truth of the matter and we all ended up in such fits of laughter no-one could speak.

Customers are the life-blood of any business, without them there wouldn't be one. So I've always tried to make everyone feel a bit special. That was one thing I did learn from Jess: it's not enough to simply do an excellent job, it's equally important to get on first name terms. It also makes work a lot more fun, with many of my best friends starting out as customers.

In those early days some customers could be pedantic, checking every little detail over and over again and coming to you to complain over the most trivial of matters. "Always listen and always do what they want," I told Malcolm.

One of the most pedantic of all was a Mr. Corbett. He had a company vehicle, a Hillman Minx, which he kept in the most pristine condition. You would never see it dirty or with a blemish on it. As he needed the car every day for work, he always asked for it to be serviced in the evening, a request which we naturally obliged. It was not a unique request and we carried out the evening duty for other customers too. The difference was that Mr. Corbett would stay whilst the servicing was carried out and always insisted on checking his own points. Without a doubt he was a perfectionist and I respected him for that.

Such was some customers' faith in us that they would seek advice on things we didn't do at that stage, like bodywork and where to go for the best paint job. Pretty soon I was compiling a list of the best suppliers and potential partners, another learning curve down the road to good business practice.

A customer that became a friend was my doctor, Doctor Brooks from Ormscliffe Road in Rednal. His surgery was actually the front room of his house. He was a no-nonsense ex-army doctor with a wicked sense of humour and a heart of gold. As he gave me, Malc and Jan free private treatment, most times we would service his Ford Capri for gratis. He had obviously been pretty high up in the forces and enjoyed some powerful acquaintances. I recall he attended Sir Winston Churchill's funeral at Blenheim Palace.

He was also a practical joker, doing tricks like springing up on you when you least expected it or pulling your legs out from under a car when you were on a trolley. He would tell us the most drawn-out of jokes which weren't really that funny, but the way he told them was. Whenever I saw the comedian, Frank Carson, on television with his catchphrase: "It's the way I tell 'em!" I would think fondly of Dr. Brooks. I reckon he was wasted in a way as a medic, as good as he was; he would have made a wonderful after-dinner speaker. The Blaster Bates of the medical world.

One memorable night, he picked up a hedgehog that was refusing to budge from the middle of the road and put it into the boot of his car, fully intending to return it to the wild. Trouble was: he forgot about it, only recalling his errand of mercy when the most dreadful smell started to fill the car. He couldn't figure out what it was and continued to drive around with it until the stench became so overpowering that it was all he could do to make the small journey to us without passing out. It was then that he remembered the hedgehog. Well, there was not a sign of it in the boot, as it had crawled down the back into a spot unreachable and out of sight, where it had expired and started to decompose badly. It took hours wearing make-shift gas masks to remove the carcass, bit by bit, sinew by sinew and spike by spike. We fumigated the car, sprayed it with everything we could think of, but it still reeked. He sold it not long after that.

IV

Work progressed on the new garage at quite a rapid pace. The forecourt and pumps remained open whilst the first phase was being built. This was a three-bay workshop complete with state-of-the-art hydraulic ramps. There was to be no more water-filled, pond life-infested and disaster-prone pit. These were to be serious service bays and I had already hiked the rates up in my mind to suit. Attached to the workshop were a little motor supplies department-come-office and an oil store.

The new garage was completed after about four months and we moved in, celebrating with a few friends and a keg of beer. We then had to close the petrol forecourt for the next six months whilst the rest of the development was completed.

I suppose in hind-sight that's when I started to get even more passionate about the future. Clark's Motor Services looked serious and I got serious along with it. With three bays we could do three times the amount of work, theoretical-ly. I clubbed less leaving that to young Malc and spent my time, when I wasn't working, making plans. I even started tying knots in socks again to remember to do something important.

The first priority was staff. It made me realise how much I missed Clive, not only as best mate, but also for the massive contribution he made to the busi-ness. So I needed a Clive replacement, a top mechanic; no, two; no, three. The best way to get top staff is to poach them. I knew exactly who I wanted and what I needed to do to get them. That was certainly not to follow Uncles Jess's example and offer them peanuts and a dream. The dream, yes, but with a wage that reflected how highly I rated them and the total commitment I expected from them in return for a more than fair days pay. So I wooed and courted and brought on board Tony Foden, a highly skilled and trained mechanic from the Rolls Royce Dealership in Halesowen. Alongside him came Terry Ashcroft who was wasted at the time in a job at British Leyland that did nothing to test his undoubted skills when it came to mechanics. They both had to adapt a little to the Clark way of doing things though. Not exactly cutting corners, but saving time by ingenuity and sheer brute force.

For example, to get to the gearbox in a Hillman Imp you had to take the engine out. This was, in my opinion, a bad design fault. Doug Clark labour-saving innovation? Stretch the engine mountings with biceps heaving and get to it that way. That little trick used to save at least four hours labour.

This was just one of quite a few short cuts I invented to get the job done quicker and the price remained the same. This was in the days before you put the accumulated work hours on a bill, but rather charged a rate, agreed beforehand, for the job. I think hourly rates are a bit of American rubbish we copied from lawyers anyway. After all, who can prove how many hours labour it takes to do a job and who queries it anyway? It reminds me of the toast: 'Here's to us and those like us, and who's like us? Damned few!'

"If you don't like what we do and how we do it and the fair price we charge," I would tell a potential customer in the nicest way, "then feel free to go to the big boys with their fancy bills and get ripped off."

We took great pride in the quality of our work and if the customer wanted to watch us stretch engine mountings and the like, they were most welcome to do so.

Jan's parents, Olive and Jim, were a great help too in those early days. Always there with a tasty Sunday lunch, the epicurean highlight of our seven-day week.

The petrol forecourt reopened and looked the dog's proverbials. Our transformation was complete. Jess, to his credit, was genuinely bowled over when he came to view it; even Dad approved, which was praise indeed. Business boomed even with the uplift in prices. The sign above the garage stood out like a beacon - 'Clark's Motor Services' flagged up with the distinctive red and yellow branding of Shell. It brought a flow of pride every time I looked at it. We were on our way.

The only downside, although I didn't see it, was that we still had the grease-monkey mentality of the old garage. The new staff had adapted to our dirty way of operating. Initially, Tony protested; after all, he was from the splendours of Rolls Royce. This was not what he had been used to. I told him: "Our motto is to give the best service for the best value and that doesn't mean our customers have to come to a five-star hotel." In the end, he just got on and did the job without further protestation, but still had the cleanest overalls of all of us.

I may be stubborn but once I realise I'm wrong then I'll admit it. It took another visit and a dressing down from Dennis Overton, the antique dealer, to make me see the light.

"Nice place, Douglas," he told me, "you must be very proud."

"I am, Mr. Overton," I responded.

"Dennis," he corrected me.

"Dennis," I repeated.

"Pity you've turned it into a pigsty in five minutes," he sighed quietly but effectively.

"We'd rather work than clean up," I confessed lamely.

"Of course you would," he smiled thinly, "very conducive to a successful business, all this grime, oil and dirt. You carry on, you'll make money, but you'll never become the millionaire we talked about, such a pity."

Then he applied the coup-de-grâce. "You can build pyramids out of house bricks if you want, you know - it may be slower, but it will endure. All depends whether you want a transient business or a legacy, I suppose. Still, if you're happy, Douglas, who am I to criticise?" and with that he smiled once more and left.

This time, although I didn't fully understand his words of wisdom, I listened. He was telling me that, by our slovenly ways, I was missing a golden opportunity. Would I like to eat in a dirty restaurant? No, of course not - so why should customers have to suffer the same fate with a dirty garage? So, with a new mission blazing away, I invested in some serious industrial cleaning materials and fluids and worked alongside my ever-increasing army of petrol-serving pensioners to restore the garage to the condition it was in when we reopened the workshops - in fact, better.

Tony Foden was delighted. Next, having got it looking pristine, I then gave instructions to Tony that he had carte blanche to ensure everyone kept it that way. Every night from then on, the workplace was cleaned before closing. It was actually a pleasure to open the shutters in the mornings. Smart, chocolate-brown gowns replaced the oily overalls and I initiated my first marketing tool by having our name embroidered on the pen pocket.

It was then that I thought up another motto which was to play a great part in the corporate image later on. When Tony joined us he said he'd been 'Clarked'. He meant it as an expression to describe the 'spiel' I had given him to get him on board. I thought, that's just what I want our customers to feel has happened to them too - that they've been 'Clarked', a two way commitment. That idea turned into 'Clark Care' our all-embracing statement of intent, which itself was expanded into the 'Customer Charter'. The customer knew exactly what to expect and we knew what we had to deliver.

V

They say it never rains, but it pours. Having got the business on the road, I decided to take Jan on a much-needed holiday to Ibiza. After all, we'd been working a seven-day week for months on end. This was at the invitation of some customer friends, Keith and June Rose, who owned the best fish and chip shop in Northfield. June was a dark-haired beauty that would set the blood racing of any male and I was no exception. We had a ball, dancing the nights away and swimming, boating and scuba diving in the daytime.

We came back nice and relaxed, only to be greeted by Malcolm telling us we had mushrooms growing under the stairs. He'd discovered these when his foot had gone clean through a rotten floorboard. It appeared my bargain dream home in Barnt Green was absolutely riddled with Merulius Lachrymals or dry rot, as it's more commonly known.

I called in the experts, Rentokil, who confirmed that it was not only dry rot, but one of the worst cases they had ever seen. The upshot was that they wanted two and a half grand to fix it. That was over half what I had paid for the house and there was no way I would consider forking out that much. So there was only one thing to do. That was to apply the 'pit mentality' once again; it was 'roll your sleeves up' time.

Applying the same spec that Rentokil had quoted, me and Malc stripped out every single floor throughout the whole house and treated all of the areas below. Then we added a damp course on the ground floor and put a waterproof membrane over the top; finally, we concreted it.

'Kill or cure', I reckoned and it seemed to work. Not that I intended staying to find out. It's like a car, if you've had a bump or a major repair; you're left with this feeling of dread lest it happens again or worse.

It was time to sell up and move on, into something more manageable for the time being. I told Jan I needed to concentrate solidly on the business for a couple of years and asked if she'd mind if we moved into a flat for a while. Bless her, she readily agreed. So began my period of growing up all over again.

7 – Reality Check

I

I got the fabulous sum of eleven grand for the house in Barnt Green Road. I'd tripled my money in just three years and learnt a salutary lesson in checking out the woodwork.

I wanted to put the money I got from the sale straight into the business and so we rented a functional, two bedroom flat in Middleton Hall Road. This was on a modest development situated between Northfield and Cotteridge, areas of the City of Birmingham.

Jan and I had the largest bedroom and Malc the other smaller one. A bonus was that we had quite a famous neighbour, Jeff Turton or Jefferson as he was better known at the time. He was the lead singer with The Rockin' Berries before going solo. He was a bit of a link to what was happening on the music scene. I enjoyed a drink or two with him on occasions and listening to his 'gig tales' of which stars, from both sides of the Atlantic, they were working with. But, in honesty, though I played lip service to his band stories, I felt not even a twinge of jealousy, as I had put all thoughts of being a rock star well to the back of my mind. So removed was I from what was happening in the world musically that I couldn't even begin to tell you who was in the top ten at that point in time. A few years earlier and I could have given you every lyric, verbatim. My business had well and truly become my new rock and roll.

II

I used part of the money from the sale of the house towards paying Shell for the land at the back of the new garage. I borrowed the rest from Lloyds Bank at Longbridge. That's when I really got to know the manager, Ray Picken, properly.

Ray wanted to know what I was going to do with the land. I told him I was going to develop it at some point, but couldn't put a timetable to it just yet. It was to his credit that he showed the faith in me at that stage to trust my long-term judgement. Those were the days of real bank managers, when you sat across the desk and eyeballed each other and the manager was allowed to make decisions on his own, rather than having to refer everything to some unseen higher authority.

"Well give us a clue, Doug," he smiled, "I have to put something solid in my report justifying why I've given you the loan. Even if you say you're going to grow Christmas trees on it."

"Now there's an idea, but no Christmas trees. I intend to build bigger and better workshops on it, but I can't really tell you when at the moment, Ray," I said honestly. "But it'll be within ten years, and I need to get the rest off Shell first, so I'll be needing a bit more for that as time goes by." I suppose it must have seemed like 'toy town' economics to Ray; I'd done some fairly naive projections of income showing we could well afford the repayments. Crude though they were, it was enough to satisfy him.

"What happens if you're ill?" Ray asked.

"I'm never ill," I told him confidently, "and if I was, there's Malcolm; he'd just have to work round the clock."

We shook hands on it and I felt chuffed at having successfully negotiated my first business loan.

I suppose my learning curve in business in those days could best be described as a mixture of innocence, simplicity and developing formulas - all be it tinged with a good dose of vision. I refer to vision in the real sense. Someone, much later when we were into company statements, mused that a mission statement is 'what the company intends to be' and a vision statement is 'what the chairman would like it to be.' Now, I find that a truism, but a cynical one. It all depends if the chairman is prepared to roll his sleeves up and get dirty to achieve his vision or just attend a few board meetings and drink pink gin at the Christmas party.

I studied the detail of the loan and worked out in my own simple way that it was costing almost three pounds per grand per week to borrow. That was about 14% per year. With a bank rate at just over 8%, it was a pretty good deal for them at 6% over base! Yes, the loan could be offset against profits, but I vowed the time would come that cash would be king. Proving once again, as if I needed further proof, how much better it was to put the profits into the business and not into toys.

III

Whilst I had given up the fancy cars and the playboy lifestyle, Malc had taken on the mantle with relish. I didn't blame him; after all, he was five years younger and that showed. He still drove his beloved e-types; in fact, he was on his third having not long taken delivery of a brand new gold one VNP 434G, as I recall. I don't think I mentioned that he almost totalled this shortly before we moved to the flat. He was coming home from the Rum Runner in the early hours of the morning and going too fast to negotiate the island by the Chalet. Instead of turning, he ploughed straight into it, landing in the middle of the flower beds. He came running in and woke me up. I went down with him and managed to manoeuvre it off the island and back to the concealment of our home garage. The next day, the local PC was round asking questions as to how it happened, but couldn't prove anything untoward. He suggested to me that we got the island sorted, which we did.

There came a time when Malcolm and I were disconnected in a mental sense. I couldn't drum my vision into him and I suppose I was quite happy to continue going through this new learning curve on my own.

IV

There was, I discovered, as much, if not more, money to be made in parts than there were in repairs, if you bought at the right price that is. For instance, a simple thing like a spark plug could be bought for twenty five pence and sold on for a pound. A 400% mark up. It all depended upon where you bought the parts from. They had to be quality, that was what Clark's was all about - quality. So I drove 'all over the Wrekin' sourcing quality parts at rock bottom prices. I took pride in honing my negotiating skills, going over what I had done in my head and examining ways of how I could strike even better deals. Trouble was, whilst I was off doing that, I wasn't there to supervise what was going on back at the ranch and I didn't like that. I suppose I was in the early stages of becoming a total control freak, which in honesty, I remain to this day.

A few miles away from our garage in Rednal, two guys who were to play a major part in those early days of development had started a revolutionary small business of their own. Slade Arthur and Paul Johnson, young entrepreneurs, had the vision to start up a parts supply business in a shack they had rented from a jeweller who had ceased trading due to ill health. He in turn rented it from British Rail. It was right by the railway bridge in Northfield and shook as the trains rattled past. In that tiny building they prided themselves on being able to provide any motor part to trade or public at rock bottom prices. They called themselves Motaparts Tool Hire (later to be shortened to just Motaparts) and I was their very first trade customer, although I didn't realise it at the time.

I called on them the day they opened for business and rang an order in almost every day after that. It was always to us within a couple of hours and I thought they must have the most superb stock-holding as they always had everything we wanted.

I later discovered that they started the business with just £150 worth of stock. Now, considering a clutch at trade would cost them £10 and an exhaust system £6, the shelves were pretty empty. So they had the bright idea of filling them with carefully labelled, but empty, cardboard boxes. This gave the impression of being able to supply anything even if they couldn't, which was mostly the case. What happened was that, as soon as I rang in an order, one or the other of them would 'hot foot it' to the manufacturers' trade counters in Birmingham in their Ford Anglia Estate and have it to me within an hour and a half. They could buy cheaper than I could by using the credit and the buying power of Slade's Uncle who owned Swan Motors in Yardley and had a massive parts department. They only put on a small mark up, which left them favourably comparable with the prices I had been paying when I was doing our buying.

Like us at that time, they put every penny back into the business and it was not long before the empty cardboard boxes were replaced with full ones. They opened seven days a week, from nine until seven thirty. At weekends, they had a queue of DIY motorists waiting for the door to open.

From those tiny beginnings in 1970, Paul and Slade next built a Motaparts supermarket in 1972, just a hundred yards from the original. That was on a plot of disused allotment land they bought from British Rail. They went on to launch a formidable chain of motor shops over the next few years. In fact, they mirrored our own growth in so many ways.

Over the top of the main shop they started another company called Motaproducts. Here they developed, patented and manufactured a revolutionary brake adjustment kit for drum brakes, which took the market by storm as a 'must have' product and which they sold out a few years later for a fortune, along with the shops. They were astute enough though to retain ownership of the properties.

Slade's father was an inventor, Evan Arthur. He owned and ran a company called Lightening Tools, where he personally designed and produced many labour-saving ways of carrying out motor repairs. One of his most successful was a special type of hose clip, which was simple and totally effective. He was your original 'mad professor', but with the bonus of being an astute business-man to boot. Evan made it clear to Slade that he intended leaving all his money to the State and didn't help him financially when he started up on his own, apart from buying them a Ford Anglia estate. But he revelled in and chuckled at his son's success all the same. Not unlike my own dad, I suppose, which made Slade and I somewhat kindred spirits.

So, nearly all of my buying was done through Motaparts. I was their big-gest trade customer, in fact, the only one for quite a time. Although I naturally drove a hard bargain, it was a relationship that worked for both of us for many years. Paul, Slade and their wives Sandra and Judy (who were sisters) socialised together with Jan and me. We even went on holiday with Slade and Judy once to Spain and he tells me there is eight-millimetre footage to prove it. They came to a couple of wild parties we threw at the house in Barnt Green Road and we were all reunited at my sixtieth bash at the Chateau Impney.

Whenever the men were on their own, the conversation would quickly turn from sex to how we could drive our respective businesses forward - brain-storming sessions over a few pints. We had a 'settlement night' once a month on a Friday evening at the flat, where we would protest, laugh and I would pay up. That was after a very careful scrutiny of every single invoice. It was a great arrangement and left me free to spend a lot more time at the garage. It saved me at least three hours a day.

They were, without a doubt, the two most enterprising and inspiring friends I had. They saw a gap in the market, took it and closed it. I helped them on their way by never being late with a payment.

V

Once, I very quickly needed two batteries. It was six thirty on a Saturday evening and Paul delivered them himself. He was eager to get off as they were going out to the Cedar Club, whilst I was going to work 'til midnight at least. Unfortunately, they were the wrong batteries and so Paul was not best pleased when I demanded he went back and replace them immediately with the right ones. He exited like a bat out of hell in his 1275 Cooper 'S' which was made up of two 'write-offs' welded together. In fact, the two sections hadn't even been sprayed, having a red front and blue back. It went like a rocket though and you could hear it coming from a considerable distance.

He stormed back inside thirty minutes, banging the batteries down and without any words being spoken took off flat out and noisily, in a cloud of dust, angrily making his point. About fifteen minutes later, he staggered back into the garage in a total state of shock. He was shaking like a leaf.

In his anger, he had been travelling so fast that, when he encountered a car overtaking another on the wrong side of the road, he was left with the choice of a head on pile-up or taking his chances by driving off the road. He wisely took the latter option and ended up careering through a wooden fence into Cofton Park. His welded-together machine spun over and over until it broke into two, becoming a total write-off, forever this time. Paul was thrown clear, landing head-first in the bushes and escaped with barely a scratch, but couldn't comprehend what had happened - temporary amnesia.

In panic, he just decided to leg it back up the hill to our place. I sat him down, calmed him with a cup of tea then took him back to the park, which was by now full of people with torches searching for the dead body of the driver. We explained that Paul was not a ghost, but flesh and bone and thankful to be alive. I helped him with the police and retrieved the pieces of his car the next morning.

Paul never made it to the Cedar Club and we didn't fit the batteries until Sunday. A good mate needed cheering up and after a few pints at the Hare and Hounds, he ended the evening laughing at what was a lucky escape with no harm done except to metal and a bill for the hole in the fence.

Incredibly, it was to be just one week later when he was to return the compliment. I was driving to Motaparts along Station Road in Northfield when a Vauxhall HA Viva came tearing down the hill called Woodlands Road and shot straight out, not stopping at the halt sign. It's a blind junction and I couldn't see him till he jumped the sign and I had no chance of stopping and so hit him head on.

The collision shunted the Viva across the road, straight into the path of a lorry. I'm afraid I just panicked and ran from the scene in a state of confusion, legging it under the bridge to Motaparts.

Paul and Slade calmed me down this time and returned with me to the scene of the accident where the police and ambulance were now in attendance. Sadly, the driver died on impact; his wife, who was in the passenger seat, was badly injured, but survived. Paul helped me with my statement to the police and I stayed with him the rest of the afternoon.

In the evening they took Jan and me out to dinner and did their best to console me, but I couldn't eat. I just kept going over and over what had happened and no matter how many times they all told me it wasn't my fault, it seemed to make little difference. I was however grateful for the company, it's at times like that you learn what friendship means.

VI

Two years passed by and it was 1967 already. Two years of solid dedication, implementing systems and of operating a clean and profitable business. Business, business and more business. I couldn't tell you what was on at the cinema, who was singing what and I must be the only bloke in England that didn't know we'd won the world cup in '66 until a customer told me three days later. I was obsessed, possessed even, and all-controlling.

Everything was running smoothly - except for one thing, Malcolm! I missed not being able to talk to Malc, as we used to, about plans for the future. Oh, we talked on occasions, but his head was elsewhere and then, he committed the cardinal sin. He started to turn up late, day after day. Even in the crazy period of living at The Barracks and our all-night partying, we always opened up on time. Malcolm's tardy timekeeping rankled to the point where I couldn't let it go any more without saying something. So, one fateful morning, when his e-type rolled in some forty five minutes late, I tackled him.

"What f-ing time do you call this? I yelled at him. "What?" He responded incredulously. I hadn't spoken to him like this in years. "You heard! I'm fed up with carrying you; we're supposed to be partners, something you seem to have forgotten."

"I pull my weight," he argued.

"That's a joke; you've lost the plot, Malc," I told him.

"I'm not standing for this shit from you," he raged. I'd never seen him this angry before. He was literally shaking with rage and I'm afraid that just made me madder too. There was no way I was going to back down. With fists clenched, we eyeballed each other and were seconds away from a physical confrontation when, with a barrage of four letter words, he turned, got back into the e-type and roared off so fast that he narrowly avoided piling into the tram station.

Malcolm didn't come back that day, nor home that evening either, nor the next day or the next. I heard from a customer that he was shacking up with a girl he'd been seeing from the Cedar Club, a barmaid. The weekend came and no word from him at all. Another week went by and still no sign, not even a phone call. Rumours were rife; the Fabulous Clark Brothers had split up. Malcolm was going to start his own business in competition, he was moving abroad, all rubbish, but my attitude hardened. If that's how it was, then so be it. I was running the business single handed as it was, so no loss. Actually, that was far from the truth, but when you're in that kind of mood you can only see the bad.

After three weeks I seriously thought it was indeed the end between us when Margaret, Jess's wife, turned up at the garage. She'd heard what had happened and took it upon herself to see first Malcolm and then me, in an effort to mediate or broker a meeting.

"You've done so much together, Douglas," she sighed. "Look at this place and what you've achieved together. Remember how you brought Malcolm up. He told me he used to think you were his Dad."

"Yes I know," I smiled.

"Look, I've suggested to Malcolm the two of you should have a meeting at our place. You haven't been to Little Glebe, our nice new house in Belbroughton, have you? (They'd moved from Hagley.) So, if nothing else, I can show that off to you. See what I made Jess spend our ill-gotten gains on. What do you say?"

"OK," I agreed and we arranged to meet that evening.

As luck would have it, we both turned up at the same time and rang the doorbell with not a word or a glance passing between us. Margaret kissed us both and treated us as if nothing was wrong. She put us in the dining room with a table and a pot of tea between us. Neither of us spoke for a few moments and then Malc broke the silence.

"You've got Jan," he said.

"Sorry?" I replied.

"You've got Jan and I'm a single bloke."

"What's that supposed to mean?"

"It means you've almost forgotten what it's like to have fun," he told me.

"Oh, bollocks! I'm having more fun now than I've ever had in my life," I protested, meaning it.

"You don't involve me," he said.

"You haven't wanted to be involved," I replied.

"You haven't asked me to."

"I shouldn't have to," I countered.

"Yes, you should. Has it occurred to you that I might want to be more than the brother who's just the monkey under the car?" He said quietly.

"Is that what you think I think you are?" I asked incredulously.

"It's how you treat me sometimes," he responded.

There was a long silence and it was Malc that broke it. "Sorry," he said.

"Sorry for what, storming off for weeks?" I asked.

"No! For taking the piss, coming in late and that, I was out of order."

This was the first time I had heard Malc talk like this. We were both proud, arrogant buggers and it took a lot for him to do it. All the venom passed away and I was looking at my kid brother again, not a stranger.

"I've been a bit out of order too Malc, not involving you, treating you as

'Baby Malc' in all senses of the word. I'm sorry too," I told him.

There were tears in both our eyes now and spontaneously we got up and hugged each other long and hard, sobbing away.

"I've missed you," he said.

"And I've missed you too," I told him.

"Fabulous Clark Brothers, right?" He whispered.

"You've got it!" I laughed. "Now, are you ready to talk about the future - our future?"

We talked for over an hour. I told him my plans and he listened with an intent I hadn't seen in a long time. He shared the vision and was ready to move on it with me. We agreed that our next move was to buy the lot off Shell. To achieve that, every single penny earned would go into the business. Most of all, we agreed that it would be him and me forever; no kids coming into the business, no outsiders, just the two of us, brothers, partners and best mates.

That was the only major falling out we have ever had in our lives. Without the intervention of Margaret, who knows where it would have ended? As it was, the bond was strengthened to the point where it remains today, that of unbreakability.

8 – Blueprints And MOT's

I

We started, as we intended to carry on, with a formal board meeting. There hadn't been any board meetings in the true sense of the word for some time. Really, they were just sessions where I'd try to bring Malcolm up to date with what I was doing and him not showing the interest I thought he should be giving. I suppose I was telling rather than discussing, so now, with our new-found united direction, all that changed.

After the first meeting we started to spend hours together after work pouring over the future, just like we used to do in the clandestine days. I gave Malcolm not only an equal share of the decision-making, but also a 'to do' list. Things like dealing with suppliers, including socialising with Slade and Paul, who I wanted him to get excited by too.

Interviewing staff was a new task for Malc and I found him to be very adept at it. He was growing his business skills by the day. Once focused, he was like a terrier on heat and I became more and more proud of him.

This was 1967 and the year the M.O.T. testing was introduced. I applied to the Ministry of Transport for a license and they came out to inspect us. No way would we have got it before the Shell refurb, but we received official approval in just a few days.

It was in fact Malcolm that saw this as a twofold opportunity.

"We should have a dedicated bay," he said. "That way we can really show we mean business; there's going to be an awful lot of money in M.O.T.'s, Doug, and I want to make sure we get more than our fair share."

"I agree, but the dedicated bay can't happen overnight," I told him.

"Yes, but we can plan for it. If the punters come for an MOT, they've almost certainly got to have a service as well; there's oil level top up at the very least, not to mention body work which we can pass on at a nice commission," he gushed.

"OK," I told him. "We'll use one bay of the workshop just for MOTs. How's Alan Blundell working out?"

"Well, for a painter and decorator, he's turned into a bloody good mechanic," he laughed. Alan was a customer and one of the guys that used to learn by hanging around watching us work. He'd serviced his own cars in the past and I recognised in him the skills of a natural mechanic. He had joined us just after the refurb was completed; that was two years ago now, back in 1965.

"I agree," I told him. "Why not send him on the MOT course and put him in charge of the bay when he finishes?"

Indeed, Alan made a fabulous MOT manager, running it like clockwork. He went on to become a highly valued member of staff and spent the rest of his working life with us, right up to his retirement in 2006; much of that, in the later years, in charge of all our painting requirements. He was the Van Gogh of Magnolia Emulsion and I mean that earnestly and respectfully.

Pretty soon the MOT side was a nice little earning profit-centre in itself. It was turning over anything up to thirty MOT's a day. I prided myself on the fact that it was regarded as the finest MOT centre for miles around. The inspectors who visited periodically always wrote us up in glowing terms.

I just love government legislation; always a buck to be made if you know where and how to go about it. Conservative or Labour, it really doesn't matter. It's just the same bunch of white-collared civil servants in Whitehall behind them, churning out the paperwork for the new rules to keep themselves in velvet boxes - bring it on!

In fact, the money we made from MOT's went a long way towards paying for the early stages of the new development.

II

I had now been having meetings with Shell for some time with a view to buying everything off them. That's why I impressed on Malcolm that, not only had we to plough everything we could into the kitty, it was necessary to pay ourselves a not exactly frugal, but vastly reduced wage for the time being. He was fine about it, understanding completely that where we were going next was so much more important than living for today.

This reduction in earnings had the added effect of boosting up the balance sheet and endearing the bank to our blueprint for ownership. Ray Picken even complemented me on the business plan. This was a first; in truth, I had been studying examples and tailored the best I came across into my own ideas. When I look back today it was still a naive document, mostly figures without any supporting argument. That came when Doug Clark's enthusiasm filled in the details verbally.

Shell agreed to sell us the workshops, but they wanted to retain the forecourt. This suited me fine; yes, there was profit in petrol, but it was a more or less a determinate figure - with servicing and repairs and MOT's it was a movable feast. Effort in, costs adhered to, results out. Hey presto!

I also had my eye on the six cottages to the right of the garage. If I could only get those, then the vision would become reality; 'kit-form planning' I called it. If it sounds callous to say I had an agenda in befriending the pensioners that lived there, it was true, but it worked both ways: we checked up on them, provided coal and carried out minor repairs for them. In fact, we acted like unpaid wardens. This paid off in so much, as they passed on or moved in with their off-spring, they sold their cottages to us - one by one. I think I paid just under a thousand pounds for the first.

As they became vacant I used them for offices, meeting rooms, to store parts in and even let staff stay in them. Malcolm took one for himself where he lived for nigh on three years. Tony Foden and his family lived in another for quite some time too, whilst they were between houses.

I actually tried to rig up a fore-runner of closed circuit TV, so that I could watch what was happening at the garage whilst working or playing in cottage number two. It wasn't terribly successful, just shadowy, ghostly figures, but served the purpose by making the staff think Big Brother was indeed watching them.

I must admit to having a few dangerous liaisons in those cottages. All work and no play didn't exactly make Douglas a dull boy, but it did set the testosterone levels running a bit high with some of the customer's wives. This was when they brought their cars or their husband's cars in for service, dressed to thrill in the scantiest of clothing.

I should explain that, as Austin Rover prospered, our customers now came from two main areas. Down the hill to the right were Longbridge and Northfield, both areas full of solid working class people. The Longbridge workforce in those days was over 40,000 strong and growing.

To the left stood Barnt Green and Blackwell where all the rich folk lived.

The directors of Austin Rover, lawyers, accountants, entrepreneurs and old money like Colonel Terry. This is where the 'customers' wives' came from, with their mini's as second cars. We didn't get much of the big stuff like the Rollers, they went to the main dealers, but we got pretty well a 100% of the wife market. Most didn't work; it was tennis at the Priory Club in Edgbaston or squash in Barnt Green; then there were the bridge and gin parties and a lot of decadency of lifestyle. Barnt Green was swinging before the word was invented.

Most times I resisted what was on offer, but there was one I simply couldn't. No names, but she was the stunning young wife of a leading city businessman with an hour glass figure and a tantalizing plan. She suggested huskily that I should hide in the boot of her husband's Daimler whilst she drove us back to her house for a session. Well this adventure was too much to turn down and I shamefully acquiesced to her enterprising offer. It was one of the most erotic encounters of my life and yes, I felt guilty, but not as much as I felt elated.

It's true that I have never been monogamous by nature, a trait I neither revel in nor apologise for. We are not talking of affairs, purely good old fashioned lust.

III

The next big innovation or, should I say, revolution was the advent of self service on the forecourt. This was the time of the start of fibre optic technology. An electric motor was fitted to the pump so that it could be switched on and off from the shop. This was combined with some sophisticated technology in the office, enabling the readings to be conveyed straight to the cash desk.

It meant less forecourt staff, though I still retained one at all times for those people that didn't want to fill up themselves. The attendant was under no circumstances allowed to take any money, except tips. This forced the customer into our little shop where they were encouraged visually to buy cigarettes, sweets, batteries and motor cleaning materials. The mark-up on those was very high. Indeed there was more profit in the extras than there was in the petrol. To the 'kit-form' plan I added a much bigger shop in my mind for the next stage of development.

With that thought in mind, and once the deal for the workshops with Shell was complete, I started on the marathon task of excavating the bank I had bought at the outset. This seemed a never-ending process and even with countless lorry loads of soil taken away, the bank didn't appear to ever look any smaller.

The soil was good quality stuff though, very sandy and I arranged with the park warden of the Lickey Hills to deposit it where they needed some in-fills. It was an arrangement that worked for both of us. We also advertised the top soil in the shop and sold many a load to private customers for their gardens. It was my way of making the project partially self-funding. All in all, it took three years to remove that bank, during which time we took away over 40,000 tons of soil and sandstone before it was levelled. The back of what had been the bank was now like a cliff face, which we bevelled and planted with long-rooted brush, covered in netting, so as to bond it and form a natural barrier.

IV

If 1967 was a year of innovation for us, then 1968 pretty nearly surpassed it. It all started with a visit from Alan Proctor of Car Care delivery service. They were a specialist vehicle distribution company whose main customer was Henley's with a massive fleet of company cars. I had first got to know Alan as a customer for his own vehicle.

"I've got a proposition for you, Doug," he said to me one day. "How would you feel about taking on a major job for Henley's?"

I was naturally all ears. "Excited, of course," I told him. "What is it that you want us to do?"

"Apply your exacting standards to the vehicles we supply by doing a pre-delivery service. Quite frankly, at the moment, there's only a one in two chance of the cars we get straight from British Leyland being up to standard. Their final checking service gets worse by the day and we haven't got the resources, time or inclination to do that. We are first and foremost a delivery company; so, what we need is a middle man to make sure that what we deliver is perfect. What do you think?"

I thought it a wonderful opportunity and I grabbed it with both hands. It was common knowledge that, with the success Longbridge was enjoying, an unhealthy degree of contempt was creeping in like a cancer. Strikes were frequent, even though wages were way above the national average, and quantity as opposed to quality was very much the benchmark. They couldn't turn out cars fast enough to meet the demand and no-one was picking up the early warning signals in that. Across the water in Germany, ears were picking up and, even further afield in the Far East, a dragon was awakening. All this was of only academic interest to us; the worse the quality of the new cars, the more work there was for Clark's Motor Services

The Henley's contract turned out to be a bigger deal than even I imagined it would be and meant us taking on yet more staff and quickly. British Leyland delivered to us and we got the cars ready by cleaning them, checking basic mechanics, tyre pressures and fuel levels and then Car Care delivered them on to Henley's branches all over the country. For this we would get £30 per car - great regular money for very little work.

In fact, the demand rocketed so quickly that it wasn't long before the volumes were such that I had everyone working overtime and we were in a state of almost constant recruitment. We prospered shamelessly and I was now striding around my ever-growing empire like a proverbial 'Jack the Lad'.

As they say, pride comes before a fall. And it was only a matter of time till I learnt another salutary lesson - never get complacent.

It started with a phone call from a grave Alan Proctor: "You've let me down, Doug," he said.

"What's the problem?" I asked

"I said to you that I wanted you to apply your own exacting standards," he started.

"And we have and do," I told him.

"They've slipped Doug - badly!"

I wanted to say "G't'ell!" but I bit my tongue and listened as his words started to sting.

"Now my neck's on the line, along with yours. Several cars have gone through with all sorts of faults lately and the Henley's management are baying for blood," he elaborated.

"First I know about it," I said defensively.

"Therein lays the problem. You don't seem to have control. Anyway, I see no point in us arguing about it. If you want to stand a chance of keeping the contract, you need to be in a meeting at head office in Salisbury at nine o'clock sharp tomorrow morning."

I didn't sleep too well. Failure was not a word in my vocabulary. I mulled over what had happened and told myself: "There is no smoke without fire, Doug." On the basis of the Henley's contract, we had taken on six more people and perhaps they hadn't been properly 'Clarked'. Heads were going to roll, that was a certainty, but there was no getting away from the fact that Doug Clark had taken his eye off the ball. My mind raced away; if we lost this and started shedding staff, the reputation we had so carefully built up could all but be destroyed overnight. I rehearsed what I was going to say over and over again in my mind.

I was up by six, showered and shaved. Jan had taken special care ironing my one and only crisp white shirt. I wore my wedding suit, cleaned my shoes and set off with butterflies in my stomach.

On arrival I wasn't kept waiting, but shown immediately into an impressive boardroom. There were the obligatory handshakes and the atmosphere was cold, but businesslike. Pleasantries over, it was time to do my bit. I felt how an actor must feel on first night, ready to give one's all then wait for the audience reaction.

The panel from Henley's consisted of George Liddle the fleet director, Ron Larkham the manager of fleet operations and Mrs. Ball the company secretary. They listened in silence as I started my rehearsed script then deviated and talked from the heart. I admitted that mistakes had been made, stressed how highly I valued the contract, not just in pecuniary value, but because of the credibility it gave to our business. I stressed that, given the chance, I would put matters right and there would never be an occasion when our work would be called into question again.

It was a few moments before anyone spoke. I felt that I had been given a fair hearing, done the best job I could of redeeming an almost lost situation and waited for the verdict. It wasn't forthcoming immediately and I was asked to leave the boardroom whilst they discussed their decision.

I sat outside reading a copy of the 'Financial Times' without absorbing a word. It was just me and a horn-rimmed receptionist who smiled occasionally. In reality I was probably kept waiting for no more than ten minutes, but it seemed like ten hours.

The door opened and I was called back in and told by George that I was to be given another chance. Firm handshakes all round and I was on my way back to Birmingham with a mission.

Malcolm and I had what was our version of an emergency board meeting. He comprehended all the implications and was as eager as me to make sure it didn't happen again.

"We've got to sew the checking procedure up so there's no daylight," I told him. "Then we put belt and braces on it Malc, belt and braces," I repeated. It was an expression that I was going to apply to everything we did from now on.

I fired the members of staff that were not up to scratch immediately and set Malc on the case to get first class replacements, no matter what the cost. Next, I implemented a check and double check quality control system, so watertight nothing could get through. There were never-to-be repeated any meetings like Salisbury, the volume kept on increasing and, every time it did, we staffed up accordingly. We held that contract for many years and, alongside it, added another massive one - British Aerospace. At the peak we were turning round in excess of five thousand cars a year.

9 – Building A Business And Badgers

I

For the next couple of years I implemented different systems in every arena of our operation. The Henley's lesson had been a salutary, never to be repeated one, but it had been good for me in many ways. Not only were the quality checks on the pre-delivery business as tight as a duck's backside, it gave me a blue-print for checks on everything from servicing through to stock efficiency. Planning and implementation was to become paramount in every aspect of what we did - a directive which I shared equally with Malcolm who caught on very quickly, adding practical and solid ideas of his own.

I made a decision to give up doing any of the manual work in order to focus solely on managing and expanding. This was actually a momentous decision to make and my first big step in delegation. If we were to move up a league then I had to change and so did others. I embarked on a new learning curve and started to visit numerous trade and motor shows looking for innovations and products that could improve our business. These were great places to make new contacts. Over that period I started to sketch out my grand master plan for how 'Clark's Motor Services' would look once we owned all the cottages, completed the bank excavation and could build the dream. This was even to include space for car showrooms at some stage in the future. What I wouldn't have given for a BL franchise. But that arena was a closed shop with scant prospect of ever coming to fruition. Yet my instinct told me there would one day come a point where all possibilities would become realities. "It's just a question of finding the magic key to unlock the door," I told myself.

We were now servicing a large proportion of all British Leyland vehicles in the area. Our workforce had tripled to thirty since 1967. The cottages heaved with stock and we were creaking at the seams. It was definitely time for the next stage. I was hungry for it, starving in fact. But I needed one more cottage first, the final piece of planning in my kit-form jigsaw.

II

Opportunity comes in many ways and guises; it's just a question of having the motivation to reach out and grab them and then, once grabbed, exploit them right up to the hilt.

Longbridge was turning out a colossal amount of cars which had to be stored, often for months on end before final delivery. Storage land was at a premium and it was in conversation with one of the Rover managers, who had called to discuss even more pre-delivery work, when I thought of Dad and his scrap yard back in Chaddesley. "I know somewhere where you can store at least four hundred," I told him, "safe, secure and accessible."

I set off back to the village where I had grown up to be the bearer of tidings to Dad that I was about to make him a rich man. I hadn't been there for a long time and so decided to use the visit to look up some old haunts. I treated myself to lunch at The Talbot where I used to do the carol singing at Christmas as a child. It was now a splendid country pub and restaurant, which did the greatest smoked salmon sandwich, with a bowl of chunky chips that's my idea of lunchtime heaven. It was a strange feeling, but a pleasant one. I went into St Cassian's church and sat in silence remembering Mom. I went back to the old house and sat in the car looking at it, reliving childhood memories. I could see myself crossing the road, catapult in pocket and with the backside hanging out of my pants. On my feet were the ever present wellies. I could hear Nan calling us in for some 'good 'olesome tack' and Grandad Morris telling me to use my 'gumption.' I must have sat there reminiscing for over an hour, the spell broken only when a well dressed young girl came out of the old house and got onto her bike.

I drove along the High Street and up the hill to Dad's; instead of turning left into his drive at the crossroads though, on impulse, I turned right and into the countryside. I wasn't ready to see him yet; my head was still swimming with memories, not all of them good where he was concerned.

About half a mile down the narrow road was an overgrown makeshift drive which I decided to explore; at the end of which, looking like a miniature version of the overgrown castle in Sleeping Beauty, lay Badgers Cottage.

I got out of the car and fought my way through the undergrowth like the fairy-tale prince to take a closer look. The building was all but derelict and hadn't been lived in for many years. I knew the last occupant had been the infamous and glamorous young village schoolteacher Miss Bithell. She was a Marilyn Monroe look-alike who, as legend had it, lived an equally outrageous lifestyle. Badgers Cottage had been the setting for many an orgy in its heyday and was the topic of much conversation by the men in the village pubs. Mostly pious jealousy, I reckon, as the majority would have stood no chance of getting in on the action. It crossed my mind that Dad, in his killer days, might have been a participant though.

Unloved and neglected as it was, the cottage reeked of magic and mystery; you could hear the laughter of wood imps on the wind. Suddenly, I knew something had lured me here and I knew what I had to do. This was to be my home and it was my duty and mission not only to restore it, but to make it into a place of great beauty. Something that would endure; a haven for wildlife and a sanctuary from the insanity of the city. It was also where I would return in triumph to the village which I had left as a penniless teenager.

III

I lingered in that spot for far longer than I had intended. The grounds seemed vast and the cottage was surrounded on all sides by fields where sheep and cattle grazed. The potential was huge and challenging. It was getting dark when I eventually knocked on Dad's door. Noel answered and we greeted each other warmly. Kathleen came out from the kitchen and was delighted to see me and put the kettle on the stove for a brew as she sent Noel out to call Dad from the workshop.

Over a hearty cuppa, made from real tea leaves in a china teapot, I put the idea to Dad.

"You're telling me that Leyland will pay me just to store their cars here," he asked incredulously.

"Yes, I am," I replied for at least the third time.

"And what do you want out of it? You've proved yourself a smart person, must be something in it for you?" He queried.

"I'd like to do my Dad a favour," I told him "I don't want a cut of any kind. If it makes you feel better though, it won't do me any harm with The Austin; might help towards getting me a franchise one day," I told him.

"Ah!" He smiled, satisfied. I felt really good and although the thoughts I broached to him on Leyland, looking a bit more favourably towards giving me a franchise, were what came into my head at the time, they did have substance which I hadn't considered till then.

Another thought occurred, Dad knew everything and everyone in Chaddesley so I asked him, "What's the story on Badger's Cottage, Dad?"

"Abandoned and neglected, left to rot since young Miss Bithell left. I think Farmer Spencer lets his beasts have the run on it. Why do you ask?"

"Cause I'd like to buy it." I smiled.

"You barmy or what?" He tutted. "It's falling apart, although come to think of it, there was talk of him getting planning permission for a bungalow," he pondered.

"You know him don't you Dad, Farmer Spencer?" I asked.

"We sit on the parish council together," he informed me proudly.

"Well, could you see if you can persuade him to sell it to me please? Explain I'm not interested in building a bungalow, I just want that cottage. I want to move back here," I explained.

We looked each other in the eyes and he understood where I was coming from.

"Yes, I'll talk to him, if it's what you really want."

"It is," I said firmly, "definitely!"

"How's Jan?" Kathleen asked.

"Well, she's been a bit sick in the mornings lately," I told her.

IV

Jan was, as you've probably guessed, pregnant. We were both elated. She, even more so when I told her we were going to move out of the flat and back into a house once more. To her credit she laughed when I took her on a mystery tour to show her what was to be our new home.

"Just the place to bring up a baby," I said and she smiled as I made her trudge through the undergrowth to derelict Badgers Cottage.

"Close your eyes," I told her and she obliged. "Now, imagine this on a beautiful summer's day, restored and extended. We'll have a glorious master bedroom with French windows leading out onto a balcony where the view will take your breath away. Then I'll put in a swimming pool."

"Can I please just have running water from a tap first?" Jan interrupted. "The idea of pumping it from a well doesn't exactly fill me with joy. Oh, and electricity would be nice."

To be honest, I needed another project where I could be physically hands-on once again. It was all very well being the managing director and going to work in a suit, but I missed the thrill of manual achievement. Badgers Cottage was going to be a dream project in more ways than one.

Dad used his charms on Farmer Spencer and in a matter of days we had agreed on a price of two and a half grand. For once I didn't haggle, I was getting my dream.

It turned out that Badgers Cottage had been built in the seventeenth century and, amazingly, was not subject to any preservation orders. Planning permission for a small bungalow on the grounds had in fact been applied for and granted. However, as much as I liked knocking things down, I had no intention of doing so with Badgers Cottage. Instead, I would restore it and improve it beyond recognition; that was a promise I made first and foremost to myself.

I had a child on the way; what a wonderful home it would be to grow up in. Maybe even one day my son or daughter would raise children there of their own. 'Dallas' was the big show on television at the time and I had visions of creating our very own 'Southfork' and Doug Clark would be the Chaddesley Corbett 'JR'.

The purchase was completed in a matter of days as I didn't haggle on the price. It was already a giveaway in my book and I wasn't looking to get into protracted negotiation, just get it done. So, with the deeds hot in my hand I was ready to roll. The first thing to organise was the water. I got permission to connect to the main supply up on the lane about 400 or so yards away. I knew George Smart had a little old digger at the back of his amusement arcade, which I think he had taken in lieu of a bad debt at some point in time. I borrowed it off him and, along with Malcolm, excavated a trench over several weekends. The digger had a mind of its own, going left when you turned the steering wheel right and vice versa. This created a few hairy moments when we forgot to turn the wheel the wrong way to go the right way. The Water Board then laid the pipes down to the cottage and connected us up. Likewise with the electricity company which put some overhead cables in to get power to the house.

So we had electric and water, light, heat and the ability to wash and cook. Primitive, but it was enough to make it habitable whilst I got to grips with all the major work. I even used an old Morris Minor estate, which I'd bought off a customer and had run into the ground until it was falling apart, as a chicken pen and soon we had fresh eggs for breakfast every day. The good life personified.

By the time my daughter Julia was born on the 22nd of May, 1970 we were living the dream.

V

In fact, at the start of the seventies there was an awful lot happening on the business side too. The preparation contract with Car Care Delivery was rocketing into seemingly ever-increasing volumes. The difference was: we now had the systems in place to deal with it effectively and efficiently. Another learning curve for building a bigger business had been accomplished and although I didn't look upon it at the time as such, it was a major leap forward, being able to handle quantity whilst retaining quality.

One factor in this was the use of bespoke systems for keeping a handle on everything, from stock control to worksheets and delivery records. Whilst visiting a motor show I met Roy Drinkwater of the Chequered Flag Sports Car Company. He was developing a unique control system designed specifically for the motor trade; he had called it EGO Computer Systems. I was so taken with it that I agreed to take it in its raw state and for Clark's to be the innovators and guinea pigs. 'EGO' did in fact revolutionise us in many ways. We had computer-produced invoices, absolutely revolutionary back then - everyone else was still typing them. The extra special thing was that you could produce a complete narrative, along with the invoice, detailing everything that had been done to the customer's vehicle. All the information had to be inputted and so I spent hours and hours producing an encyclopaedia of everything that could possibly be done during service. All this was added to the database and we had bespoke software - especially for Clark's and light years ahead of any other garage I knew of.

I was also invited to attend conferences and seminars arranged by Shell. There, I discovered how they treated and involved their own staff, which, in turn, made every employee (regardless of rank) take pride in the Shell corporate status. This gave the company a transparent identity through and through; employees at every level knew the company structure and mission and the part they played in it. This encouraged me to work on our own identity and reward schemes. A party at Christmas might create the goodwill, but I wanted them to fly the flag of not only what great blokes and bosses Doug and Malc were, but also of what a forward-thinking company we were. The staff were encouraged not to be afraid of throwing in ideas of their own.

With this thought in mind, I started creating reward schemes, writing mission notices for staff and promise notices for the customers. Signage like: 'If you think we've done a good job tell your friends; if you don't, then tell me, Douglas Clark.' At first, this approach was greeted with amusement, but when staff and customers saw I wasn't laughing they took notice. I became almost obsessive about tidiness in every aspect of the business. I insisted the floors in the workshops were always so clean you could eat your dinner off them. The office was organised so that there was never a file unfiled that wasn't being worked on and full use was made of every bit of organisational technology we had. From index files to job sheets, information was to be readily accessible. The garage forecourt was immaculate with the pumps even gleaming and not a scrap of litter to be seen. The shop was spotless and structured. Everywhere had a system and a schedule, 'belt and braces' applied to everything.

Yet, once all this was done, we swiftly became the product of our own success. Once again, there wasn't room to swing a cat and it was obvious we needed to expand. There was still one cottage to go before we owned the whole block and the excavation, although in its last stages, was still a few lorry loads away from completion. Then there was the question of obtaining planning permission, which would be a lengthy process. So, what to do?

Salvation came once again - through Shell. The Forge Garage at Hagley, once a prestigious car showroom, had laid empty for a couple of years, being the product of another era. I had, however, mused over possibilities for it many times as I had driven by. We were at the point of turning away work at Rednal; it would be economical to spread the load to another garage and there was certainly space to put in at least three service bays at The Forge. I approached Shell with a view to purchase and they pondered for a couple of weeks whilst I pressed them. I had a bee in my bonnet and wanted a swift answer. I even told them I had somewhere else in mind and needed an answer quickly. This worked and they came back saying they would be willing to rent it to us initially with a view to later purchase. This was on the condition they would supply the petrol. Well, that was fine by us.

Malcolm was ready for a new challenge too and we agreed that he would take on sole responsibility for setting everything up at Hagley and running it as replica of Rednal. It was decided that, until it built up its own customer base, we would ferry all of the excess work across from Rednal - with the owner's permission - having the vehicles back, serviced and ready for collection at the agreed time.

In the midst of the move to The Forge, I heard the sad news that Mrs. Stratford, the final owner of cottage number six, had passed away. As soon as it seemed respectful to do so, I approached the family to buy it. A bit like playing Monopoly, the final piece of property to make up the set is always the most expensive. This one cost me twenty four grand; far more than it was worth and twenty four times what I paid for the first. In fairness, I would have paid even more if pushed. On purchase, I obtained an order to say it was unfit for human habitation; it was in a dreadful state, no one had ventured upstairs in years.

I hadn't allowed any major repairs on the other cottages either, except in the ones Malcolm and Tony Foden and his family had used. Tony had moved a few months before and Malcolm vacated overnight to a house he had bought in Dodford. So, having them all empty, I set about making them all unfit for human habitation, breaking the stairs and knocking a few holes here and there. I even encouraged vermin. Very soon, this enabled me to obtain the same order on the others that I'd got on number six.

That's when I would have left them alone to crumble further into decay for the time being. After all, we more than had our hands full with the renovations at Hagley. Doing up Badgers Cottage was time consuming too. Then I got wind of the fact that some historical society was to attempt to take out a preservation order on them the very next week. Win or lose, it wasn't a risk I was prepared to take and so I had the lot condemned on that Friday and demolished over the weekend. Come Monday morning they were rubble. The local history society members were left scratching their heads in disbelief.

All the stores we had kept in the cottages were moved en-masse to Hagley at the same time. That was one hell of a weekend.

VI

In fact, 1970 was one eventful year. Into the world came singer Mariah Carey, the gorgeous super models Naomi Campbell and Claudia Schiffer, the actor River Phoenix, the cricketer Darren Gough and our Olympic rowing medallist, Sir Mathew Pinsen. We lost the most famous stripper ever to shed her clothes, Gypsy Rose Lee, the prolific writer E.M.Forster, the renowned conductor, Sir John Barbirolli, the most famous, ex French President and war leader Charles de Gaulle and the incredible music talents of Jimi Hendrix and Janis Joplin. On TV we watched the zany antics of The Goodies and Monty Python's Flying Circus and at the cinema, 'MASH' and 'Love Story'. The 'must have' toy for all ages was a Stylophone and the miniskirt sadly ended its fashion era. The teenagers, who got the vote at 18 in 1970, wore Afghan coats, bell bottom trousers, tank tops and crippling platform shoes. Topping the charts were Simon and Garfunkel with 'Bridge Over Troubled Water', Tony Christie sang of his 'Yellow River', Freda Payne her 'Band of Gold' and actor Lee Marvin had an unlikely hit growling 'Wanderin' Star'. The first ever Glastonbury festival was held with a £1 entrance fee and a free glass of milk. The NatWest Bank opened for business in the UK, Concorde made its first supersonic flight, Alexander Solzhenitsyn was awarded the Nobel prize for literature, Edward Heath was elected Prime Minister, The Beatles disbanded and Queen started up.

Clark's Motor Services turned in a magnificent £300,000 pre-tax profit and my beautiful daughter Julia was born. Indeed, what a year 1970 was and I loved every challenging minute of it.

Part Three 1970 -1980

10 – Thinking Outside The Box

I

As I'm sure you've gathered by now, I didn't benefit from the greatest of academic educations. I've always regretted that. I advise youngsters that working life is so much easier with the basics behind you rather than, as in my case, having to learn and build a knowledge-base the hard way, via the education of life. I had to learn to write business plans, expand my vocabulary so that I could hold my own with the most eloquent in the top echelons of business society and learn to communicate the message I wanted to get across to my own employees in an inspirational manner.

I've never been too proud to ask questions or listen to people and I believe that is still true of me today. I still retain a thirst for knowledge and am constantly on the look-out for alternative ways of doing things. Watch, learn and listen - to me, the three most wise and powerful instructions in the education of life. Whether that learning process is achieved by watching your Grandad lovingly putting an engine together or by listening to a Shell executive emitting words of motivation, whilst addressing an audience of key workers and dealers, is irrelevant. It is the process of learning that is key.

I once attended a conference, held by Shell, out of a sense of duty. Then, finding I had picked up so much useful information that I could plough back into Clark's, I couldn't wait for the next. During a break for coffee, one of the Shell executives paid me a compliment saying, "We like you at Shell Doug, because you're prepared to think outside the box."

II

Rather than just accept the compliment, I asked him to explain. He took a napkin and put nine dots in the form of a square onto it.

"Join those dots together without taking your pen off the paper or going over the same dot twice," he asked, thrusting a biro into my hand.

Now, unless they were of a sexual nature, I'd never been one for party games but, realising I was being put on the spot, I didn't want to make a prat of myself. So, before putting the pen to the paper, I thought about the dots. "Remember how you looked for ways of saving time on the Mini engines", I told myself. "He's expecting you to stay within the box and, when you reach a certain point, you'll have to take your hand off because they won't join up; that's obvious. What if I go outside the box with the pen and ignore the symmetry?"

The best solutions come quickly if you set your mind to ignoring the obvious. Now, I'm sure many of you have seen this puzzle solved or have been shown the solution before, as it is a classic business mind teaser. However, I hadn't. I ignored the box and in my mind looked at other shapes, circles, rectangles and a triangle. I took the pen and started from the bottom right dot, up the middle to the top, down the left side, cross the line without touching the dots to the top right and back across the top line to the top left. Hey presto, job done.

"I knew you could do it," he told me. "Not many people can because they can't think laterally. You think outside the box, Douglas. People at Shell talk about what you've done at Rednal; you turn mediocre solutions into great solutions. You are prepared to ignore assumptions. Look at what you are doing with that bank behind you that you bought off us. To anyone else it would be just a bank; to you, it's an opportunity. You don't start from the obvious premise that a car has to have four wheels and a motorbike two, now do you?"

I know this ability to think outside the box stood me in good stead in the 70's. While most of the business community thought we were in recession, therefore, we need to batten down the hatches, I thought what recession? All I can see are opportunities."

III

The 70's were the exact opposite of the 'swinging' 60's for the United Kingdom and indeed the western world. If the 60's represented innovation in everything from motor cars to music, when it seemed everyone had a bundle of notes in their pocket and a smile on their face, then the 70's was the hangover after the party. The 70's began with a poor economy, high inflation and, as the decade went on, the problem was made worse by war and oil supply difficulties and compounded by wage and price controls. We had a recession and stagflation (inflation combined with a stagnant economy). The average annual inflation rate from 1900 to 1970 was approximately 2.5%. From 1970, however, the average rate hit 6%, rising to 13.3% by 1979 (the prime lending rate hit 21.5% in December 1980, the highest in history). The 70's was perhaps the worst decade of British and American economic performance since the Great Depression of the 1930s.

In the 70's, OPEC was in control of oil supply whereas, previously, America had ruled the roost on both supply and price. In the 70's, war in the Middle East had a drastic effect on the price of oil. Syria and Egypt attacked Israel in 1973 resulting in a backlash of support from the US and other western countries. In retaliation, several Arab oil exporters imposed the 'Arab Oil Embargo' resulting in a dramatic increase in the price of oil and proved to the Arabs the power they now had. By the end of 1974 the price of oil had quadrupled.

I will return to the impact of all this later, but I think it is important to mention it at the outset of these next few chapters as the background to this period of my life. I remained for the most part oblivious to national and international problems, but rather saw the whole decade as one of opportunity.

IV

From 1964 to 1970 Harold Wilson had successfully led the Labour Party and the country. When the economy started to go wrong and it was clear that the Trade Unions actually held the real power, he was ousted at the 1970 general election by Edward Heath and the Tories. Try though he did, Heath failed to quell the power of the unions and the misery continued to the point that Wilson was returned to power in 1974. A rot had set in at Longbridge which they would never fully recover from although no one, me included, could see it at the time.

One of the desperate and really arse-covering legislations brought in by the first Wilson government was that of stock relief. The belief was that, by allowing stock to be offset against taxation and rolled over, it would fuel manufacturing. What it did in fact was to create false demand and lead to over-production and unrealistically cheap prices. For Clark's though it was almost a licence to print money. I bought up vast stocks of top-name tyres, multi-thousand Ferodo brake shoes and pads, starter motors, alternators; you name it I bought it. Ah! The beauty of inflation, the value just kept going up. I actually started selling to Motaparts and carving fifty-fifty deals with them on storing specialist stock. It's difficult to say where my customer base actually came from as it seemed to find me rather than the other way round. I became the first port of call and more often than not, I could supply it immediately and cheaper.

V

This Doug Clark buying initiative happened at the same time that Malc was starting up his operation at The Forge. The poor chap had hardly been in situ a week when the first pantechnicon arrived on the forecourt along with a load of scaffolding and wooden planks. I had in fact forgotten to tell him to expect it, such was my haste to do the deals, but he took it all in his stride.

Let me tell you a little about Malcolm's life at this point. He had a regular partner, Valerie, who had been a grass-tracking fan of his in our heyday (they married in 1971). He was also now racing Formula Ford cars in the rare spare time that he had. His work and play ethic was to start at eight in the morning, finish at ten at night, party till two or three in the morning and start all over again. The five-year age gap meant that he was now living the life style I enjoyed before marriage and the thrill of nonstop partying was replaced by the lure of building an empire. When he first saw The Forge at Hagley he rang me and said, "Bloody hell, Doug, it's a dinosaur. What are we going to do with all that space?" Well I suppose that was the catalyst for my buying spree. On this visit he met the Shell tenant who was under notice, Brian Jones, a balding hippie in a sheepskin jacket who grumbled about his lot and told Malcolm he was leaving. Malc didn't let on at that point that he was taking over, but shocked him a few days later when he swept in majestically as the new king. Brian Jones was livid and told him: "You'll do no good here mate, we're opening a business down the road and all the customers will come with us." How wrong he was. Malcolm had John Davis in tow with him, who Brian Jones knew, which made him even madder. John was the forecourt specialist for Shell and was all set to do a complete redesign and revamp of the one at The Forge. Naturally, this was to include a big, bold, illuminated Clark's sign. Shell had been reluctant to do anything to improve the look under Brian Jones & Co., but had total faith in us. I was itching to be involved in all this, but stayed away and let Malcolm have his head.

They started work on the forecourt within days and managed to keep it open at the same time as the shiny new pumps, signage and shop were going up and in.

VI

Inside the massive showroom and workshops were all sorts of equipment that was left over from the days when the building had indeed been a forge. This included a giant lathe which looked like something out of a Jules Verne or H.G.Wells novel, a beautiful monstrosity far too good to break up. Malcolm decided to utilise it by attaching brushes to the turning parts and it became the ultimate brake shoe cleaner. There was also a control panel on the wall which he rigged up to perform many labour saving touches.

At the start of the second week Malc drove the first job from Rednal to Hagley, it was a Rover 2000 which was misfiring and he discovered on the run that this was due to a burnt-out valve. It's funny how, with all the thousands of vehicles you work on, certain silly facts like that stick out in your mind.

VII

Malcolm started Rob Pinches on with him, straight away too, along with three other staff. Rob was quite an introvert by nature; we had taken him on at Rednal after giving him a practical test which proved him to be a natural. In fact, I would go so far as to say he was the most brilliant technician we ever had working for us. Malcolm obtained special dispensation from the Ministry of Transport for him, so that he didn't have to complete paperwork (because he couldn't). Rob had also just lost his licence after a stupid drunken binge, embarked upon following a row with his girlfriend. He was on a slippery slope and the move to Hagley saved his bacon. Initially, Malc would pick him up from Bromsgrove in the mornings and take him back at night, but Rob bought a bike after a couple of weeks and, to his credit, cycled to Hagley and back most days. I put Tony Foden in his place at Rednal when he left so it worked out well for both of us.

VIII

By the time a fortnight had passed I decided I was long overdue for a visit. First stop was the workshop which was going flat out. Most of the space was taken up with the mountain of stock I'd sent, precariously stacked to the ceiling on the make-shift scaffolding. Another Clark innovation that would never pass the health and safety rules of today.

"I don't know, Doug," Malc grinned, "I was expecting to have acres of space here and we can barely get round the bloody cars to service them without bumping into a stack of tyres or batteries."

I hadn't the heart to tell him I had an even bigger load on the way within the month. It was time for quick thinking and so out came a note pad.

"Tell you what," I said, sounding for all the world like I'd planned this all along, "we'll have a mezzanine gallery put in on stilts. A big solid construction that will hold three times the stock and you can kit out service bays underneath."

He loved the idea and so did I. I got on to Stratford Storage the very next day and explained what I wanted and how soon it had to be done. Two days later they were in and building it. It actually increased the available space by 40% with judicious streamlining and stacking; it took everything I'd bought up to date. I also purchased a fork lift truck with a pallet handler on it so that the stock could be moved easily.

IX

On that same visit I took a look at the accounts structure in the forecourt office. It didn't take a genius to see that many of the so-called 'valued customers' of Brian Jones were not averse to taking forever to pay, along with providing the odd dud cheque. We knew all about those from the Uncle Jess days at Rednal where he would let his cronies cash a cheque and if it bounced, as they often did, he was too proud to ask them for the cash. So, the account customers were put under notice that, if they wanted to keep their accounts, they had to deposit with us a month's average spend in advance with the carrot that, if they paid within ten days rather than a month, they could enjoy a half percent discount. As expected, we lost a lot of customers. However, with the new self-service pumps now open and the new look blazing - along with the extended opening hours - it was more than compensated for by passing trade. In fact, I introduced the same system at Rednal, just to be fair.

X

Malcolm had lots of ideas for Hagley, one of which was offering a breakdown service. The next garage down from us was owned by Malcolm Smith. It was an old family business called, not unnaturally, Smiths, and did a bit of everything including breakdowns. Our Malcolm met Malcolm Smith and suggested that they work together on the recovery side. Their Malcolm gave our Malcolm very short shrift; he told him he hated the garish new look of The Forge and was positively rude to him. Rather than going away with his tail between his legs, Malc vowed to teach him some manners. Not as he would have done in his young days, with fists flying, but rather in business. He made it a priority to start up the breakdown business and made it cheaper, quicker and better. In a very short space of time he also had the majority of their service business. The terrier was fast becoming a Rottweiler like his big brother.

XI

Along with the garage at The Forge, we inherited a disused 1930's house; no-one had lived in it for over fifteen years. Malcolm decided to have it made habitable so that he could literally live on the job; deja vu of the old 'Barracks' days. The windows were replaced, a bit of new carpet laid, the services connected and he was happy. He actually stayed there for two years and even spent twelve months of married life there.

One night, he was asleep in his bedroom when he heard an almighty crash outside. It turned out that a woman motorist had spun off the road whilst checking herself in the mirror and careered straight into the supports of our beloved giant sign, bringing it crashing to the ground. Malc sat bolt upright, thinking either he was under attack or the Martians had landed. He went outside and found a damsel in great distress and did what any gentleman would do. He made her a cup of coffee and calmed her down. The damaged sign meant an insurance claim which Malcolm dealt with. The insurance company took it away to get it repaired or replaced. It was back within a week, but when he went to test the lights on it he discovered they hadn't been put in. Then followed a series of it going back and forth with other faults that subsequently became apparent. Every time it would be delivered by this huge gorilla of a chap who would try to use his size to bully Malc into acceptance. But the little terrier was having none of it and when 'Bull Neck', as he dubbed him, returned for the sixth time and it still wasn't right, the fireworks really set off. Bull Neck lost it completely and set off chasing Malc round the workshop threatening to tear his heart out and other niceties. So dangerous was the situation that the police were called. They calmed the situation and asked Malc if he wanted to press charges? He said: "No, I just want my sign fixed properly". Three months to the day from when it was demolished, Malc finally accepted the replacement as satisfactory. It wasn't Bull Neck that delivered it though; he never saw him again.

It wasn't the only time he was threatened. A company called Jewells, a butchers in Longbridge, had an account with us for servicing, which had run into a very heavy deficit before they went bust. All the warning signs were there and I should perhaps have seen it coming. When they went to the wall we had two of their vans in for service at Rednal. Well, I felt it was fair game to claim them to recoup some of the loss. When the receiver came a-calling they were nowhere to be seen. Malc and I had them carefully hidden at a friend's barn in Redditch. The nice debt collectors were replaced by heavies who, getting nothing from me, called over to attempt to persuade Malc to come up with their whereabouts. Fortunately, they didn't realise we were brothers and when the strong arm tactics didn't work they tried to bribe him with fifty quid.

"Mate, I wish I knew," he told them, "I could really do with fifty quid and that Douglas Clark is a right bastard to work for."

They left empty-handed and, a few months later, we sprayed the vans and moved them on in the trade. They didn't fetch as much as we were owed, but I felt justice had been served.

XII

Another amusing incident whilst Malc was living at The Forge was when a cyclist knocked on his door fairly late at night and asked if he could leave his bike there overnight, as he had found a lift with some mates in the warmth of a car. Malc agreed and then, as soon as he was gone, started riding it in and out of the pumps. So carried away was he with doing stunts that he failed to notice a police patrol car had pulled up on the forecourt. The copper was new to the area and didn't believe Malc when he said he lived there; he was all set to arrest him for disorderly conduct when he was persuaded to ring me and I vouched for him. We still laugh about that today.

XIII

The one area of our business Malcolm and I had often discussed was getting into bodywork. This wasn't just for the extra revenue it would introduce, but also because we were never really satisfied with the work carried out by the companies we recommended. It was therefore a natural part of the plan to introduce a body shop at Hagley at some point. In the meantime, the best freelancer we found was a neighbour of mine at Chaddesley Corbett, Charlie Pettit. He worked in his barn at home most of the time. Malcolm got him the business and we went evens on the profit. Charlie was a charmer with the women, which was a problem as, at the first sniff of a skirt, he would down tools and be off having nookie. This meant that Malcolm could never promise a customer a definite collection time, which went against our business ethics. Also, skilled as he was, when totty was on the scene the standard of work dropped and, more often than not, Malcolm would send the work back to be redone. After all, it was the Clark reputation on line.

Inside The Forge workshop was a bay that had at one time been used for washing cars. I discussed with Malcolm the idea of bricking up the sides and ends and turning it into a spray booth, thereby taking the first major step to bringing the bodywork in-house. So, he duly ordered up the bricks, bags of cement and a concrete mixer and was ready to start when he had an unexpected visitor. This was Rex Chamberlain who was the real estate manager from Shell and whose job it was to make sure Shell tenants were displaying the image that head office would wish to see.

He was delighted by the cleanliness everywhere, it was as spotless as Rednal. We had learnt that lesson long ago. He was also impressed with the smart gowns worn by the staff. In fact, his check-list was all going smoothly till he discovered the bricks and building materials all ready to make a permanent fixture in the workshop. Malcolm thought he was going to have a heart attack such was his distress.

"No, no, no!" Rex exclaimed. "You can't do this, you need planning permission and head office will never agree to it. No, no and no again!"

"I'll show you the plans," Malc told him innocently and proudly presented the drawing I had done which brought about even greater palpitations.

Malcolm rang me in distress whilst Rex was still saying "No!" over and over again. I told him there was nothing we could do, but give up on the idea and so that spray booth never did get built.

However it sparked off another idea in my mind. The old car showroom at The Forge was unused and this I thought would make an ideal spray and body shop. I had seen a state-of-the-art spray machine at an exhibition. It was made by 'Burntwood Engineering' and what impressed me was that Rolls Royce used one. So, without telling Malcolm, I contacted them and discussed a purchase. They said that it would need to have the floor dug up for air circulation underneath. This was a major structural change to the building and I knew

Shell would not agree to it. And so I suggested that they could have an order if they raised the machinery up on grids. They protested a little, but conceded it was possible. The low-bake oven arrived, much to Malcolm's amazement and delight, within a week. I had the windows painted out and an extractor fan put in the roof. It worked like dream; the paint was literally baked on the car and dry within forty minutes. The finish was perfection itself. We employed a manager, Graham Taylor, to run it and, within the month, it was chock-a-block with work. Within six months we were getting nearly all the insurance business around. Malcolm had put another nail in the coffin of rival Malcolm's business down the road.

XIV

Within twelve months of Malc taking it on, The Forge had become the local garage of choice. Whilst this was the medium-term plan, I hadn't anticipated it would become a short-term reality. Whilst it was a great achievement, it also brought corporate problems in so much as The Forge could no longer handle any work from Rednal. We were once again in the position of having to turn work away.

Salvation came in the form of planning permission for the big development at Rednal being granted. I wasted no time in getting cracking.

It's a truism that success breeds success. So delighted were Shell with what had happened at The Forge that they approached me with another massive opportunity. Their biggest petrol garage in the Stourbridge-Kidderminster area was The Cross Keys at Hagley. Again, this was a deal brokered by Rex Chamberlain.

"Do you fancy adding the crown jewels to your empire Doug?" He asked me. "The potential at The Cross Keys is huge. It's already our biggest local turnover and we want to at least double the pumps, expand the shop and make it even bigger. Are you up for it?"

Well I've never been known to say "No" up to this point and, despite the fact that there were already not enough hours in the day to manage what we had, I jumped at it. It made sense when he said that if we take on Cross Keys then the proviso was that Shell would take the petrol out of The Forge and, with their interest gone, sell us the premises. 'Actually, that would be a blessing and another notch on the bedpost for total ownership of everything,' I thought to myself. 'We'll knock that house down, expand the shop and rent out the forecourt to a used-car dealer.' And so we did, within weeks of the pumps going. The icing on the cake was that I managed to get them to agree to sell the freehold to us at the same time, for the princely sum of forty grand.

I went out to celebrate and chill out with Jimmy Fletcher, who was now thriving with the onset of the fruit machine craze and the relaxation of prize money laws. He had banks of fruit machines at the Copper Coin and an over 18's area which took big money. We went over to Bridgnorth to see ex-Chalet Country Club owner Robert Cresswell who had opened a pub there. That night I smoked fag after fag, got home with heaving lungs and was actually physically chucking up obnoxious bile. I made my mind up there and then to quit. I've mentioned before that when I make my mind up there is no back-tracking. Bearing in mind I had been at it since I was eleven, it was a real test of will-power in those early days. I do have a Romeo and Juliet cigar once in a blue moon, as a special treat, and I really savour that.

11 – A Leap Into The Deep End

I

There were three big things going on in 1973: the development at Rednal, taking on Cross Keys and the birth of Treble-S. As number three is something I haven't mentioned before, I'm going to start with that.

In essence, it was the birth of the forecourt shop as you know it today, a sort of mini supermarket with a captive audience, some of which are now open 24/7. Back in the 1970's though they were mostly just kiosks which sold cigarettes, bars of chocolate, batteries and a few motoring accessories. We were already doing all these plus bundles of firewood. The story here was that I was talking to my neighbour and noticed that he had got a massive pile of wood offcuts. These had come from a window manufacturer and he used them to feed a burner for his greenhouse. He told me that there was far more than he needed, so a deal was struck whereby I provided him with plastic bags and he put bundles of this soft wood into them. I paid him 32p a bag and put them out on the forecourts at £1.99 a bag. They flew off as soon as I put them out. You have to remember that, in those days, everyone had an open fire at home. Over four years, I made fifty-seven grand out of those little bundles of wood. I also sold a range of handmade rustic garden seats and bird tables (these were made by a lovely husband and wife couple, Mr. and Mrs. Doolittle) and at Christmas the little tit boxes went down a treat, again at £1.99. Next came grow bags, I did a deal with a company to have forty tons of grow bags a year delivered to Badgers Cottage from where I would load them up into the van in the mornings and take a dozen to each of the garages. I paid 99p and sold them for £1.99, one hundred percent profit. I added to this: ladies handbags, clock radios and Casio watches. Then, on a visit to the Spring Fair at the National Exhibition Centre, I wandered on to the stand of a Dutch company called Curver. They made a revolutionary range of storage boxes, plastic buckets, laundry baskets, bowls, jugs and all sorts of other kitchen and household utensils. The difference between Curver products and any other plastic range on the market was that these were sturdy and of a quality you wouldn't mind having on view.

II

Curver was the start of my forecourt revolution. I obtained, there and then at the exhibition, a contract to secure for the next twelve months with an option of another twelve. Within a week, the first cross-European pantechnicon rolled up at Rednal and we unloaded enough plastic products to cram what little storage space we had to the rafters. That was after putting them all over the forecourt. They sold like hot cakes. The entire stock was gone within the week and I doubled the order for the following week and also had a separate load sent across to The Forge as well as to our newest addition, Cross Keys, where the sales success was repeated. The word got around, retailers wanted to stock them and it was only a matter of weeks before we were supplying all over the country.

III

It was all a question of logistics. I applied the logistics and the money just kept rolling in.

Shell was well-impressed with this evolution, so much so that at the next Shell retailer convention they set up a mini-meeting between myself, Ray Slater, Tom Cox, Ken Barwell and Ron Nicholls. These were other garage owners that had the same idea as me, not plastic buckets, but each had thought outside the petrol 'box' and added innovation to their forecourts.

"Gentlemen," said an executive from Shell, Peter Scott Simmons, "welcome to the Grand Council of the SSS."

We looked at him inquisitively.

"Shell Saver Shops," he explained; "you innovated it and we want you to run it under a Shell corporate banner, nationwide. From now on, all of our forecourt shops are to become Shell Saver Shops and, just like it says on the label, we want you to provide the Shell Saver goods."

A plan was hatched and the company was born. We all got on well from the outset and took on buying areas and lines; each complimenting the other. Tom Cox already had connections in the Far East, so that was an obvious choice for him. He went on buying expeditions and soon we were selling digital watches, clocks and all sorts of electrical and electronic gadgets. So popular were some of these, such as the watches which we purchased for 99p and sold for £1.99, that we linked them to pump promotions such as: only one watch per visit and the motorist had to buy a minimum four gallons of petrol to qualify. Some people even filled up the four gallons, got their watch, went round the block and did the same again thinking they were being smart. Often they stopped working in the first few days, but that was easily solved as we handed them a brand new one with a smile.

Ken Barwell, who had possibly the biggest garage and stores of us all at Yardley, concentrated on motoring accessories: everything from spark plugs to de misting cloths. Tom Cox, took on garden furniture, fancy goods, electrical goods and more. Ron Nicholls, who had a huge self-service garage at Bearwood, took on fancy goods. This included everything you can think of as fancy. Glassware from Italy, beer mugs from Germany, umbrellas from somewhere else and multi-coloured, flashing cigarette lighters by the boxful; he also made sure that the product range was constantly changed. Ray Slater, whose garage was at the Maypole, took on the more sophisticated areas of electricals, such as car and domestic radios, the first small portable televisions and van hire.

IV

In addition to my contract with Curver, I was also responsible for other parts of Europe where I sourced garden furniture amongst other things. So now the motorist would walk through an array of patio furniture, buckets and storage boxes into an Aladdin's cave of novelty, domestic and motoring goods. It was rare that they left without buying far more than just the petrol they had put in their tank. To accommodate the logistics of all this I implemented an array of systems which were all displayed on a wall map. We supplied not only garages the length and breadth of the land, but retail shops, schools and hospitals. The deliveries ran into many van-loads per week with potential for disaster, yet it ran with the efficiency of a Swiss railway. Rarely was a delivery not in or out on time. I applied what I call my three-legged stool approach. One leg was the customer who wanted good value, innovation and satisfaction from his own customers with stock delivered on time. The second leg was the staff; I now had a small army of dedicated office staff who were well paid and 'Clarked'. It was no longer a one-man logistic team. The third was the company; despite the fact that this could have been a separate business in its own right, I treated it as part of the whole Clark Empire and never lost sight of the fact that our core business was servicing and repairs. Nor did I rob Peter to pay Paul or gamble with the finances; everything had to be self funding. I was seeing too many companies come crashing down through under-funding and over-trading in the mid seventies. That's why I made sure the three-legged stool never even wobbled. The Treble-S team worked together for the next decade and made a small fortune in the process. We met often and fed off each other in terms of mental agility. Looking back, I was really lucky and proud to have them as partners.

V

Back in our own little empire of Rednal, we added another prize: College Service Station in Bromsgrove - another Shell, high-volume, self-service, huge forecourt business. Along with The Forge (even though it was now a garage without petrol) and Cross Keys, by the time 1974 ended we were getting a thousand motorists a day onto the forecourts. At Cross Keys we achieved the seven-figure milestone of 1,000,000 gallons of fuel sold per annum.

Then came the oil crisis I referred to earlier. What a marketing opportunity; thank you Mr. Nasser! At all four garages we issued special window screen stickers to our service customers displaying the legend 'Clark's Priority Customer'. In fact, you can still see some of them on classic cars today. What it entitled them to was fuel over and above the passing motorist. They were badges of pride and honour.

VI

So, with planning permission granted for Rednal, the last lorry taking soil away from the bank and the cottages razed to the ground, all was ready to make the next dream come true. Almost, that is, for there was still one little piece of the planning jigsaw I needed to solve. I had, for a couple of years, been trying to buy the hot-dog stand and the detached house that stood to the right of the garage in order to complete the horse shoe shape I had in my mind, and on bits of paper, for the new building. It was owned by the sister of George Smart, the fairground man. She lived in the house and the hot-dog stand was run by her nephew, George's son. It was George who had put the 'mockers' on any deal by insisting she asked silly money. I went behind his back and did a deal with her directly. George was not a happy man and, as the rumours of people who had crossed his path over the years and had ended up regretting it were legendary, I must admit to being a little nervous. George ranted and raved at me, stating that I was taking the bread out of his son's mouth, but confined his anger at that, much to my relief. However, I knew I was on his list of enemies and that wasn't good.

Was it just coincidence that a few days after completing the deal I received a frantic call from Malcolm? He had tracked me down to the Albany Hotel in Birmingham where I was attending a meeting.

"You need to get back here quick," he told me. "There are police all over the place with a warrant to search everywhere!"

I made my apologies and hot-tailed it back to Rednal. My mind was racing away, going through all the possibilities. "You run a clean business," I told myself. "Walk in tall and show them you have nothing to fear." They searched every nook and cranny and came up with nothing that we did not have a receipt for. My over-engineered ledger system was immaculate proof that everything was above board.

"I'd like permission to search your houses," the officer in charge told me when they had finished.

"On the condition you tell me what this is all about," I told him.

"That's fair," he pondered. "We've had a tip-off that you're using stolen parts from Longbridge."

"I think not," I told him. "Do you honestly imagine we would risk that after building a solid business like this? Or, for that matter, risk the relationship with our biggest customer. Go ahead and search where you want."

So they searched everywhere and came back with nothing. It was getting dark when they returned empty handed.

"Boots of your cars?" He asked.

I sighed, but told him to go ahead.

There, in the boot of Malcolm's car was a lone ignition coil that we didn't have a receipt for.

"I think we needn't worry about that," the officer said. "I'm very sorry to have troubled you, Mr. Clark; it seems someone has it in for you."

'Yes!' I thought to myself. 'And I have a pretty good idea who that can be.'

Life is too short and there would have been no mileage in starting some sort of vendetta, so I just chalked that one down to experience. Good job too, in hindsight! As, a couple of years later, I discovered the name of the real culprit and it wasn't George.

VII

At the same time as the development was about to start, I was nearing completion of the renovations at Badgers Cottage.

It's rather important that I mention this as part of that construction work was to have a profound effect on my thinking for the Rednal building.

Internally at the cottage I hadn't just gone out and ordered materials simply to get the job finished; rather, I sourced what I had in mind from far and wide. Such as the sandstone pillars for the inglenook fireplace: they came from The Shoulder of Mutton in Bromsgrove (now a superb live music venue, The Wishing Well). The elm beam support above the inglenook came from another friend, Phil Morgan. Jack Oddy, who was a customer and once the highest ranking pattern maker in Longbridge, got me the granite for the driveway from the Strathalan Hotel in Birmingham. I built a new lounge with an upstairs conservatory leading off the master bedroom. A spiral staircase from the lounge was space saving and a joy to the eye. The staircase was also via Jack, who got that for me from the old Central Post Office in Birmingham City Centre; I swapped him a tractor for it.

Badgers Cottage became just as I had imagined it when I first set eyes on the sad, animal-inhabited dwelling on that fateful visit to see Dad.

VIII

I put in a swimming pool; well, it was the same price as a Mini in those days so it wasn't so much extravagance as choice - new car or pool - no contest really. This was actually delivered by police escort and was the talk of the village. I also had a large summer house built by the pool which would double as changing rooms. All-in-all, it was becoming our dream home.

Now, as I said, there was something which happened when working on the cottage that helped my thinking on Rednal. I had a yen to build a stable block; Jan was into horses and I wanted to get a pony for my daughter, Julia, and so I designed a steel-framed building on my usual note pad and instructed the work to commence. The trouble was: I got the load-bearing calculations wrong; this caused major structural errors. The roof sagged through lack of support strength. I admitted to myself that this would not have happened had I had it designed professionally, a lesson I took on board when commencing 'the big one' at Rednal.

IX

There was a company at that time called Redpath, Dorman, Long, they were designers and builders of steel fabricated buildings and one claim to fame was that they manufactured the structure for the Sydney Harbour Bridge. They had so much work to do at Leyland that they opened a permanent office there. They were forever taking buildings down and erecting more efficient ones space-wise. One of the employees there was Dave Fletcher (later he was to start his own company, DGF Engineering); he was also a customer of ours. I recall we looked after his Morris J2 van. In conversation with David, when I was telling him about my problems with the stables, he told me that what I was trying to achieve was a portal-frame building. That is the terminology for a steel-framed structure that supports itself by everything leaning on itself, thus spreading the load evenly and giving it what I now know to be structural integrity. It means that as long as you have the structure right, you can do whatever you like with the building itself.

Dave introduced me, at my request, to their senior structural engineer, John Campbell. I immediately warmed to him and engaged him to design the portal frame for Rednal. It was a relationship that was to last many years. I engaged him on permanent contract from Redpath, Doorman, Long to Clark's. Rednal was just the start; together we built all sorts and shapes of garages, still from my drawings, but with him providing the steel infrastructure plans to make it happen correctly. John was in charge of calculations, but went on to become senior design and structural engineer alongside John Fisher and Dave.

X

Another key player who came on board at that time was Mike Chapman. He was a superb architect who developed the knack of quickly comprehending what I couldn't put into words and transforming my rough sketches into detailed plans. He also knew his way round building regulations and made me legal in that sense too. I first met Mike through Dad; we were both at a cheese and wine function in Chaddesley at the back end of the sixties. Mike gave me his card which I kept and, when I rang him a few years later, he knew exactly who I was; Douglas, son of Noel.

XI

So the work began. As the ground was sandy, Mike insisted the foundations would be particularly sturdy. They were two foot deep and made up of vibrated concrete. We were actually grateful for the sand, this served as an excellent moulding base. When the concrete was being poured into the mould, Malcolm came across to watch it gently flowing in. We had a chuckle or two as we recalled the wooden planks we had used when concreting the pit back in the bad old days.

XII

Sadly, Jess never got to see the completed Rednal garage; he died aged 85 in 1974 and his wife, Margaret, two years later. I regret that neither of them witnessed the miracle, but I'm sure they sat on a golden perch somewhere, smiling down. I imagined Jess turning to Margaret and saying, "Taught him everything I knew and now look at him."

And she would respond with a twinkle "Yes, our Dougie, Lord of Lickey Manor."

XIII

I had one overwhelming criterion in the design of the Rednal complex, which was to be able to see everything. With this in mind, I insisted that my office would be open-plan and sited with my desk in the window, from where I could see across into the new reception - about to be built. I also wanted to see down into the workshops and, across from where I was seated, to all the sales and purchase desks. Nothing was to be obscured from my all-seeing eye.

XIV

The work was to continue until 1980. It started in phases: the first being a service road which would eventually surround the entire complex. Next came the new workshops, right behind the old ones and right up to the service road, which in turn now edged the bottom of the bank we had excavated. Above this were to be built the new offices. It took a little over twelve months to realise this phase and during that period we continued to use the original front bays right up to the last minute. It was a momentous day for us when that first phase was finished. Not only did it look good, it contained some fabulous new gear - some of which is still in use today. In particular, I had a really expensive brake disc skimming and resurfacing machine that was the first of its type in the Midlands.

In fact, you couldn't get that kind of work done at any garage that I knew of; the brake discs had previously been sent away to a specialist firm. So, what we offered the customer was quite unique.

I got my wish with the office too. From my 'throne' I could survey my whole domain and communicate with anyone and everyone through a microphone I had rigged up to the desk. I delighted in being able to say "Customer waiting!" or "Car registration number 'so and so' obstructing the forecourt!" The customers loved it but, as you can imagine, the staff were not too keen. It was a little 1984 and big brotherish, but it paid dividends and gave me many a chuckle. In fact, so awesome was the power of my microphone that I only had to run my hand over it and make it crackle to bring about a reaction.

Some devious members of staff got together clandestinely and forged a cunning plan to rid me of my megaphone of power. I was anonymously reported to the council. Surreptitious sound levels were recorded and I was ordered to stop using it or face hefty fines for breaching the noise abatement act. My eighteen months of broadcasting came to an abrupt end. I never found the saboteurs, though I spent days watching the faces for giveaway signs of merriment. Seems everyone had a happy face but me. Deep down I chuckled too, but didn't let it show. Looking back, I say "Well done guys, good call."

XV

In my team of office personnel I had four ladies who were all gems; the three M's: Margaret Pash on the purchase ledger, Marg Wathen on cash control, Margaret McCall on sales ledger and also, Eleanor Rigby (yes, her real name) as management accountant. I made them all managers and they, in turn, had staff reporting to them.

It was 1976 and we reached another landmark. Throughout the company we now employed over one hundred people, not to mention the part-timers.

XVI

The transformation continued ever-onwards in the latter half of the seventies as cash allowed. We built a new MOT bay complete with a rolling road, brake tester and a 4-post lift.

Next to the lower workshops (going to the left as seen from the front), came a steam-cleaning bay and a valeting room. I designed this in such a way that it was accessible from either: in front from the forecourt or behind from the service road. The steam-cleaning room was really well appointed with powerful pressure washers; so powerful, in fact, that they would occasionally take the under-seal off the cars. Next to that was a tyre fitting bay and between this and the valeting bay, was a staircase going up to what was to be our sales offices. In the tyre fitting bay I introduced a real revolutionary idea - a turn-table. What this meant was that a car could be driven in frontwards, have its tyres changed and then turned round on the circular turntable (a bit like the ones used for trains) and driven out again. This was not a gimmick or an extravagance, but a time-saving piece of mechanical ingenuity. I reckon we got at least three more cars through a day because of it. You have to imagine that Rednal was now like Piccadilly Circus on a bad day. Cars were coming in continuously for petrol, service and MOTs; then there were the deliveries, not to mention all the construction vehicles and the contract cars. It could have been a permanent traffic jam, but for most of the time it was free flowing.

At the back of the tyre fitting bay there was a staff room where the troops could have a brew at break time. There were also separate staff toilets in this area. I earnestly believe that a toilet says much about a person or a business. If you go to the loo and find you have to pull a piece of string to flush it, or it's filthy dirty and cold, then what does that say about what they are doing to your car? So, both customer and staff toilets were kept spotless, had bowls of pot pourri to make them smell nice, and yes, I did inspect them personally.

Coming down from the tyre fitting bay were a series of workshops; these formed the left-hand side of the horseshoe. Each bay was fitted with 2-post lifts and had its own set of service tools. I invited customers to watch their cars being serviced by our team of mechanics, all neatly dressed in their brown service coats with 'Clark Care' embroidered on the breast pocket. It never failed to impress. I nearly always wore one myself in case I needed to stick my head under a bonnet or two, but also to convey a message of equality, though I admit to being more equal than others.

At the end of the service bays were the service reception and communications rooms; these comprised the last phase of all. Up to the end of the decade, part of this function was carried out from a port-a-cabin sited on the forecourt, near to the shop.

For heating and air conditioning, I had heat pumps installed in the roof. The siting of them was contrary to the advice of the manufacturers, who were concerned they might fall and tried to insist the exchange units be located outside. This was totally impractical and I insisted they be sited where I planned or I'd cancel the order. They conceded and everything worked just fine. I created a very pleasant climate-controlled environment, which meant happy staff and happy customers. Shell brought over various managers to visit us with increasing regularity: to gaze in awe at our 'monument to imagination' that had risen from the bank and also to show other dealers the standards in service excellence we were setting.

XVII

By the end of the seventies 'The Headquarters', as we now referred to it, was complete. However, there was more to come. I wanted room for another reception for a new innovation, the 'U Can Hire' business, which I will come to in a later chapter. For now, let me leave you with imagining the satisfaction I experienced when we were appointed as main service agents for Rover in 1982.

12 – Hot Nights, Horses And Sunroofs

I

Now, by this point I think you might have got to know me quite well. I hope I don't come across as conceited or smug, because I feel I'm not. I believe I remain to this day a modest man. For what I have achieved I am not only grateful, but thank God. Looking back, it seems like a dream - but happen it did.

So there were times when I would take a reality check and time out for a breather or a bender. One of those occasions was in the hot summer of 1975 when the swimming pool was in situ at Badgers Cottage and Jan and I decided to throw a launch party.

What a party that turned out to be. We went to the Cofton Country club on a prearranged meet-up with several couples we had socialised with on and off over the past few years. Like us, they were all fairly successful business couples who worked so damned hard that the need to let off steam became overwhelming once in a while. We danced the night away at the club and then everybody piled back to ours for supper and to see the new floodlit pool, which had been the talk of the club that evening. It was gone midnight and the gin and tonics were flowing freely; the night was still very hot. So it came quite naturally when a large-breasted brunette was the first to divest herself of all clothing and, to a round of applause, jump into the pool, re-emerging seconds later with a smile and engorged nipples which bobbed up and down on the surface of the water, enhanced by the glow of a full moon.

This was a sort of unseen signal as everyone was soon shedding clothes around me and diving or jumping into the pool. The laughter was raucous and wild. Summer frenzy took over; pool games became poolside games, which in turn became garden games. Couples swapped partners, made up threesomes and moresomes, as I gazed in awe at this spectacle of nymphs and nymphets engaging in all sorts of gymnastic permutations and activities. There was a tug to my arm and I gazed no more, but joined in my very own Roman orgy. What a way to host a house warming party. I'll name no names, but you know who you are and wasn't it fun?

II

Everything in Doug Clark's garden was truly wonderful in the mid seventies. 'Put the right systems in place, invest in the right people, pay them well and give them responsibility, then make them accountable. Look after your customers, give them what they want, when they want it and at a fair price. Finally, communicate your message to staff, suppliers and customers clearly and precisely.' This was written in my office, by my bed and by every telephone I had. It was my law unto myself and it really worked. So when a friend and customer, Tony Bird, came to see me, suggesting a new business venture, outside of Clark's and my safety zone, I thought applying the same formula would bring about more instant success. How wrong I was!

Tony's wife had a small business manufacturing and supplying horse head collars (eventually to become a world-wide business). He asked me to go into partnership with him in a venture at a closed-down shop I had bought to convert into flats in Barnt Green on the High Street. I had already done the first floor, but hadn't started on the shop and so it was currently just lying empty.

The idea was to sell his wife's products and lots of other horse tack. He even had a name in mind: The House of the Cavalier. Well, as Barnt Green village was the small, but thriving shopping centre for all the rich and famous that lived in the surrounding large houses, complete with stabling, I thought it a great idea. We struck up a partnership and converted the premises.

III

I made contact with Harris Meyer who was the Rolls Royce of equestrian attire, fully stocked the shop out with the finest saddlery; then, in a blaze of publicity we opened the The House of the Cavalier for business. The show jumper, Anne Moore, cut the ribbon and we did moderately well. We soon realised however that, although it would chug along, the business was never really going to make us worthwhile money. I also had a good offer on the whole premises from George Smart and, as the two remaining cottages by the garage had come up for sale, I could really do with the funds. So I talked to Tony and he agreed we should close. The only problem was that we were left with an awful lot of unsold stock. In my usual purchasing manner I had bought in bulk to get the prices down.

IV

Doing some research I had discovered that one of the biggest horsey exhibitions was held bi-annually in Germany. It was called 'Essener Equitana' and, looking at the attendance figures over the years, was an established winner with the riding community on a Europe-wide basis. I had an idea: to divest ourselves of the stock and recoup the losses. We would attend the show as exhibitors and sell it off. But we needed a gimmick. What better way to attract the customers than to personalise the tack with engraved brass name plates, done there and then on the stand.

"It's really only a matter of logistics," I told Tony. "We hire a bloody big lorry and drive the gear over ourselves."

"We'll need a massive stand if we're going to start engraving name plates," he countered.

"No we won't; we'll set all that up in the truck outside. Just have a good display on a small stand, take the orders and have them call back to collect their wares within thirty minutes. It's only like servicing cars," I laughed, "and that I do know a little about, unlike horses." I knew that the government was very keen to promote export through trade shows and that there were many grants available for that. I cheekily contacted the Department of Trade and Industry and, after being put through to several people, convinced the white collar manager with a plum in his mouth at the other end of the line that The House of Cavalier was ready to expand and export. He had no idea that we were shutting up shop.

Grant negotiated, pantechnicon booked and kitted out with an engraving machine and supply of brass plaques, Terry Bird (Tony's son) and I set off on our European adventure, loaded to the gunwales with all the stock from the shop and everywhere else I had it hoarded.

V

Well, Doug Clark's two-man invasion of Europe was, unlike the shop, a storming success. The aisle to our stand was blocked with visitors ready to part with their Deutsch Marks for saddlery and brass plates with their horse's name on it. What a souvenir of their visit to the show.

We sold out of everything before the show hit its final day and went out into the despotic nightlife of Essen to celebrate with schnapps and steins and Fräuleins.

Although it turned out all right in the end, financially, this episode taught me another valuable lesson: stick to what you know best, diversify from the core, don't start another core.

VI

Now sunroofs were different. They were part of the car, so therefore, part of the core. I theorised this to Malcolm over a pint at our now-regular weekly meeting at the Robin Hood in Drayton. Malc, since being seconded to Hagley on a permanent basis, had told me he was feeling a bit isolated. Even though we had put a direct line between the two garages, it was not face-to-face; so I introduced these get-togethers as a way of addressing that problem.

They were great sounding-boards and a chance to have some much missed brotherly bonding, as since he now had a house and family of his own, we didn't have anywhere near as much contact outside of the business as both of us would have liked.

This was the same hot summer of the infamous pool party and the weather was still roasting. Very few cars had sunroofs fitted as standard and it hadn't escaped my attention that there was a thirsty market for them.

"I've got this contact through the guys at Treble-S," I enthused to Malcolm. It's called Skylark Sunroofs and they are based in South Africa. We're going to import them and sell them as a kit in the Saver Shops."

"Where do they get them fitted?" Malc asked me.

"That's the clever bit; every one sold will include a discount voucher for fitting at Rednal. I've got it all set up there and then, if it takes off big time, you can do them at The Forge too," I smiled. "I think at Cross Keys would be better," he pondered. "We don't have the space at The Forge, the bodywork is going through the roof, it would be an attraction at Cross Keys and you'll get much more traffic. We don't have petrol there, remember."

I looked at him with a new respect; he wasn't challenging me, he was telling me and what he said made sense.

"You're dead right, Malc," I said, "and I know just the bloke to do it for us at Cross Keys when we're ready to move."

VII

So the next venture began. We imported and fitted them; it was a huge overnight success. Then suddenly, there was one massive problem. Those sunroofs were made for the South African market, where the sun nearly always shone, not like our fickle weather. The rubber seal that went round the aperture was like a sponge; instead of keeping the rain out, it sucked it up like blotting paper until it couldn't soak up any more. What happened next was it poured into the car, drenching the driver and any hapless passengers. It didn't drip, it poured.

I managed, very quickly, to get a new seal manufactured that was up to the job. We had sold hundreds and I was determined they wouldn't besmirch our good name. We told everyone that we would refit the offending items free of charge. Of course everyone wanted it done at once, which was understandable, but a logistical nightmare. For days we had vehicles queuing down the road from opening time to closing time.

Meanwhile, I ranted and raved at Skylark in South Africa to get their finger from up their backside and modify the seal. They did this and we were soon selling them again, but the brand name was tarnished and it was time to find another supplier.

To make matters worse, John Tibbots, our sunroof fitter, had a disaster when he was taking a load of rivets to Cross Keys from Rednal in his old, rotting Vauxhall Viva. Upon opening up his boot on arrival, he found that the contents had disappeared on the journey through a hole in the floor. Rivets had been dispersed like the Pied Piper's peas all over the roads leading to Rednal. By the time he got as far as Lickey, they had all gone save for just one 'born survivor' little rivet who made it all the way. For days these little things were everywhere and deadly to tyres; seemed like they lay in wait for the motorists to embed themselves into every available aperture.

Cars were queuing up again, not for replacement seals this time, but for puncture repairs. We did a roaring trade and certainly did not let on that it was one of our staff that had brought about this puncture plague.

VIII

Having dipped our toes in the water and, despite getting them burnt a little, there was absolutely no doubt in my mind that sunroofs were excellent business. We needed to legitimise them though; the selling-through-the-shops notion was tainted and so was the name Skylark. So, what better company was there to get a franchise from than the brand leaders: Britax Weathershields?

They didn't give them away willy-nilly either. You had to prove that you had a dedicated space and qualified staff before they would even consider you. However, who could not but be impressed with our prestigious Rednal Head-quarters?

We passed muster with flying colours and soon had the sought-after yellow and black Britax Logo on the windows. I even ensured it had its own reception and waiting area.

The Britax product was superior in every way to anything else we had sold and fitted. Not only did we get to fit them to 'on-the-road' cars, we also got contracts to fit them to brand new ones from Rover, for customers who had ordered them as an extra.

It was time to expand this particular operation to the highly successful petrol business we had at Cross Keys. I negotiated a Britax franchise for there as well. The garage was already tight on space, as it had ten pumps, a shop and a jet wash, but I figured there was enough room at the rear to build a covered way big enough to fit the sunroofs in. So, in true form, I got it transformed in no time.

Once ready to roll, the man I brought across to head this was Alan Blundell who was our most experienced sun roof fitter at Rednal. That left Richard Dodd, who Alan had trained up, running the sun roof and vinyl operation at Rednal. In fact, so successful was Cross Keys that I had to move Richard across as well, within two months, as Alan couldn't cope with the demand. At the same time, up for overdue promotion was our Rednal forecourt manager, Dave Price. He made sure that we never ran out of fuel and that everything was pristine. Customers and staff all liked Dave and he took my ranting at him, when traffic flow held up the day, in good heart. I suppose he was more in fear of me than in awe, and that is something on reflection that I regret. Age does indeed mellow. I gave Dave a raise and put him in charge of all of our forecourts. Dave increased the gallonage at Cross Keys by 25% in the first three months that he was in charge. This once again proved that customer care pays dividends. A smile and good service and you'll go back, often making it your local; a scowl or disinterest and you won't go out of your way to return.

It incenses me today when I go to fill up at any garage in England and, as I go into the shop to pay, the cashier is on his or her mobile. They swipe your card without looking at you, gesture to put your pin number in the machine and thrust you a receipt without a please or a thank you. Call me old-fashioned, but this is downright rude as well as bad business.

So Dave was Mr. Charm and all our forecourts were thriving under his management. That is, until he decided to run off with the cashier. His wife came in to see me in floods of tears and after consoling her, I was off on the warpath to find our errant manager.

I told him what a prat he was; by all means have some nookie, but don't rock the domestic boat.

"I'm not like you Doug," he said, "I fall in love." My lower lip quivered.

I warned him that further philandering with members of staff would have dire consequences all round. Yes, I know it was the pot calling the kettle black, but I didn't get caught did I? Nor did I have any intention of leaving my family.

IX

So well did we do with our sunroof division, that in 1979 we were awarded first prize for the 'best sunroof achievement of the year by any Britax Weathershield dealer'. It was a cheque for £400, presented to us at a dinner by Derek Peatey, the managing director of Britax. It was a proud moment and tangible justification for having and maintaining the highest standards. "Reach for the stars, not the moon," I told the staff at the next briefing.

X

In the latter part of the 70's I achieved a personal status in the industry I never dreamt was possible. Amongst many memorable events, three stick out. Firstly, the dinner I was invited to by the Bank of England at the Botanical Gardens in Birmingham where I dined amongst the captains of industry, including more 'sirs' than you could shake a stick at. I went in style, in my chauffeur-driven Rolls Royce and accompanied by Tony Bird who had also been invited and was building an extremely large and successful business himself. We drank champagne all the way there.

The next, was being invited to leave or sell my share in Clark's' and become CEO of Service Operations for 'Evans, Halshaw', who claimed to be the UK's leading car and van retailer (better known as P.J.Evans). They offered me a staggering three and a half million pounds spread over five years. The trouble was the payment was to be made out of increased profits and with more penalty clauses than a minefield has mines. I told them: "Thanks, but no thanks", but I was dead flattered to be asked.

The third was an amazing helicopter trip I was invited on by Shell to visit their oil rig operation in the North Sea. I loved the sense of danger when we were briefed on what to do if the helicopter crashed. I was thrilled to wear an all-over survival suit and I was just blown away by getting out of the helicopter onto the rig and shaking hands with the rig boss, just like I was the prime minister.

The trip was hosted by the regional director of Shell, Stan Thomas. I was, in fact, the only dealer to be invited and the reason became apparent over dinner when he said: "Douglas, I can see what's happening with your business and everyone at Shell is extremely impressed with what you've done with the Treble-S shops so far."

I waited for a sting in the tail. Were they about to take them away from us and manage them themselves?

In fact, nothing could be further from the truth as he expounded: "Our investment in Lucas Batteries hasn't been all we would wish it to be. Would you like to take on battery sales for us nationally?"

"Would I? Don't be silly," I thought. With a name like Lucas, I would also have the muscle to bulk-buy starter motors, alternators and other electrical car components.

"I'll not only consider it, but give you a definite 'yes' now, if you're offering me the whole Lucas battery contract and not just the bits you can't shift," I told him.

He beamed and said: "I wouldn't have expected you to ask for anything less. Consider it done, the 'full monty', the whole of the Lucas B90 range." That was the catalyst I needed to become a wholesaler on a far larger scale than ever before.

13 – The Beautiful Body Shop

I

Cross Keys had gone from being a pretty unclean, old fashioned, three-pump business to a twelve-pump, spotless, recipe for success under Clark's. Whereas they opened 9-5 previously, we now opened 7-10; we also introduced another first, hot food, hot drinks and sandwiches!

Meanwhile back at The Forge, whilst I was running everything in what could best be described as a military operation; Malcolm was getting to grips with his pride and joy - The Baking Body Shop. This proved so successful that it wasn't long before once again, he had more work than he could handle.

Malcolm's mission was to not only provide at The Forge the best service around, but the best body-work repairs as well. Our state-of-the-art machine put him in a different league to anyone else. The spraying technique of acrylic, as opposed to cellulose, was a 'no contest' when it came to re-finishing. It was more environmentally friendly too, not that anyone bothered about the environment back in the 70's. We didn't realise what problems we were storing up for the future generations. Now we do and I'm not only an advocate of environmentalism, I'm a practitioner in everything I do.

Malc had taught himself to weld soon after the move to Hagley and had become pretty proficient at it. He had built a great little team of professionals around him, all well 'Clarked'.

"Truthfully, Doug," he said to me at one of our meetings, "anyone can use the paint machine given the training, but panel beating, hand finished painting and welding are all special skills in their own right and it takes special people, artists, to do it."

I wasn't going to argue with that.

"Trouble is," he went on, "we're right out of space and, much as I hate turning work away, we have to do it."

"On the service side too?" I asked him.

"Yes on the service side too," he ventured, "and you don't help either with your mania for buying up mountains of stock and storing it here. Did you know that a customer came in for his Jag the other day and we couldn't find the bloody thing?"

I laughed and so did he. "It took us over an hour to finally dig it out from under a mountain of Curver boxes."

II

A solution came once again through contact with Shell. Another garage was up for sale, this time The Belle-Vue at Marlbrook, near to Lickey. They didn't want it to be a petrol franchise; it was too small by their standards. They would rather just sell us the premises, which could not have been better for us.

I rang Malc on the dedicated line we had installed and told him the good news. "How do you feel about moving back over this way into new premises that just does bodywork?" I asked him.

"Sounds good to me, in fact it sounds great," he enthused, "and I've got just the bloke to take over managing The Forge for us."

This was a local guy called Chris Pardoe who Malcolm had not long taken on, but had been well and truly 'Clarked'. I liked him immediately and he went on to maintain the top standards of service Malcolm had introduced for many years.

At Belle-Vue, we transferred the low bake oven from Hagley, this time setting it into the floor as it was intended to be situated; plus, we built a superb paint shop with panel beating areas.

The only person Malcolm took with him from The Forge was 'Moaning Sid' as we called him. A good, if not great, panel beater who would not work a minute's overtime and pulled gurney-like faces at the very mention of it. Nevertheless, Malcolm needed him in the short term; he was getting on a bit and very set in his ways. He didn't last too long at Belle-Vue and took early retirement, but in the initial move, he served the purpose.

Malcolm was sorry to leave Rob Pinches behind, but there was no place for him at Belle-Vue, as his speciality was mechanics not body work. In fact, so skilled did he become that to call him a mechanic is really a disservice - master technician is more appropriate. He later moved back to Rednal and still works for us today on a personal level. When we eventually sold up, we gave Rob some specialist equipment to start up his own business and there is no one we trust more to maintain our own cars in England than Rob.

III

Malc recruited, or rather poached, the top panel beater from Tessall Garage to work alongside him at Belle-Vue as well as Moaning Sid. This was Bill Partridge who everyone said was the best around, although he would most often take the easy option, not the best one, which was frustrating. Malc cracked the whip and got his pound of flesh from him the hard way and he ended up staying with us right up to the 90's, when we sold this part of the business to MGR/Phoenix. But more of that later.

Belle-Vue emerged as a centre of excellence; Malc set and achieved the highest standards and pretty soon the order book was once again full. He would pay his staff well; traditionally, panel beaters would be on half the hourly rate of mechanics as it was a less skilled job. Malc argued their case, saying they were artists; he called it the 'fudge factor' which made me laugh and we did indeed pay them far more than the going rate. This meant that we had panel beaters queuing up to join us, so Malc got to the enviable position where he could take his pick. He had a big sign on the door of the Belle-Vue stating 'You're Welcome' and he meant it.

IV

Although it was indeed just a body shop, I did sneak in a state-of-the-art car wash - an Esquire Kleindienst - in fact, the Rolls Royce of car washes at the time. This meant car wash users had to go in somewhere to pay, so a small shop was in order too. It's always these little add-ons that put the icing on the cake.

A simple thing like putting out buckets and brushes, so that motorists queuing for a wash could give their wheels a once over, was so popular an innovation that people would come just because of it. They wouldn't dream of getting out the bucket at home though.

It was at the time of the move to Belle-Vue that Malc, taking a leaf out of my book, bought a rundown cottage in Bromsgrove called Timberhonger, after the district. It was set in fifty acres and, as I had done with Badgers Cottage, he lovingly had it rebuilt as a home for his new wife and family. Being just down a few back roads from Belle-Vue meant he could keep an eye on the building work and even do a bit himself.

It ensured that Malcolm and I were closer to each other too. He could pop to Rednal and I could pop to him and we could talk about other things (family matters for instance) rather than just pure business. For instance, I didn't realise that he had got close to Dad in the last years before he died. I didn't know that he would pick him up and they would go for a drink in Chaddesley, often joining in a 'lock-in' or two. This pleased me greatly and I'm sure Dad was proud to show him off.

V

The year 1980 approached and with it the start of a new decade. In that final year of the 70's the Shah of Persia was overthrown in the Iranian revolution and Ayatollah Khomeini returned there after fifteen years in exile. Saddam Hussein became President of Iraq with much help from the west. Margaret Thatcher became Britain's first female Prime Minister, heralding in changes which would shape the future for the rest of the century. The USSR and the USA signed the Salt II treaty limiting nuclear arms; Soviet forces, at the same time as it was being signed, were invading Afghanistan. Visicalc, the first spreadsheet software, was introduced - a life-changing development for business. Idi Admin, the Ugandan dictator, was finally deposed and no-one shed a tear over his demise. Rhodesia became Zimbabwe and what was once the food bowl of Africa was destined to start a spiral into poverty, that only gets worse as time goes by, under the despot Mugabe.

We did laugh though, as the Garfield comic strip first appeared and were saddened when the great Muhammad Ali announced his retirement from boxing. In technology, Sony introduced the very first Walkman and, with its birth, pedestrians became a liability as they crossed roads with music blaring in their ears. Pete Doherty the drug-fuelled singer, Jonny Wilkinson the Rugby hero and Michael Owen the football star were born. Sid Vicious of the Sex Pistols, Richard Beckinsale the actor from 'Rising Damp', Joyce Grenfell the actress and comedienne and forces sweetheart Gracie Fields all died. Airey Neave the politian and Earl Mountbatten were both needlessly assassinated by the IRA.

On a happier note, Britain's first nudist beach was given permission to open in Brighton.

Musically, the big hits were 'We Are Family' by Sister Sledge, 'Hot Stuff' by Donna Summer, 'Message In A Bottle' by the Police and 'Another Brick In The Wall' by Pink Floyd. On TV, we watched American shows such as Dukes of Hazard and Dallas.

The average price of a house in 1979 had soared to £13,500 and a gallon of petrol now cost seventy nine pence.

At Clark's, we celebrated a wonderful decade with a dinner for all managers at the Chung Ying restaurant in Birmingham and one hell of a party for all the staff at the Cofton Country Club. It had been a decade of expansion beyond belief; we had achieved so much and yet I knew the best was yet to come.

Photo Gallery

"A Photographic History of My Life"

Me and my first bike; aged about four, in the garden of
our first home, a rented cottage in Mustow Green.

Mom, Dorothy Morris,
always beautiful.

Mom with my sister Valerie
and me.

My brother Tony with my sisters
Pam, Val, Susan and Carol. *L to R*

Val 'cleaning up' outside
'The Little Garage.'

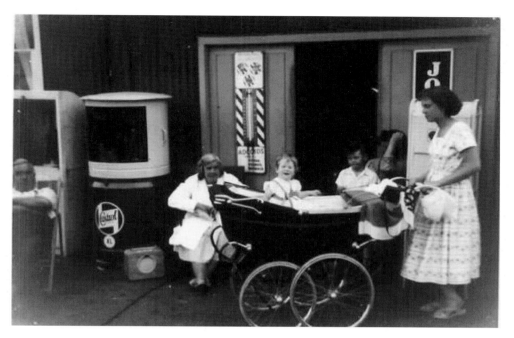

Grandad Fred and Nan (Morris) plus Grandchildren outside the Chaddesley Garage and here's the famous 'Silver Cross' pram.

Val, Grandad Fred, Nan and Mom at the wedding breakfast.

Grandad Fred's garage at Lower Chaddesley, opposite The Fox Public House. Circa 1953.

Pam and Malc with cousin Julie (*c*) braving the waves at Aberystwyth. Circa 1958

Malc promenading with Auntie Josie on the same holiday.

Pam with the ice creams.

Malc, Susan and Pam

Aunt Josie.

Uncle Morris.

Nan Morris beside one of Grandad Fred's taxis named The Queen Mary.

Mom and Dad's Wedding Day, St. Cassians Church,
Chaddesley Corbett 1941.

Mom at Val's Wedding.
St. Cassians again.

Grandad Fred at Aunt Josie's
Wedding.

Nan Morris and Auntie Maude,
Grandad's sister.

Pam and Nan at Val's wedding.

Bluntington Cottage, my dad's home. Note the petrol pump on right at the top garage.

FALSE DAWN: Prime Minister Neville Chamberlain made his 'peace in our time' address after meeting Hitler in September 1938; a year later Britain was at war

Prime minister Neville Chamberlain, Mom drove for him when he visited Kidderminster.

Group photo at Chaddesley Corbett Endowed School. Left adult, Headmaster, George Cotterill, right adult, Headmistress, Miss Mathews.

Me, relaxing in Grandad's garden.

Here I am, a proud choir boy outside St. Cassians Church.

Carol and Lionel's wedding day.

Val and Terry's wedding day.

Tony, Sue and me. Borth holiday, 1952.

Grandad Fred at Aunt Josie's
wedding.

Malc at Borth.

Malc again, outside
'The Little Garage.'

Malc outside Bill Turbott's cottage, next to The Little Garage.

I was proud to give away Carol on her wedding Day.

Original Badgers Cottage. Circa 1804.

My Father Noel Clark, (*CF*) on duty with the RAF during WWII.

L to R. Dad, Gramps with their Austin 7 and Ernie with his M.G.T.A.

Dad, on leave, at Bluntington Cottage posing with Ernie's
M.G.T.A.

Hazel Havard, a friend from
Rednal. Early 60's.

Me, outside Grandad's house
(Now the dining room of The Fox.)

Camping holiday in Aberystwyth with friends John Stone, Maurice Reeves, and Patrick Moulder

John Stone in 'Charles Atlas' pose.

Patrick Moulder testing the cider.

Early Citizens gig. The Crown at Wychbold.

Ford Falcon Special and Grandad's
King John Taxi.

Malc getting early motor bike
experience.

My M.G.T.C. 1960.

Malc sitting on the bonnet of my
hand-built Ford Falcon special.

The Barracks Pub, Rednal. This was the site of the future Rednal Garage, which today are dealerships for Rolls Royce and BMW motorcycles.

The Hare and Hounds Pub at Rednal. One hundred yards up from Rednal Garage at the Lickeys. Nice early photo. Circa 1912.

My 1961 Austin Healey Sprite.
Lickey Tram Terminus in the
background.

The 'Sprite' in action.

Tax disc for KAL 587, the M.G.T.C. my next car after the
Ford Falcon.

Form No. 69

Telephone No. 2211

WORCESTERSHIRE CONSTABULARY

COUNTY POLICE STATION

Bromsgrove.

25th September, 1959

Road Traffic Act 1930.   Section 4 (1)

Dear Sir,

It has been reported to me that at 3.0pm. on Saturday 5th September 1959, you being a person, who was not the holder of a licence, did drive a motor vehicle, reg. no. W.W.P. 781 on a road at High Street, Bromsgrove. Contrary to the above Act and Section.

No further action will be taken in this case, but I am to inform you that if you are reported again, it may be necessary to take proceedings against you in the later case.

Yours faithfully,

Chief Inspector / Superintendent.

for   25/9/59

Douglas John Clark,
Lower Chaddesley Corbett
Near Kidderminster.

4,000. 6019.

This taught me a salutary lesson.

Very rare photographs of Buddy Holly and The Crickets.

Buddy Holly and The Crickets.

Jolie's Pit, at the rear of The Fox Pub. Also The Little Garage to the right.

Me and Malc on our first grass track practice session where minutes after this
was photo was taken, I broke my collar bone!

Noel in practice session at the Prestatyn Trotting Track.

Dad, Noel Jr. with his manufactured bike,
Malc and Cousin Kevin on crutches.

Newspaper photo:
Caption 'The fabulous
Clark Brothers - they
build them and race them'

Fun days in the grass track season. Gossip mongering. Circa 1967. Front,
Clive Godbolt, our close friend, who died tragically in a car accident.

Me practicing at Prestatyn Trotting track for what would be a first, racing
with famous riders like World Champion Ivan Mauger. Circa 1969.

SPARKLING PERRY IS CHAMP AGAIN

TAKING FULL advantage of the absence of reigning champion Cyril Jones at the Evesham Club's meeting at Penvin, Worcestershire, on Sunday, Tig Perry (441 Elstar) regained the Worcestershire championship grass-track title that he had lost to the Welshman last year.

And only a puncture on his 250 cc model spoiled tireless Tig's chances of yet another clean sweep. But it allowed Phil Corin (250 Hagon) to win his first final.

In a poorly supported sidecar class, burly Glyn Lloyd (1,000 Vincent) won two out of three finals, but only after two razor-sharp struggles with Peter Davies (650 Triton).

The third race was a side-by-side scrap between these two round the dry, but not too dusty, 550-yard course.

Davies led by a whisker for four of the six laps, then Lloyd, his big twin slightly quicker than the supercharged Triumph, raced past to win by a wheel.

Steadily improving Doug Clark (500 Hagon) gated best in the championship final, but Perry led after a lap and Clark's second place was in danger from Brian Evans (500 JAP) until Evans overslid.

RESULTS

250 cc: 1 P. B. Corin (Hagon); 2 B. Evans (BES); S. C. Perry (Elstar).
350cc: 1 A. F. Perry (Elstar); 2 M. G. Hill (Fontargen); 3 P. B. Corin (250 Hagon).
Over-300 cc: 1 A. F. Perry (441 Elstar); 2 D. Clark (500 Hagon); 3 S. Ellis (441 BSA).
Worcestershire Championship: 1 A. F. Perry (441 Elstar); 2 D. Clark (500 Hagon); 3 B. Evans (500 JAP).
Local Riders: 1 B. Evans (500 JAP); 2 P. M. Spires (500 Bewley); 3 W. C. Jones (500 JAP).
First Sidecar: 1 P. Davies (650 Triton); 2 J. Pork (700 Triumph); 3 J. Chapman (650 Triumph).
Second Sidecar: 1 G. Lloyd (1,000 Vincent); 2 P. Davies (650 Triton); 3 P. Hill (650 Triumph).
Third Sidecar: 1 G. Lloyd (1,000 Vincent); 2 P. Davies (650 Triton); 3 P. Hill (650 Triumph).

I came second in the 1969 Worcestershire Championship.

PETER COLLINS (above) became Britain's youngest-ever grass track champion when he won the 350cc title last summer. From Frodsham, Cheshire, and only 18, Peter is sponsored by talent-spotter and Duckhams enthusiast Jimmy Rowlinson.
432 Doug Clark 1971/1972

Second again in 1971, this time to Peter Collins who went on to become World Speedway Champion.

Clark notches four for charity

DOUG CLARK (350 and 500 Hagons) notched four wins in the solo class at the Bristol Grass Racing Combine's charity meeting held in cool, windy conditions on a 550-yard circuit at Marshfield, Wilts, on Sunday.

Despite being harassed by John Webb (500 Elstar), Mike Davis (500 JAP) and Bill Jones (500 JAP), Clark reappeared success in the 500cc experts and both invitation races.

Gerald Wheeler (650 GSER) finished his best ever season in winning vein. Gerald won three of the four sidecar races

with Peter Robson (700 Sabre) winning the other when Wheeler retired with a broken chain.

Bob Jones rode a borrowed 500 JAP to victory in both Stars of Yesteryear races with ex-Bristol Bulldogs speedway team skipper Billy Hole runner-up in both encounters.

PROVISIONAL RESULTS

350cc: 1 D Jefferies (KMB), 2 R Horner (BSA), 3 M Lucas (Elstar), 4 T Freegard (Elstar), 5 G Pitcher (Elstar), 6 P Mitchell (Elstar). **Heats:** Horner, Jefferies. **500cc:** 1 D Clark (Hagon), 2 J Webb (Elstar), 3 P French (Freegard), 5 J Husband (Antig), 6 K Davis (JAP).

Heats: Husband, Webb.

350cc: 1 Husband (Antig), 2 J January (Camel), 4 A Hodge (Erskine), 5 Freegard. **Heats:** Hodge, Husband, R Clarke (Elstar), Wilmott.

Unlimited to open: 1 Clark, 2 Davis, 3 N Webb, 4 Jones, 5 M Burton (BSA), 6 French. **Heats:** Husband, A Moss (Hagon), Webb, Clark.

Grass track machines only: 1 Clark, 2 Jones, 3 Webb, 4 Burton, 5 Moss, 6 K Davis (JAP). **Heats:** Moss, Clark, Perkins, French.

Scramble machines only: 1 T Phillips (350 Greaves), 2 E Wisstanley (500 Metisse), 3 C Marsh (500 Metisse), 4 R Hopkins (500 Metisse), 5 A Giddings (500 Triumph), 6 P King (250 Triumph). **Stars of Yesteryear; first race:** 1 B Jones (500 JAP), 2 W Hole

(500 Hagon), 3 M Beacoce (500 JAP), 4 P Evans (500 JAP), 5 R Wilmott (500 Hagon), 6 B Hopkins (500 JAP). **Second race:** 1 Jones, 2 Hole, 3 B Taylor (500 Hagon), 4 Wilmott.

First sidecar: 1 G Wheeler/J Boit (650 GSER), 2 T Robson/D Hopes (700 Sabre), 3 R Gooding/R King (1000 JAP), 4 S Degrappaday/O Schofield (650 Triumph), 5 O Spurway/B Salter (650 Triumph). **Heats:** Wheeler, M Morgan/A King (650 Metisse-Wright).

Second sidecar: 1 Robson, 2 Degrappaday, 3 Morgan, 4 J P O'Keefe. **Heats:** Wheeler, Robson. **Third sidecar:** 1 Wheeler, 2 Robson, 3 M Ham/L Macfluer (650 MCB), 4 O'Keefe. **Heats:** Wheeler, Robson.

Fourth sidecar: 1 Wheeler, 2 Ham.

Celebrating a semi-final win with neighbour Frank Verlic (Ex Midland Sidecar Champion).

Still celebrating at Hereford.

LEFT:
Pre-75 racing at Bewdley. Midland veteran Doug Clark enjoyed his day, finishing fifth. Here he leads Shropshire's Vincent Priestley and new-to-the-class Simon Ashworth.
Photo: Ron Hinsley.

Returning to the past, great fun.

Mixing it at a Cheltenham meeting.

Practice session. Shrewsbury. Circa 2002.

Midland honours upheld

DOUG CLARK (500 Hagon) and Glyn Lloyd partnered by Peter Cave (1000 Vincent) upheld Midland Centre honours at the Rugby club's grass track on Sunday against strong visiting opposition from neighbouring centres.

At the well organised meeting on a fast oval course at Kilsby, near Rugby, half-a-mile from the South Midland Centre border, there was a great battle in the unlimited final between Clark and stylish Roger Collins (500 Callow) who had walked the 500cc final.

Held up by a poor start, Collins got on Clark's tail but just could not get past.

Visitor Dennis Lemon (Hagon) won the 250 final ahead of a scrap between Rob Homer (Basmer), Mick Nicholson (BSA) and Phil Corin (Hagon). Lemon won the 350 event as well but 27-year-old Leicester rider Nicholson, on his home-brewed 250, pressed him very hard.

Leicester sidecarrist Dave Hallam and John Lorimer, now with a blower on their 650 Triumph, got to grips with the mighty Vincent in the first chair final but only had their nose in front for 10 yards before Lloyd re-passed.

Birkhamstead clubman Mike Vangucci (350 Velocette) took one vintage race and veteran Bill Davies 500 Rudge the other two.

PROVISIONAL RESULTS

250cc: 1 D Lemon (Hagon), 2 R Homer (Basmer), 3 M Nicholson (BSA), 4 P Corin (Hagon), 5 L Oakes (Greeves), 6 R Gibson (Elstar). **Heats:** Oakes, Lemon, Nicholson, Corin.

350cc: 1 D Lemon (Hagon), 2 M Nicholson (250 BSA), 3 J Husband (Antig), 4 R Perkins (Antig), 5 R Homer (250 Basmer), 6 D Clark (Hagon). **Heats:** Homer, Nicholson, Clark, Lemon. **Semi-finals:** Nicholson, Lemon.

Over 340cc: 1 R Collins (500 Callow), 2 D Clark (500 Hagon), 3 M Nicholson (500 Jap), 4 P Corin (500 Hagon), 5 R Perkins (350 Antig), 6 B Lewis (500 Erskine). **Heats:** R Parker (500 Elstar), Collins, Nicholson.

Unlimited cc: 1 Clark, 2 Collins 3 Lewis, 4 Nicholson, 5 Corin, 6 J Husband (350 Antig). **Heats:** Clark, R Gibbons (500 Hagon), Collins, Lewis, Husband, D Lemon (250 Hagon). **Semi-finals:** Collins, Lemon.

First sidecar: 1 G Lloyd/P Cave (1,000 Vincent), 2 D Hallam/J Lorimer (650 Triumph), 3 P J Brown/P Shearsby (700 Cobra), 4 J Cork/R Wood (750 Triumph), 5 F Verlic/A Prescott (650 Triumph). **Heats:** Cork, Brown, Hallam.

Second sidecar: 1 G Lloyd, 2 Hallam, 3 P Hill/C Barnbrook (650 Triumph), 4 Cork, 5 D Lloyd/L McBean (650 Triumph). **Heats:** Brown, G Lloyd, Hill.

Sidecar confirmation: K O'Hare/R French (650 Triumph), 2 D Lloyd, 3 Verlic, 4 G Bale/A Weston (650 Triumph).

First vintage: 1 M Vangucci (350 Velocette), 2 W Davies (500 Rudge), 3 E Edwards (500 Ariel), 4 R Elmore (500 Douglas), 5 J James (500 Rudge), 6 W Goodman (350 Velocette).

Second vintage: 1 Davies, 2 Vangucci, 3 Elmore, 4 James, 5 J Lidgate (350 Velocette), 6 Goodman.

Third vintage: 1 Davies, 2 Vangucci, 3 Elmore, 4 James, 6 Lidgate, 6 Edwards.

GEOFF MAYES

GEOFF MAYES, Martin Webster, Ricky Davies, David Thorpe once again dominated the racing in their classes in the Cotswold YMC schoolboy scramble at Long Compton on Sunday, with most of the opposition coming from John Dee and Terance Harvey. Although second in the senior class, Chris Everett still leads Geoff Mayes for the CYMC championship.

PROVISIONAL RESULTS
Senior production: 1 G Mayes

Results from the Motorcycle News.

Racing go-karts in Jersey (note the number 7).

The winner!

Malc at Rednal Garage (note the Jack), before we made the infamous pit.
Circa 1961.

Crash results from the infamous lapping nights. Dick Eggintons' Lotus Cortina
quick body change, at least we got the job. Circa 1966.

Original Rednal Garage, closed for demolition. Circa 1966. See page 165 for redevelopment, also the remains of The Barracks pub porch supports, still standing.

New Rednal Garage. Circa 1968. This was the second redevelopment of Rednal Garage.

My good business friends Paul Johnson and Slade Arthur. They were a great inspiration back in the day.

The Citizens appearing at The Locarno Night Club, Birmingham. Finishing second in the Midland Rock'n'Roll Competition. (Great experience on the revolving stage). Circa 1963.

L to R. Keith Mustow, Dennis Reeves, Me, Pete Snipe, Twink and Neil Welsh.
The Citizens at The Locarno.

The Suedes at the 'Silver Blades', Digbeth Birmingham. A great Saturday
night venue. Circa 1966. L to R. Me, Joe, Terry and Colin.

The Suedes photo shoot for our 2 I's audition.

The Suedes photo shoot for 2 I's audition.

R. F. COATES, LL.B.

CONSULTANT.
J. H. DEREK YOUNG

ASSISTANT SOLICITORS
G. J. LEWIS, LL.B.
D. L. PARTINGTON, LL.B.

BULLER JEFFRIES

SOLICITORS
COMMISSIONERS FOR OATHS

48 TEMPLE STREET · BIRMINGHAM B2 5NL

TELEPHONE
021-643 8201-4
021-643 0202

TELEGRAMS
PACTUM BIRMINGHAM
AND AT
3 QUEEN VICTORIA ROAD
COVENTRY CV1 3JS
TELEPHONE 28734/5

YOUR REF.

OUR REF.

1st March, 1978.

CB/BM/77/477

D.J. Clark, Esq.,
Clarks Motor Services (Rednal) Ltd.,
466, Lickey Road,
Rednal,
BIRMINGHAM, B45 8UU.

Dear Mr. Clark,

Forge Garage.

We write to confirm that we have safely
received from you the Conveyance and Mortgage deeds
duly sealed, together with your cheques for £36,000.
and £1,149.10. You can regard the matter as
completed at 28th February, and we will, of course,
be forwarding the deeds to Lloyds Bank, Longbridge,
in due course.

Yours faithfully,

Buller Jeffries

The purchase of Forge Garage Hagley, a big move.

Ann Moore arrives at Barnt Green, by pony and trap, escorted by two mounted 'Cavaliers' — Don Mills, of Halesowen, and Terry Bird, of Wychbold.

ANN MOORE OPENS SHOP

It was an even busier than usual Easter Saturday morning in Hewell Road, Barnt Green's main shopping street.

Crowds of people lined the already busy street to catch a glimpse of international show jumping star Ann Moore. The numbers were further swelled by the bright spring sunshine.

Ann Moore was in Barnt Green to open "The House of the Cavalier," a sadlery, equipment and riding wear shop.

She came to the shop from the Barnt Green Inn, in a horse and trap escorted by two cavaliers on horse back. For two hours Ann stayed and talked to customers and at the same time signed autographs for young admirers.

Afterwards the 1972 Olympic silver medalist, who has now given up competitive riding for motor racing, was collected in a horse and trap.

Business diversion, House of the Cavalier! Saddlery Shop Barnt Green. "Nothing ventured nothing gained, but keep an exit route!" Circa 1975.

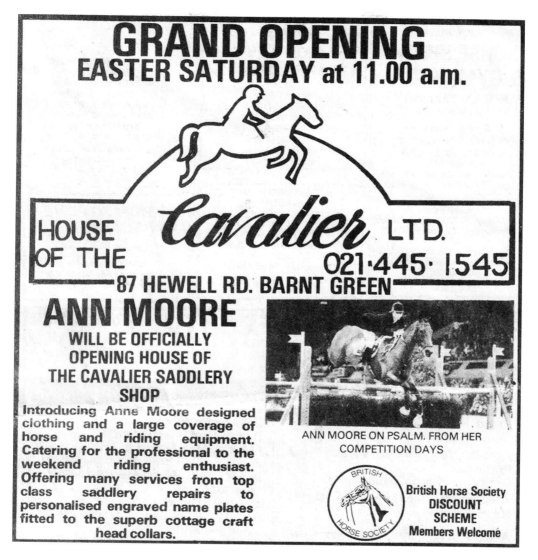

Advertisement from the opening of House of The Cavalier LTD.

Ann Moore with Don Mills and Terry Bird at the grand opening of
The House Of The Cavalier.

OUR GROUP LOCATIONS

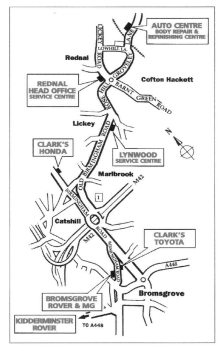

BROMSGROVE - 29 Birmingham Road **Tel: 01527 579630**
KIDDERMINSTER - Worcester Road **Tel: 01562 862822**
REDNAL - Lickey Road **Tel: 0121 453 7127/8/9 & 3117**
AUTO CENTRE - Groveley Lane **Tel: 0121 477 3838**

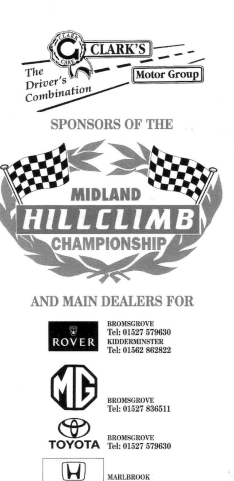

SPONSORS OF THE

MIDLAND HILLCLIMB CHAMPIONSHIP

AND MAIN DEALERS FOR

ROVER
BROMSGROVE
Tel: 01527 579630
KIDDERMINSTER
Tel: 01562 862822

MG
BROMSGROVE
Tel: 01527 836511

TOYOTA
BROMSGROVE
Tel: 01527 579630

HONDA
MARLBROOK
Tel: 0121 445 3020

WITH OUR UNIQUE PROGRAMME OF
'CLARK CARE'

Clark's marketing brochure. Sponsoring the Midland Hill Climb
Championship for many years.

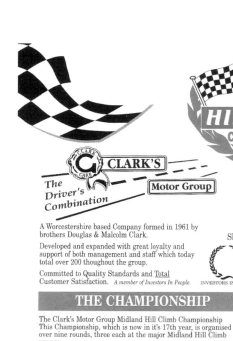

MIDLAND HILLCLIMB CHAMPIONSHIP

CLARK'S Motor Group

The Driver's Combination

A Worcestershire based Company formed in 1961 by brothers Douglas & Malcolm Clark.

Developed and expanded with great loyalty and support of both management and staff which today total over 200 thoughout the group.

Committed to Quality Standards and Total Customer Satisfaction. *A member of Investors In People.*

INVESTORS IN PEOPLE

THE CHAMPIONSHIP

The Clark's Motor Group Midland Hill Climb Championship This Championship, which is now in it's 17th year, is organised over nine rounds, three each at the major Midland Hill Climb venues.

Classes are organised for Modified Production Cars, Sports Libre Cars and Racing Cars. The Championship is so designed that it is possible for a car from any class to win outright. These vary from cars that are driven to and from the meeting on the road to grand prix type cars with 600+ bhp engines.

DATES & VENUE

April 7/8	Loton Park	Aug 10/11	Shelsley Walsh
April 13/14	Prescott	Aug 17/18	Loton Park
June 1/2	Shelsley Walsh	Aug 31/Sept 1	Prescott
June 8/9	Loton Park	Sept 21/22	Shelsley Walsh
June 29/30	Prescott		

LOTON PARK — Alberbury

Shrewsbury

Bromsgrove

Kidderminster

SHELSLEY WALSH

Worcester

PRESCOTT HILL — Gotherington

Cheltenham

LOTON PARK

Situated eight miles west of Shrewsbury in the village of Alberbury this venue is the longest in the Midland Hill Climb Championship. Winding through a deer park the hill is very much a driver's course requiring precision as well as speed. Run by the Hagley and District Light Car Club since 1970.

BROMSGROVE

CLARK'S Motor Group

The Driver's Combination

This is Clark's Test Drive Centre where we have a range of vehicles to test drive from MGF, ROVER & TOYOTA. Also Pitstop Services Available.

PRESCOTT

Prescott Hill is situated on the edge of the Cotswolds near the village of Gotherington, 5 miles north of Cheltenham.

Excellent spectator and viewing facilities are a feature of this venue. Like all the hills it is possible to stroll round the Paddock and view the cars at close quarters and talk to the drivers. Owned and run by the Bugatti Owners Club since 1936.

SHELSLEY WALSH

The oldest and fastest hill in the Championship, Shelsley Walsh is 10 miles west of Worcester in the Teme Valley. This famous venue was first used in 1905 and is the oldest motor sport track still in use in the world. Speeds of 140mph are reached at the 'home' of Speed Hill Climbing which is expertly run by the Midland Automobile Club.

VIII WEEKLY MAIL, FRIDAY, NOVEMBER 20, 1987   MH

Clark's Motor Services (Rednal) Ltd.

AUSTIN ROVER

For Hire

An impressive fleet of around 100 vehicles makes up the U-Can-Hire range operated by Clark's Motor Services from Rednal, Hagley and Marlbrook.

And whether you want to move furniture, arrive in style at a business meeting or simply want a carefree self-drive day out, you can hire the perfect vehicle to suit your requirements.

The full range of reliable Austin Rover cars are at your disposal at competitive rates —

and excellent service is standard.

Vehicle hire has grown steadily from the beginning with helpful and attentive staff ensuring many satisfied customers return.

Two Rover Sterling's are the 'flagship' vehicles in the hire range for executives and the company can also provide chauffeur-driven cars.

And the Extra Value plan means just that, with great deals on long-term hire rates and reduced rates for customers with vehicles in for service or repair.

Fast Fit Service

Speed and efficiency throughout customer services is a Clark's hallmark — and nowhere more so than at the Fast Fit Tyre Centre.

The on-site tyre bay at Rednal is fully-equipped to cater for all requirements.

And with Semperit and Michelin among the top tyre brands stocked, motorists know they will soon be safely back on the road.

The average time involved in pulling into the tyre bay and leaving is half-an-hour or less — and competitive prices make the service even more attractive.

Great value-for-money deals, including free valves and balancing on every four new tyres bought, add to the complete Fast Fit package.

U-Can-Hire manager Mr Lee Shepherd puts a customer 'on the road'.

Doug and Malcolm Clark at Clark's Motor Services headquarters in Lickey Road.

Regional Director of Shell UK Ltd., Mr. Stan Thomas, presenting award to Clark's Manager, Dave Price.

Receiving the National Award Prize Cheque from Britax Sun Roofs Manager,
Derek Peatey. We were their top UK dealer.

Clark's Motor Services (Rednal) Ltd.

Directors: D.J.CLARK (Managing), C.M.A.CLARK, A.P.FODEN (Servicing)

V.A.T. No. 109 5790 52

FORGE GARAGE
KIDDERMINSTER ROAD
HAGLEY
Tel: 288 4873/2234

CROSS KEYS
FILLING STATION
KIDDERMINSTER ROAD
HAGLEY
Tel: 288 2234

BELLE VUE GARAGE
(Auto Refinishing Centre)
492 BIRMINGHAM ROAD
MARLBROOK, Nr. BROMSGROVE
Tel: 021-445 4268

HEAD OFFICE
REDNAL GARAGE
LICKEY ROAD
REDNAL, BIRMINGHAM
Tel: 021-453 7127/7128/3117

Approved Fitter Dealer

Weathershields
SUNROOFS

Your Ref:

Our Ref: DJC/LW

20 June 1985

Mr Taylor
Austin Rover Group Ltd
Sales and Marketing
Canley Road
Canley
Coventry
CV5 6QX

Dear Mr Taylor

I wrote to you on the 16th of May 1985 asking for your comments regarding my Companys future with Austin Rover Group. In your reply Tracey Stokes indicated that Mr Harbour would be contacting me, I have not heard from him to date.

I would greatly appreciate some news on this matter as I do have some pressing decisions to make related to the outcome by way of staff and premises.

Thanking you in anticipation.

Yours sincerely
for Clark's Motor Services (Rednal) Ltd

D J Clark
Managing Director

cc Mr Harbour

Tyre agent for SEMPERIT · HENLEY · FIRESTONE · AVON · PIRELLI

Follow up letter from me concerning the Austin Rover Franchise application for Bromsgrove.

Austin Rover Group Limited
Sales & Marketing
Canley Road
Canley
Coventry CV5 6QX

Telephone: Coventry (0203) 70111
Telex: 312571

Our Ref: JDC/MS/1892L/19

14th December, 1987.
(Dictated 11.12.87.)

PRIVATE AND CONFIDENTIAL

Mr. D. Clark,
Managing Director,
Clark's Motor Services (Rednal) Ltd.,
Rednal Garage,
Lickey Road,
Rednal,
BIRMINGHAM.

Dear Doug,

BROMSGROVE MAIN DEALERSHIP APPOINTMENT

My colleagues and I at Austin Rover are delighted that after such protracted and difficult circumstances we have now agreed a firm basis upon which we may proceed to appoint you as our new Main Dealer for the Bromsgrove marketing area.

In order to clarify matters in such a complex situation we have taken the liberty to send you three separate letters - this one with respect to Bromsgrove, another with respect to Tessall and the Birmingham South West Territory, and yet another with respect to the termination of your Services-Only Franchise at Rednal.

So far as Bromsgrove is concerned, as we stated to you in correspondence 20th July and 6th August 1987, we are happy to award your Company the Main Dealer Franchise for the Bromsgrove marketing area once you have completed your development at the Bus Garage site at Bromsgrove, which you confirmed to me today will be completed for full trading occupation by no later than 1st August 1988.

In the meantime, as separately confirmed to you, your Company will continue to hold the Austin Rover Service-Only Agreement in repect of your Rednal premises until the date of the official opening of your Bromsgrove premises provided that this shall be on or before 1st August, 1988.

The support proposals agreed between us in respect of Bromsgrove are as follows:

- We have already paid to your Company our agreed bridging cost support in respect of Bromsgrove from the date the acquisition up to 30th November 1987. We will continue to pay in full your interest costs on the acquisition price of Bromsgrove from 1st December until such time as building work, (excluding demolition/excavation work) is begun on the site. You today advised me that this building work would commence no later than 1st March, 1988, on a schedule which would guarantee full trading occupation by no later than 1st August 1988.

Cont'd.....

D-Day! The acknowledgement of the Austin Rover Franchise for Bromsgrove.

Displaying some of our trophies amongst our growing collection
of classic cars.

Unveiling a very rare Austin Healey 3000.

Receiving the Bugatti Owners Club trophy for his hand built
Clark-Caterham.

Me, driving my treasured Austin Healey 3000 at the Bugatti Owners Club
Concours event.

Presenting the trophy to a class winner at the Prescott Hill Climb.

New state of the art Accident Repair Center, Longbridge.

Groveley Lane Development, built by Clark's building division. One of the best body shops in the country.

The Clark's winning team, that won the M.G. Rover Award for customer service. L to R. Paul Jeavons, Adrian Smith, myself, Matthew Smith, Chris Rixom.

Happy times with Leigh.

The knight and his maiden.

Sea Rover, my home in Malta for a time.

The Senior Citizens (L-R) Dennis, Pete, Twink, Doug Valinder, and myself.

My guitar collection in Canada, Gretch White Falcon and a pair of 60's
Gibsons.

The Senior Citizens recording CD at Pato Bantons Studio. CD called 'Live and Still Gigging!'

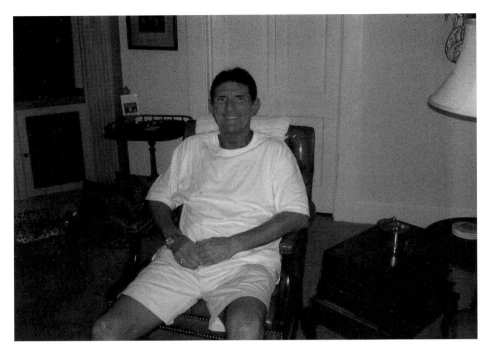

A great friend Hugh Efird, successful guitar dealer from West Palm Beach.

Cousin Kevin with 14lb Carp
caught at Badgers.

New Smyrna - Florida.

Senior Citizens - photo call. Rob Walkden depped for Twink.

Me and front cover fame.

Me topping out the new dealership sign at Bromsgrove.

Cartoon drawing of the infamous 'Wheelie-Bin Trip'.

Badgers Cottage across from the duck pond.

Have Porsche will travel.

My BSA Gold Star 500CC. BSA ex-works T.T. Bike, featured in
'The Little Giants of Small Heath'.

Out for an early spin and a Little Chef breakfast. Harry Hombach
taking photo.

Leigh and I 'biking it' at the Isle of Man T.T.

Hunters Lodge, my home in Calgary, Canada.

Skiing, Canada.

Posing at the end of Brad Pitt's drive, at Bragg Creek, Alberta,
Canada.

Photograph of Chinook rising up from the Rockies, taken from the rear of my home in Calgary.

My ultimate Aston Martin.

My Denali 'mean machine' just the job for Canadian winters.

My Porsche 911 Cabriolet complete with winter hard top. Calgary.

Morning greeting of Mr. Peacock at Badgers Cottage.

My good friend and neighbour Frank Verlic at Badgers Cottage

Hanging basket display at Badgers Cottage.

Badgers Cottage facing north.

My cat Pepper.

My favorite chicken having a word
in my ear. Badgers Cottage.
Circa 2002.

Preparing for Halloween.

Miami Boat Show, photo taken from the hotel window when I visited the show to order Mission Accomplished.

Mission Accomplished. Home port, New Berne, North Carolina, USA. 2005.

Mission Accomplished. Spring in the Bahamas at West End Marina.
Circa 2005.

Master state room on Mission Accomplished.
(Note the mirrors on the ceiling.)

The 'Rupert Suite', one of three guest rooms on
Mission Accomplished.

Mission Accomplished, docked for refueling, Florida.

Mission Accomplished, leaving port from St. Augustine, Florida.

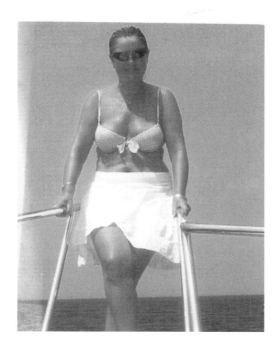 

Yvonne.   The Titanic Pose.   Doug.

Transport aboard Mission Accomplished, a great shopping trolley.

Malc and me in the salon Mission Accomplished.

Aft deck dining.

Malc and me powering across the Bahama Bay.

Banff Springs Hotel, Canada.

Dinner at Ella's in the Bahamas. Lobster and conch at just 16 dollars.

Beachcombing.

Dinner is served.

Enjoying the bracing Canadian air.

THE ST. AUGUSTINE
RECORD
SINCE 1894

50¢ — **FRIDAY** AUGUST 15, 2008

Two Million Dollar Man

Kevin Parry, of St. Augustine, swims in the ocean north of Vilano Beach with his dogs, Lilly, left, and Jackson Brown, on Thursday afternoon. Parry, who owns a local stucco company, won $2 million in the Florida Lottery last week. **By DARON DEAN**, daron.dean@staugustine.com

Mega Money winner says he doesn't intend to change a thing

By CHAD SMITH
chad.smith@staugustine.com

In a way, Kevin Parry is already a millionaire.

He has all he needs and then some. The beach is just a few hundred yards east of his home, and the Tolomato River, where he spends many afternoons fishing, is just a few hundred yards to the west.

The 47-year-old St. Augustine native has been married for the past four and a half years, and for the past 15, he's owned his own stucco business, which has afforded him a nice home, which he built. A few refrigerators hold his catch before it becomes homemade fish chowder.

"This is the glamorous life, right here: two dogs, the beach, two boats," Parry said in his dining room Wednesday.

As of a few days ago, he's also got $2 million.

Parry won the prize in Friday's drawing of the Florida Lottery Mega Money game. Only he didn't know it until Sunday.

He checked the newspaper on Saturday and compared his ticket with the numbers on the front page: 22-29-4-16. They matched.

But the winning Mega Ball number — 7 — didn't. So he went about his day, going fishing on the river, happily thinking he had won about $2,000.

However, Parry said, he woke up Sunday morning not knowing whether winning a few grand would heal the wounds he has suffered in the current economy.

Like most firms in the construction industry, business has been slow lately for Parryman Stucco, and he was wondering if he would be able to keep himself and his seven employees afloat.

He also was worried he'd have to cut back on his weekly tithing to his church later that morning.

He told a deacon at the church about his stroke of luck with winning the $2,000.

Parry remembered him replying, "It's God saying, 'Stay loyal, stay faithful, and we'll take care of you.'"

After church, Parry's sister and mother stopped by his house. They had seen on the news that someone from St. Augustine had won the Mega Money jackpot Friday and wanted him to check his ticket again. They didn't think it could be a coincidence.

Check if it was a 7, his sister said. He got the ticket from his China cabinet and looked at it.

"Why'd you say 7?" he remembered asking.

He had the winning number all along, but he read the numbers in the paper without his glasses Saturday and didn't think he had the winning Mega Ball number.

Naturally, his sister started crying. His mother started flailing her arms.

His father, Ed Parry, a retired maintenance man from the Florida School for the Deaf and the Blind, was a little more subdued.

The elder Parry has been playing the Lottery just about since it started in Florida in 1988 and has always talked about taking a limousine ride to Tallahassee to claim the jackpot, his son said.

"I feel like I'm stealing from him because he's probably got $50,000 invested in it," he joked.

But someday next week, Ed Parry will get that ride, in a stretch Hummer, to claim his son's winnings.

PLEASE SEE WINNER/8A

WINNER
CONTINUED FROM PAGE 1A

The younger Parry knows that after taxes, his prize won't nearly be $2 million.

But he doesn't care.

"If you can pull something negative out of this, you're going to have a long life," he said.

He doesn't plan to change a thing.

A friend brought him a bottle of 1998 Dom Perignon to celebrate. A nice gesture, but he's more of a beer or bottled wine kind of guy — nothing fancy.

His deck is decorated with nautical trinkets and street signs. It's not cluttered with junk, but it's original — it's his.

And, he said, he doesn't need to buy a big, sterile house or a shiny Ferrari to have it all. He has his two dogs — Jackson Brown and Lilly — his boats, his chowder and his wife, Serena.

Of course, he knows winning $1 million and change won't transform his life a whole lot. But even if it would, he said, he doesn't want it to.

It will, however, help him keep his business going. But, he insisted, there's another reason his daily trip to the Kangaroo on the east side of the Usina Bridge for his newspaper, coffee and lottery ticket paid off.

He said he thinks there's a reason he won, and he thinks he's meant to pay it forward. He's just not sure how yet.

Serena Parry said they are hoping to use a part of the money to fund a foundation, Shannon's Hope, they started in December in memory of her sister.

Her 30-year-old sister, Shannon Carol Holzer, was murdered in December 1997 by a man who robbed her family's store on County Road 13 in Colee Cove. The murderer, John Calvin Taylor II, an ex-convict from Arkansas, was convicted in 2004 and is awaiting execution in Raiford.

In December, the Parrys bought more than $15,000 worth of toys and clothes to give to needy children for Christmas. They are hoping to do that again this year.

Other than that, Kevin Parry said he doesn't have any grandiose plans for the money.

"The sad thing is it doesn't take a dime to do what I'm doing now," he said about spending time on the water in a motorboat his father built or swimming in the ocean with his dogs.

But he'll figure out what to do with the money. He's convinced of that.

On Saturday, his brother-in-law went fishing and found a small buoy floating in the water he thought Parry might like.

He grabbed it from the water and brought it to the home Saturday night. It didn't seem strange until Sunday, when he saw the word that had been painted onto the buoy in black letters:

Karma.

My friend, Kevin Parry from St. Augustine, used my number 7 for his mega ball number and won 2 million dollars on the lottery, a great way to help a friend.

Celebrating Kevin's lottery win with a trip to Tallahassee in a limo.

Making friends with the wildlife in Florida. Found the tortoise in the middle of the road and put him safely back into the undergrowth.

Me and my truck. St. Augustine.

The Fabulous Clark Brothers enjoying a pint at The Wharf in Holt Fleet.

My in-laws, Olive and Jim.

My visit to Chaddesley Corbett Endowed School, to meet teachers and class and talk about the old days there in the 40's and 50's.

The Austin Healey 3000 at Bugatti Owners Club Concours show.

A mannequin of me and my racing bike. My 60th bash at Chateau Impney.

Bromsgrove Dealership used for Austin Seven meeting.

My yellow E-Type, left and Malc's D-Type at a classic car meeting in
the Isle of Man.

Once used to house Midland Red West buses, this Birmingham Road depot is set to become an auto service complex, with garage,

Ex Midland Red Bus Garage bought by Clark's, demolished to build state of the art M.G. Rover Dealership.

Risk = opportunity?
www.glegal.com

The Birmingham Post • TUESDAY October 16 2001 27

Risk = opportunity?
www.glegal.com

Business

Clarks has driving ambition

By James O'Brien
Business Staff
james_o'brien@mrn.co.uk

Worldwide over-capacity US car plants idling, big challenges confronting the industry in Europe as production is scaled down – it is becoming a familiar scenario.

But it is a long way from the other end of the automotive industry's spectrum which sells the cars.

Franchised dealerships with a sound and astute business record are operating in a different environment. Business is good and can even be said to be booming.

One of those companies on an upward curve is Clarks Motor Services which has a dominant position in North Worcestershire and south Birmingham.

More than 5,000 cars a year pass through its pre-delivery inspection operation at Bromsgrove before going out to its nine dealerships which include new premises at Ambercote, Stourbridge, and another due to open in January at Halesowen.

The Ambercote investment is worth £2.35 million which has been financed by the company while the Halesowen site developed with Honda is another large, modern, grey and glass building due to open in January.

The chairman of Clark Motor Services is Doug Clark who started out in 1961 with his brother doing repair jobs on cars at their father's garage at Cradley Corbett.

Now it is a business with a turnover in excess of £60 million annually.

But yesterday in the conference room at Clarks' new Volkswagen dealership at Ambercote, Doug traced the process of selling cars.

"There is a strategy, and an understanding of timing and put that alongside the fact that selling new cars is a seasonal business," he cautioned.

"Couple that with the high cost of premises to sell cars with a brand name.

"Oh, and then there is the accessibility of the showroom and repair facilities and another important factor is that the location should allow the business operation to be seen constantly by the public.

Chairman Doug Clark (right) and Trevor Wilcox, brand manager at the Stourbridge VW centre

"I might as well mention that the economics of the square foot is important as well. Costing has to be right and then all that goes into a business plan that gives profitability. Then comes that crucial ingredient called 'viability.'"

The dealerships which have kept these factors in sight have been those which have survived the harsh economic climates over the past ten years.

They are now benefiting from prudent housekeeping.

The emphasis now is on the dealerships that can call themselves a group and have two brand operations on a single site.

The showrooms at Kidderminster, Bromsgrove and Redhall have two dealerships side-by-side.

One of the constraints on Clarks business has

been Doug's insistence that despite whatever financial and business advice he has received it has been imperative to remain as a "regional group".

"That has been my aspiration, never to move out of that position but making sure the retail premises are in the right place.

In addition to the nine outlets, Clarks has a pre-delivery inspection operation at Bromsgrove which serves all the outlets. The longest journey to a Clarks' showroom is 20 miles.

The pre-inspection facility and the storage area – soon to become a multi-storey secure car park for the group's cars which will replace the present open air compound – has given the group a greater retail opportunity by freeing space at the showrooms.

This means money is not tied up as "wooden dollars" as the trade calls it.

Even as recently as three months ago it looked very tight for September registrations and doom and gloom and the prospect of a recession was not helping, said Doug.

"But events have influenced what I see could happen over the next six months and if it has been brought about by a drop in the bank rate.

"Without doubt it is a major encouragement to keep people in the frame of mind where they can afford things, and that means cars as well.

"It is like mortgages for houses, it is about gauging the time to repair the business. It is a cheap time to borrow money.

"There is also a reduction in the price of oil. There is an over-supply of oil."

He said the motor trade had gone through

hard times during the past three years but the realignment of car prices, over-production and manufacturers reshaping themselves had influenced how dealerships saw themselves.

They had to meet the demands of the manufacturers with investment, training and quality premises.

"This is the time to concentrate on the immediate opportunities and I would predict – short of the unknown – that the road is well and truly open for a good trading period with excellent deals for the motorist," said Doug.

Since the Government's Competition Commission report on car prices and criticisms of the relationship between manufacturers and dealerships, the figures for pre-registration of vehicles to help massage sales and give manufacturers a growing picture of how they were doing in their league table has been spiked.

"That is what the manufacturers would like the public to think, but the job of the dealers pre-registrations has now fallen to the dealers

A pre-registered car in a showroom can be a very good deal even though technically with one registration on its log book – the garage's – it becomes a nearly new car.

"The pre-registration cars distort manufacturers figures but for the man in the street they are one of the best buys he can get.

"Dealers are now part of the mechanism of pre-registering cars. We are doing it because it is a development and a process of balancing the market place and manufacturers' selling objectives.

"September was a great month for Clarks Motor Services but the success of a car can also have its pitfalls.

Nearly 700 cars were sold that month, many of them MG Rovers, indeed so many that the car manufacturer couldn't keep up.

"They were simply unable to deliver them all so there were some disappointed people about.

I don't think they can keep up with the model demand.

"But Rover, Volkswagen and Toyota have helped to take our business forward," said Doug.

But another manufacturer will take the business forward as Clarks seeks to get customers in the location shortly. It has won the TVR franchise, a pure British thoroughbred car.

Clark's acquired this site and built the dealership themselves within nine months.

231

FUTURE VISION: Architect Mike Chapman with developer Douglas Clark. Ref:D03709

Driving on for success

Hundreds of jobs if town becomes home to a Midlands' motor village

EXCLUSIVE
BY KATE HUGHES

A MULTI-million pound deal and hundreds of new jobs could be coming to the town thanks to a Bromsgrove businessman.

Douglas Clark, of Clark's Motors, has applied for planning permission to build a unique motor village spanning nine acres on the Buntsford Gate industrial park.

Bromsgrove was chosen as the perfect site in the south Birmingham area because of its excellent motorway

and reputation for business development.

According to Mr Clark it will be a 'one-stop shop' with more than 60 per cent of the top car manufacturers represented and facilities such as a shuttle bus to take people into town after they have dropped their cars off for a service.

"I have been to Calgary in Canada where they have these motor villages and it inspired me to set this one up.

"It is a fantastic opportunity for the town," he said.

Mr Clark estimates 360 jobs will be created on the site giving a massive

Now Bromsgrove District Council will have to decide whether to allow a change of use of the land from industrial to retail.

Dealers such as Renault, Peugeot, Fiat, Rover, Toyota, Honda and Suzuki have been sizing up the site.

Mr Clark has asked Bromsgrove architect, Mike Chapman, to design the state-of-the-art buildings for the motor village.

If all goes to plan the proposed scheme could be up and running in 18 months time.

The proposal is set to come before the town's planning committee on

Today, this site features three high class dealerships: Toyota, Peugeot and Nissan, with more to come!

arage boss claims Euro
ıles forced him to sell

·········
O'Brien
ff
n@mrn.co.uk

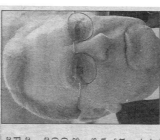

Doug Clark – forced to go with flow of events

G Rover Group has bought Midlands dealership Clark Motor Services as idge manufacturer solidate its position in market alongside its

ut comes in the wake Competition Com- ges to bloc exemp- hich has seen manu- w up new franchises, stronger control and nore investment from

sition, for an undis- does not include the any property where ture Motors – part of Group – will run the perations it takes over

Phoenix Venture Motors also takes over the large Clark accident and repair centre in Gravelley Lane, Bromsgrove.

The businesses will be signed under the Phoenix name.

Doug Clark, chairman of Clark Motor Services, who is in Canada, told *The Birmingham Post* last night that he had been forced "to go with the flow of events".

"The retail sector is now being monopolised by the manufactur- ers who have taken an opportunity presented under the new block exemption rules. It is a forced change and not evolution.

"We have been kicked out and are sensitive to what is happening. The EC rules will not do the job they anticipate in the medium term.

"The particular pressures on the motor trade today are leaving the entrepreneurial type of trader out in the cold. They are under tre- mendous pressure and still have so much to offer the public.

"There is now a cloned-type of representation coming, through from the manufacturers," said Mr Clark.

The changes have caused sig- nificant problems for other dealers

> The particular pressures on the motor trade today are leaving the entrepreneurial type of trader out in the cold

Doug Clark

south and west of Birmingham and has dealerships in Rednal, Bromsgrove and Kidderminster.

The business was started by Doug Clark – later joined by his brother Malcolm – who worked as a mechanic in their father's small garage at Chaddesley Corbett, near Kidderminster.

Mr Clark took over a petrol station at Rednal in 1959 where he started to sell and service cars. It marked the start of what was to become a significant business.

The Clark dealer- ships, which 18 months ago had an annual turn- over of £64 million, have been affected by some decisions coming down from manufacturers' fol- lowing the start of new bloc exemption rules towards the end of last year.

Clark Motor Services turnover

as the manufacturers tighten their hold on franchised operations.

The Clark business, which now becomes a considerable property owner, operates mainly to the

was almost halved due to the changes manufacturers demanded as they put more pressure on the dealerships.

Mr Clark, who has been in the motor trade for more than 40 years, built up a business with 460 staff – about 140 are transferring to Phoenix Venture Motors.

Recently Clark Motor Services ended its franchises with Honda and Volkswagen at Halesowen, TVR and Toyota, both at Bromsgrove.

Clark is keeping its Kia fran- chises at Rednal and Kiddermin- ster, its BMW Motorcycle busi- ness at Rednal and Honda dealership at Kidderminster.

The remaining part of the com- pany, which is still Clark Motor Services, is seeking planning per- mission for a ten-acre site it owns at Buntsford Gate, Bromsgrove, where it proposes to build a "mo- tor mall" of showrooms. Six major manufacturers have already expressed interest in the project.

Time to call it a day.

233

Clark's corporate logo.

License disc holder from hire department.

Clark's
Austin Rover
dealership
opening in
Bromsgrove 1988.

AUSTIN ROVER

The Birmingham Post

★ TUESDAY October 16 2001 **19**

Page 27

Motor
dealer is
going
places

Business

ANDERSEN

The world
at real
and
virtual **war**

Page 23

Clark's *Motor* Services (Rednal) Ltd.

A SPECIAL EIGHT-PAGE ADVERTISING SUPPLEMENT ON CLARK'S MOTOR SERVICES

AUSTIN ROVER

Where Good Service Pays Dividends

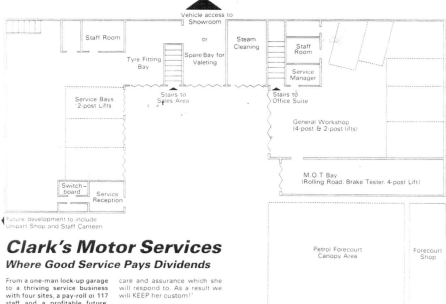

Vehicle access to Showroom

Staff Room

or

Steam Cleaning

Staff Room

Tyre Fitting Bay

Spare Bay for Valeting

Service Manager

Service Bays 2-post Lifts

Stairs to Sales Area

Stairs to Office Suite

General Workshop (4-post & 2-post lifts)

M.O.T Bay (Rolling Road, Brake Tester, 4-post Lift)

Switch-board

Service Reception

Future development to include Unipart Shop and Staff Canteen

Petrol Forecourt Canopy Area

Forecourt Shop

Clark's Motor Services
Where Good Service Pays Dividends

From a one-man lock-up garage to a thriving service business with four sites, a pay-roll of 117 staff and a profitable future. Such is the progress of Clarks Motor Services.

Last year their headquarters site at Rednal in Birmingham was appointed a Service Only outlet and immediately became the subject of a massive £300,000 extension and redevelopment programme. Service magazine visited the Rednal garage to look at the new purpose-built workshops, which form the bulk of the development, and also to speak to the man behind the success of this newcomer to the franchise – Managing Director, Doug Clark.

When I arrived, Doug was hidden from view – buried in the engine compartment of a customer's Maxi on the forecourt.

'It happens occasionally,' he told me, 'but not often thank goodness. We had this car in to replace the wheel bearings. Sent the customer away confident we'd done a good job and two days later the car is back again. This time the engine is misfiring and the dear lady owner is convinced it only happened because we changed the wheel bearings.'

'How do you get over that one? She doesn't understand cars. She wants her Maxi running smoothly again – and she still thinks it's our fault that its not.'

'This type of customer is a challenge. It's our job offer a level of care and assurance which she will respond to. As a result we will KEEP her custom!'

Doug has one overriding philosophy towards his customers – to give each one the attention and service he would want for himself. Today this philosophy is epitomised in the Clark-Care logotype which graces all their stationery.

It works, and Clark's Motor Services are the proof.

In 1960, when Doug started working at the Rednal garage, the facilities were sparce – just two petrol pumps and a very small lock-up garage. Built to service a bygone age.

Doug and Malcolm Clark.

In 1965 Shell bought the premises and installed Doug as their tenant. Business grew, so younger brother Malcolm Clark joined Doug. Shell expanded the site and Clark's Motor Services were on their way!

Today the Rednal Garage is very different. A modern, purpose built Service Centre, designed for the business environment of the 1980's.

Independent specialist bays cater for routine servicing, tyre fitting, MOT testing and steam cleaning, together with a small but well equipped general workshop. The principle behind the 'U shaped' design allows bay operators a certain autonomy of operation and ensures that the main workshop is kept free from the congestion created by short-stay vehicles.

But the creation of these attractive new facilities posed constructional problems.

Super clean, super efficient. Bob Hart and David Bird at work in the Leycare Service bays.

4

Service December 1982

This is when it really started to happen, with the service only franchise at Rednal.

FEBRUARY 1996 Vol 9 No 4

Redditch & Bromsgrove

Chamber of Commerce & Industry

Briefcase

BUSINESS NEWS

Crack down
on bad
debtors

Cleverdon
to speak
at AGM

New loan
schemes
launched

Studley
overhaul
in sight

Business
premises
disappoint

Focus on
Enfield
Estate

HONDA

→ PARKING

→ SALES

→ SERVICE

CLARK'S

Clark's clinch Honda deal

COVER STORY

CLARKS'S CLINCH HONDA DEAL

Advertising Feature

Honda Dealer Principal Mike Wollacott

HONDA is the latest in a line of top car manufacturers to select Bromsgrove based Clark's Motor Services as their main dealer in the area.

Clark's, which already operates Rover, MG and Toyota dealerships, will change the face of Marlbrook with their impressive Birmingham road site, which is currently being transformed. The development will also bring much needed jobs to the area when the purpose-built showroom is completed next month.

The Honda Dealer Principal, Mike Wollacott, is already operating from the main road site. The old car wash has been torn down to create space for the Used Car Display and the old buildings behind that, demolished to make way for the showroom. The specially designed workshop is already in operation and a range of the Honda cars, including a new design Civic range and used cars, are on sale.

"It's a very exciting move for us and for the area," says Mike, who has worked with Clark's MD Doug Clark for ten years.

"It's good for the area because of the extra jobs, great for car buyers because of the wider choice and a welcome move for current Honda owners because the nearest Honda dealer has been in Halesowen."

Clark's now become the main supplier of Hondas in an area from Northfield to Worcester. The specially trained staff will offer the extensive car range - from the new Civic models through the Accord, the Prelude and the Shuttle - and parts and servicing facilities.

Mike, fresh from years working on the Rover dealership, is delighted with his new project. Honda are known for selecting dealers with a sterling reputation.

"Doug has built up a reputation for second-to-none customer service. To do that you have to make sure the right staff are employed and the right training given," says Mike "We were attracted to Honda because they match our reputation well, for quality and reliability."

Mike, who lives in Bromsgrove with his wife Emma and their seven month old daughter Lucy, says the success of Honda cars lies in their reliability.

'The product is so reliable it's amazing," he says "One man told us he'd had seven Hondas and in all that time the only thing that has gone wrong was that a bulb had gone. Customer satisfaction is very high."

Mike has been impressed with the ranges too. Honda are looking for an increased market share through their 180 or so dealers.

"The appeal of Honda cars is their reliability, style and quality. There really is something in the range to appeal to everyone; there are sporty cars, estates, saloons and people movers - the shuttles."

Honda do not offer a diesel engine, but there is a Vtec economy engine which claims around 60 miles to the gallon.

Mike has been driving the Aerodeck (the Accord estate) and is vastly impressed.

"It's a quality product, but the thing is it's reliability. The cars are absolutely fantastic."

Mike has an excellent background in the motor trade. He started working with Doug Clark when he was just 18. Doug was then selling cars from a temporary showroom in Rednal. Since then of course, the business has gone from strength to strength, operating from showrooms in Bromsgrove and Kidderminster.

The Marlbrook site is open to customers from 8am to 6pm weekdays, 8.30am to 5.30pm on Saturdays and 10am to 2pm on Sundays.

The busy staff - which includes After Sales Manager, Paul Jeavons and Workshop Foreman, Mike Staley - are working round the clock however, as the business gears up.

"I love the job," smiles Mike, "I enjoy working with people and get satisfaction by giving a quality service - all things in-bred by Doug."

Honda UK will open the new showroom in March, but in the meantime anyone interested in testing out a Honda will be made very welcome.

"They will be very impressed," Mike says confidently.

For further details please contact: Mike Wollacott on 0121-445-3020. 492, Birmingham Road, Marlbrook, Bromsgrove, B61 0HS.

Clark's M.G. Demonstrator, managed to get an appropriate registration number.

DRIVING TRADITION TODAY

Clark's Motor Services sole distributor for MGF throughout Worcestershire

ADVERTISING FEATURE

Above: Fond memories. Doug Clark in 1979 with a 1955 MG 1500 TF. Below the new MGF 1.8i VVC.

CLARK'S Motor Services of Bromsgrove has achieved a top accolade in being selected as the sole distributor in Worcestershire for the sporty new MGF.

Motor enthusiasts have given the new car, launched at the Geneva Motor Show in March, a terrific reception and orders are already coming in.

The model will be on sale at Clark's Motor Services, Birmingham Road, this summer with the demonstrator MGF arriving early in June.

Rover's MGF project fuelled great excitement from the start and succeeded in delivering the goods - the creation of a superbly styled marque combining contemporary design with classic hallmarks.

It will be available in two versions - the MGF 1.8i and 1.8i VVC with prices around £16,000 and £18,000 respectively.

Deliveries of the 1.8i are expected late August and the VVC in early September.

The traditions of the MGF are epitomised by the use of a reversed version of the famous MG Octagon badge- carefully redesigned to combine nostalgia with modern impact.

But it also boasts superb handling and agility, achieved through a mid-engine, rear-wheel drive configuration, double wishbone suspension and front and rear disc brakes.

Speed-sensitive power assisted steering and ABS are standard on the 1.8i VVC model and optional on the 1.8i.

Rover, which unveiled the marque almost exactly 70 years after the launch of their first MG, took four years to develop the MGF and it marks their return to fully productionised sports car manufacture after some 15 years.

Rover have appointed just 120 specialist dealers nationally and emphasised the importance of retaining a high level of specialist sales and service personnel to support the marque comprehensively and provide dedicated attention to MG customers.

Clark's Motor Services has been a Rover main dealer since 1989 and has built up considerable experience with most MG models over the past years.

Doug Clark, Managing Director of Clark's, enjoys a lengthy association with MG after buying an MGTC in the 1950's and subsequently building up a small collection of MGs.

Doug said: "The link up with MG really does signify ' driving tradition today.'

"The response to the MGF has been quite outstanding. We already have a good number of orders ,all of which are subject to road testing,and we are running a very fair and precise sequence order procedure.

"Having tried the car I can say it is a real thoroughbred.Although it has all the benefits of latest technology it has retained a specialised feel only possible in a car of this stature.

The electronic assisted power steering is phenomenal and combines with a strong, sporty response."

Doug has managed to secure, an instantly collectible number plate for his keenly awaited demonstrator car - M4 MGF.

On hand to take assist prospective customers will be Clark's MG specialist Rob Sherrey.

Doug said: "Rob is well established with us and has an excellent understanding of MGs. We selected him as Sales Representative for this new marque because of his specialised skills."

The MGF's power is provided by new variants of Rover's award-winning K series engine. The 120PS MGF 1.8i derivative has a top

speed of 120mph with a 0-60mph time of 8.5 seconds.

The 1.8i VVC version, featuring a unique Variable Valve Control System, achieves 145PS with a target 0-60 time of seven seconds and a top speed of 130 mph, although these figures are provisional. The car has an elegant woven acrylic hood engineered by Pininfarina, which is folded up and down in a few seconds.

An optional black hard top - with full headlining and a heated rear window - can be fitted with ease and transforms the car into a stylish sports coupe.

The July issue of Briefcase will feature a special pull out supplement on the Clark's Motor Services Group.

Article from the business section of the 'Birmingham Post and Mail'.

Advertisment for another
fund-raiser.

My limited edition Fender
Playboy, Marilyn Monroe guitar.

My hero guitarist, Albert Lee, with his band Hogans Heroes

The Trade Winds in St. Augustine, Florida, USA. The Matanzas Band and my friend Troy, the base player. Great entertainment. Circa 2006.

Matanzas, performing at the Trade Winds.

Jamming in Malta?

Larry Freeman playing harmonica with Matanzas at the Trade Winds,
St. Augustine.

Drinks at the Trade Winds (L-R Larry, June, Troy, Yvonne and me.)

Playing twelve string Rickenbacker, see Playboy to the right.

Larry and me rehearsing on board Mission Accomplished for open-mike night at The Trade Winds.

And the performance!

Getting my kicks - on my Route 66

Lots of serious snakes in America.

Customer waiting!

The Photo Gallery Finish

Part Four 1980 – 1990

14 – You Don't Get If You Don't Keep Asking

I

A lot had been happening down the road at Longbridge during the 70's. British Leyland was the result of a series of mergers between combinations of different British car makers. The result of this hotchpotch was renamed the British Leyland Motor Corporation (BLMC). This encompassed Daimler, MG, Land Rover, Jaguar, Triumph, Riley, Wolsey, Austin, Morris, Rover, Sherpa and Vanden Plas. It was destined to become an unmanageable monster, burdened by ineffectual management, product duplication and crippled by strikes. The most infamous name from that period was Derek Robinson, the trade union spokesman and shop steward within BL.

Robinson, as union convener at Longbridge, became the most powerful shop steward in the country. With his network of representatives in the fourty two different BL plants around the country, he led a long-running campaign of strikes. His rabble-rousing cry was that the apparent mismanagement of BL was driving the company towards financial ruin. Although there was truth in that, what he was doing in fact was to kill any chance of survival it may have had and in 1975 BL went bankrupt and was nationalised by the government.

Along with multi-billions of pounds of government money, a new CEO was brought in, Sir Michael Edwardes, a no-nonsense, hard-nosed South African trouble-shooting cookie who made it his priority to end the strikes. Sir Michael was well connected with the press and used them mercilessly to turn Robinson into a figure of hate and ridicule, calling him Red Robbo. Between 1978 and 1979 Robinson was credited with causing 523 walk-outs at Longbridge, costing an estimated £200m in lost production. The catalyst Sir Michael used to rid himself of the troublesome priest Robinson was to sack him for signing a leaflet which criticised the inept BL management. In November 1979, a ballot on a strike, in sympathy of the dismissal, went 14,000 to 600 against him and he disappeared into obscurity.

Having dealt the death blow to Robinson, Edwardes set about slashing costs and commenced a merciless round of factory closures and sell-offs. This included the MG assembly plant in Abingdon and the Triumph plants in Speke and Canley. Next, he entered into a partnership with Honda. The Japanese were desperate to make inroads into the British market and so it was a marriage made in heaven for both parties. Honda took a 20% stake in the company while the company took a 20% stake in Honda's U.K. subsidiary. Jointly, they developed a range of cars which were at the forefront of the company's revival in the 1980s. Lastly, the number of BL Dealerships in the UK was trimmed down drastically and it seemed any chance of us getting one was further away than ever.

It was a decade which saw some great new models coming out of Longbridge, where the BL name was changed in 1981 to Austin Rover Group. Firstly came the Triumph Acclaim, then the Austin Ambassador followed by the MG Metro 1300, the MG Maestro 1600 sports (shelved after one year on sale and replaced by the more powerful MG Maestro 2.0 efi., which had a fuel injected 2.0 litre unit in place of the previous 1.6 twin-carburettor) and the Austin Maestro. The big hit in 1974 was the joint-venture Rover 200. This was later followed by the Rover 800 series. So successful were these models that it came as no surprise when the company changed its name once again, becoming Rover Group PLC.

The Austin/MG Metro was one of the top five selling cars in Britain throughout the 80's. The Rover 200 was one of the few strong-selling small family saloons of its era. Austin Rover was selling around 100,000 of them every year during the later part of the 80's. Also, a range that did well was the Montego, famous as much for its advertising where the driver swung into a tight parking space on a hand brake turn. This was great for us as the work shop was full of Montegos with burnt out brakes, as the young bucks tried to emulate the stunt performed by Russ Swift. I once had the privilege of being in a Montego with Russ at Bickenhill Test Track where he actually performed the stunt with me in the passenger seat. Austin Rover's decision not to replace sports cars like the MGB and the Triumph TR7 was in line with the decrease in popularity of sports cars generally. Hot hatchbacks were all the rage, led by Volkswagen's GTI. Austin Rover launched performance variants of its MG Metro and MG Maestro hatchbacks.

With the Japanese invasion truly underway it was like World War Three out there in the car market. Toyota, Honda and Nissan were all exporting heavily into the UK and demand was all but outstripping supply. The Germans were already here and represented quality and reliability. Both the Germans and the Japanese were streets ahead of the Brits.

Following the Honda/Rover collaboration, Nissan did a deal with the British Government to build a manufacturing plant over here. In March 1984, a 799-acre green-field site in Sunderland was allocated. As an incentive, the land was offered to Nissan at agricultural prices - around £1,800 per acre. The North had suffered a period of closures including most of the shipyards on the Tyne along with many coal mines. The high unemployment this caused meant Nissan had a large, eager, manufacturing-skilled workforce to draw upon.

Nissan demanded that the plant be single-union. This was unprecedented in UK industry, but they got it. It is a fact that not a single minute has ever been lost to strike action at the factory. NMUK is the most productive car plant in Europe, producing more cars per man than any other factory. As the decade went on I was inspired by some of the methods used by Nissan to ensure productivity remained constantly high and introduced my own version of some of them. The most notable being 'Kaizen', that's a Japanese word meaning continuous improvement, where all the workforce is encouraged to look for and report any ways to improve their working environment, no matter how small. I used to have suggestion boxes and held regular meetings with staff at all levels and listened to their ideas. In fairness, I was doing the 'Clark' version of this way before I had ever heard of Kaizen, but not in such a regulated way as Nissan had introduced.

II

I had embarked upon a series of strategic partnerships myself. The success with Britax had shown me that there was money to be made in 'add-ons' that had nothing to do with our core business of servicing cars, but were an extra service and profit centre in themselves. This was a progression from Clark's own established brand of servicing skills to a point where you can use those skills on other things. This included fitting electric windows and central locking systems to vehicle models that didn't come with them. We were many activities under one overhead and that made perfect sense.

III

Ken Smith, the after-sales director of Austin Rover was a regular petrol customer of ours, as he lived in Barnt Green and we were on his way home. Every time I saw him coming in to fill up, I would make a point of going out and bending his ear. We discussed the gossip from Longbridge and I would, without fail, ask him about the chances of us getting a 'service only' franchise. The answer was always the same and he would tell me with a smile that there was "No chance." He was a good listener though and it was through him I discovered that there was, in fact, one garage which had gotten a 'service only' franchise, but that was in London.

We were already servicing a good percentage of the employees' cars from Longbridge; employees who preferred to come to us rather than travel to one of the main dealers in Birmingham, Redditch or Stourbridge - but not anywhere near enough for my liking. The problems at Longbridge didn't affect our business. I looked upon Longbridge more as a giant oasis, a watering hole with 50,000 workers, all with vehicles that needed regular care and attention, plus their relatives' cars. The dream of tapping into all that business is why I kept on and on at Ken Smith.

Then in 1981 an event happened that was to change everything. Patrick Motors, an old-established Austin Rover Dealership and service agent, closed down. I didn't know the 'ins and outs' of why or how, but nor did I care. I was only delighted that this left a massive service opening in the area. The nearest was Bryant's in Bromsgrove, who already had more work than they wanted and were far more interested in selling cars than servicing anyway. So, overnight, we picked up even more cars from the Longbridge workforce. Ken now took my requests seriously and put a proposal to the main board, which included the very astute Trevor Taylor, the then CEO (later he went on to be CEO of Toyota GB). We were in fact preparing Trevor Taylor's personal cars already so he knew of us and the standard of our work and was immediately supportive. It wasn't as simple as them just saying "Yes" though. Franchise regulations are there to protect existing dealers and so the franchise body had to examine the case and make sure none of its members was going to suffer by granting us an agreement.

Various meetings took place; members of the board and the franchise association came to see our operation at Rednal and time went on with no decision. Ken Smith was like a dog with a bone; he knew it made sense and persevered on our behalf. I was summoned to one final big meeting in the main board room at Austin Rover, this time with John King the regional director. I thought it went well and that I couldn't have put my case any more strongly. I had prepared a document showing that we were upgrading the number of hydraulic lifts that were demanded to be given 'Leycare' status. In fact, I was putting in more than the minimum requirements. Ken Smith supported me in every way possible and had provided me with the full spec of what was required, so that we were well prepared.

Two days after that meeting I had a phone call from the Regional Manager, Ron Scott, informing me that he had been contacted by Eric Willoughby, the national after-sales director at Cowley in Oxfordshire, to say that he was appointing Clark's as 'after sales/service-only' franchise. Once I put the phone down I was silent for a minute, then yelled a war whoop at the top of my voice and danced around the office. Everyone was caught up in the atmosphere and it was one of the most memorable days of my life. A milestone in Clark credibility. Malc and I had an extra pint at the Robin Hood that evening to celebrate.

"Fabulous Clark Brothers strike again", I told him and he grinned from ear to ear.

IV

Winning that franchise was like giving me the keys to Aladdin's cave. Apart from all the business which came our way from the Longbridge workers, almost overnight, something else dramatic happened in the explosion – Clark's became national.

We were asked to quote for fleet work and in the fullness of time got a contract with British Aerospace to prepare 5,000 vehicles per year. Such was our value that we were chosen by the consumer affairs department at Cowley to prepare the very special Austin Rover cars for the very special people. This consisted of government officials, including the Prime Minister, Margaret Thatcher herself, vice chancellors of universities, as well as entertainment and sporting personalities. For anyone of importance that required a Rover car, the interceptors at Cowley and Canley would send the vehicle to us and we never once let them down. I remain to this day so proud of that fact.

15 – The Start Of The Monopoly Years

I

In anticipation of things to come, I had made one or two significant moves at the start of the eighties. The first was to buy Tessall Garage at Longbridge in 1980. It was an old-established garage owned by Patrick Hawker who also had another famous landmark garage, The Spot, about a mile further along the Bristol Road towards Birmingham. He was quite a canny businessman and I'd often go to see his operation, as he was always quite innovative when it came to the latest technology.

I made an appointment and my opening words were: "I've heard on the grapevine that Tessall could be up for sale?"

"I don't know where you've heard that", he smiled at me, "and I don't know who would want to buy it."

"I would," I told him.

"And why would you want to do that; haven't you got enough on your plate already?"

"I could do with somewhere nearer to Longbridge," I told him honestly. What I didn't tell him was that, to me, it would make a wonderful pincer movement - having Longbridge works sandwiched between the two garages so we could tap even more into the 'watering hole'.

"Where will you get the money from?" He inquired.

I told him it wasn't a problem, which of course it was! But in typical Doug Clark style I knew it was an opportunity I had to grasp. The belt and braces could come later. For now, I just wanted a handshake, which I got and we settled on a quarter of a million. Cheap at the price to me and a nice pension for him. Although it was the furthest thing from my mind at that point, circumstances were such that I would have to sell Tessall within five years - actually for double the money, but that isn't why I sold and I will return to that part of the story a little later.

Patrick Hawker was a hard and abrupt, but basically honest man who insisted on being loyal to the people who had been loyal to him. So, part of the deal was that I took on all the staff, which I duly did. Some good people came out of that acquisition and over time I weeded out any stragglers, of which there were few.

In fact, as far as staff were concerned, poaching was the name of the game. I wanted the best people around and was prepared to pay above the going rate for them. At Lickey, the environment was now such that it was regarded as a centre of excellence in every sense of the phrase. From the forecourt attendant to the top mechanics and beyond, everyone was proud to be a part of the Clark organisation. That, in turn, made me proud beyond belief. Such was our reputation that we became regularly featured not only in the local press, but the national trade magazines. Clark's was becoming a brand name.

Obviously, my next port of call was the bank. We had always been with Lloyds; they were, in my opinion, the most switched-on and hungry-for-business bank around at the time; trying, as they were, to make major inroads against the big three: Barclays, Midland and NatWest. As such, they were eager to invest in 'up and coming' businesses, into which slot we fitted nicely.

One guy in particular became a major influence in the way we financed things. That was Robin Hunter, their pension's advisor. He had set up a pension fund for us whereby most of the profits went straight into the fund rather than coming to us in salaries and bonuses. We did, in fact, still live far more frugally than most owners/directors running similar-sized businesses. The big picture was expansion, expansion and more expansion. The money accumulated in the fund was used to make land and property acquisitions. The company would pay the going interest rate on the loan back into the fund. It was and remains a marvellous scheme that Robin created for us. Up until 1975 it was not possible for shareholding directors to participate in anything like this and some begrudgers might say that a golden loophole had been created. It was true that you got your cake and ate it too, but also it was a springboard to create wealth and opportunities for all those who worked for and with us. It was known commonly as an

SAS (self administered pension scheme).

Robin left in the early 80's to become an independent financial consultant, forming his own company, Hunter and Co. Needless to say, we were one of his first clients and remain so today.

With all the costs of developing Rednal there weren't vast funds to draw on, so in the short term, it meant borrowing from the bank in the general sense as well. I made my mind up that The Forge at Hagley was no longer a major player in the grand plan and so surreptitiously put it up for sale. It didn't take long, after casting the line into the water, before I got a bite. It went to Charles Clark (no relation, but in themselves, a major brand name in Wolverhampton) who were following their own strategy and put a Jaguar franchise in there - and they did very well with it too. I was happy with the £180,000 I got from the sale, a very nice £140,000 profit from the initial purchase.

The actual date of the sale was very close to the 29th July 1981. I remember it well, because it was the day on which Diana and Charles got married and that was a national holiday. So, sadly, we had to close for the day and celebrate the happy couple along with the rest of the country.

II

Now that we had the 'service only' franchise, we had to deliver, and even with Tessall Garage in the stable, there wasn't enough room to properly prepare the new cars for British Aerospace, which was all part of the deal. So I rented two unused warehouse units in the heart of Austin Rover itself - 8,000 square feet and well fit for purpose. I kitted them out with lifts and had them cleaned from top to bottom. Then I got together the best valeting team I could muster. It consisted of nine ladies and two guys, all of whom laughed and joked and worked like Trojan Horses, taking the 'Clark' standards right into Longbridge. In fact, you might well ask why Longbridge wasn't doing that itself? Well, I can only say that it was going through a period of missed opportunities, which to me were golden opportunities, so I didn't complain then or now, just kept smiling, that's all.

Another major development happening at almost the same time was the body shop at Marlbrook. Malc was turning down significant amounts of business because its order books were full for weeks ahead. Just after The Forge deal went through, I bought 12 acres of land adjoining the West Works at Longbridge for £120,000, just ten grand an acre, from A.J. Southall, a Stourbridge based engineering company. This was speculative, as I thought I might be able to sell part of it on, at some point, at a tidy profit. The only building on the land was an old factory, which was so decrepit it was a wonder it was still standing. It certainly wasn't for long; I soon had a bulldozer running through it and razed it to the ground.

I had visions of a ski slope, as this was starting to become fashionable and also our very own motorcycle scramble track. However, ski slopes were not to be. Instead, I negotiated a massive government grant through our accountants, Grant Thornton, and embarked on building a 28,000 square foot state-of-the-art body shop, which I wanted to be the talk of the industry. It was built by our own construction company, which now owned our own heavy plant equipment, as well as employing full-time carpenters, brickies, electricians and labourers. Richard Dodd was now our full-time 'Clerk of Works' for the building division.

The body shop was equipped with the latest Burntwood baking ovens, which included an infra-red drying process. This was to exactly the same standard as Rolls-Royce used in their paint shop. I also installed Black Hawk body jigs. This was a computerised process whereby a damaged car was put on a platform and the computer analysed every millimeter of the vehicle and identified, in the minutest detail, all damage. In fact, it is a three stage process: firstly it measures then stretches all the damaged metal and finally it reinstates the body work back to manufacturer's standards - a piece of technological wizardry. There was a separate piece of software for each make of vehicle. It also clearly identified vehicles that were totally beyond repair. I bought three of those jigs at forty grand apiece. In today's money that would be nigh on half a million each.

The body shop opened its doors for business in 1982, cost £900,000 to build and, under Malcolm's leadership, instantly became the jewel in the crown that I had planned it to be.

III

When we landed the British Aerospace car preparation contract we were already tight on space. I realised that, even with all the juggling at Rednal and elsewhere, we just didn't have the capacity to handle it effectively. Across the road from the new body shop I had spotted the Britannia Works which then housed the Peter Paint Pad factory. You may remember them from the late sixties, early seventies; they were quite revolutionary in DIY. "No more brushes", was the cry and it seemed everyone was using Peter Paint Pads instead of the traditional brush. Everyone, that is, except for the professional painters and decorators who knew better. The finish was not as good, the product was not cheap and had no life after use - they were disposable and expensive. With today's recycling awareness they would probably be a non-starter.

The entrepreneur that was Peter Paint Pads appeared to have spent the profits in the good times, driving as he did a shiny Rolls Royce. Well, that went along with the factory when the company went into receivership. I bought it lock stock and barrel (minus the Rolls) from the receiver for £400,000. The factory and the offices were pristine and required only a modicum of altering to suit our needs. It was a very valuable asset to me, 8000 square feet and stood out as a huge landmark to our progress in achieving the grand plan. With this in the stable we could take on everything and anyone. So over the moon was I with this building, that we decided to use it for a giant public relations night to bring all the staff and their families together under one roof. I engaged the entertainment agent, Royston Evans, to devise the evening. The place was decked out with huge statements including 'The Last Detail is the Next Customer'. It was a party with a purpose: to unite all employees together in a common mission and sense of pride. The future of Clark's promised prosperity for all. There was a sumptuous sit-down meal, nice wines, a cabaret and a great band to which we danced the night away. The existing workbenches were cleverly disguised as tables and, to all intents and purposes, it felt like a really swish hotel.

So successful was the evening that I decided there and then to host a monthly dinner for our ever-growing number of branch managers and their wives. So began our long and happy gatherings at the Chung Ying in Birmingham. With apologies to the late Humphrey Bogart, I believe that: "Of all the Chinese restaurants in all the world, the Chung Ying is and remains, the greatest Cantonese this side of Hong Kong."

So, whilst Ernö Rubik was inventing and launching his 3-D puzzle cube, which sold a staggering ten million in less than six months, we were solving problems which were the creation of our own success. But, what do problems create? More problems!

16 – Go Back To The Old Kent Road

I

We were growing like topsy! Every garage had full order books for servicing; the pre-delivery inspection business was the cream on the milk and I started yet another business which slotted in beautifully. This was a lucrative little add-on called 'U-Can-Hire'. It did exactly what is says on the label. We purchased a small number of category B cars from Austin Rover, which we hired out on a daily and weekly basis. These were cars which hadn't been passed as fit for sale through the showrooms and had minor imperfections, but were just right for what I had in mind. It needed a good person with the right customer attitude to run the division. I knew who I wanted, Lee Shepherd. He was on the front desk at Motaparts, so brazenly I approached and poached him. Don't think it went down too well with Paul and Slade, but I didn't lose any sleep over it. I wouldn't say it made a fortune, but it was a good value-added service to offer to our ever-growing customer base. I certainly wasn't in the business of offering courtesy cars - there was no profit to be had in that and they would end up in the repair shop all too often. However, if you charged a nominal car hire fee, they would be looked after – strange but true. We are talking of the days when companies issued cars to their employees like confetti. I remember being at a dinner where the fleet manager described the company car. "It's a wonderful vehicle," he exclaimed. "The company car will defy the limitations of the speedometer, run on empty most of the time, you never need to check the oil and water and it only needs servicing when the crunching noise, coming from under the bonnet, starts sounding like someone with a hammer is trapped underneath and wants to get out." It brought the house down, but certainly was a truism. I wasn't going to have courtesy cars treated in the same manner as a rep's freebie.

U-Can-Hire existed as part of the business for many years and, at its height, enjoyed a fleet of 130 vehicles including mini coaches, which we hired out to local schools and football teams. So well did we maintain those cars that often they were sold for more than we had actually paid for them.

II

Clark's now had a main board with myself as MD, Adrian Smith as Pre-delivery Inspection Manager, Tony Foden as Group Service Manager, Dave Price as Forecourts Manager and Malcolm as General Manager of the Accident and Repair Division down at Groveley Lane, which incidentally now employed eighty five people.

I also brought a new person onto the board and into the company: Stephanie Strong as Personnel Manager. Boy, was she 'strong' by nature as well as name, the nearest thing to a Gestapo officer this side of the Second World War. She took no prisoners, did Stephanie and woe betide anyone that hadn't done their homework before a meeting. She would pull me up too on any health and safety matters, such as loose handrails or obstruction hazards. Lord knows what she would have made of our 'dear old pit'.

There was a board room in every branch and I encouraged Kaizen-style internal meetings to take place (out of hours, if possible) as well as rotating the board meetings to make each branch manager the host.

The next innovation was management accounts. These had been requested by the bank for some time and, whereas I mocked their usefulness initially, as just another set of figures, I became an overnight fan when John Costin, a senior accounts manager at Austin Rover, explained how I could control the business so much better with them. He told me I could check from purchase to supply-and-fitting everything that moved within the company, down to the last nut and bolt. Nothing could escape the all-seeing eye of management accounts.

The revelation couldn't have come at a better time either as I was spitting feathers. We were flat out everywhere, into some very heavy borrowings to fund the continued expansion, the wage bill was through the roof and surprise, surprise, at the end of our financial year in 1983 we hadn't made a penny.

I vented my wrath at Malcolm though it wasn't his fault. "We made bloody money when it was just thee and me Malc. So, why aren't we doing it now?"

"Too many mouths to feed?" He ventured.

"No, it's because, despite the checks and double checks and belt and bloody braces we put on everything we do, we haven't applied the same belt and braces to the overall control," I told him. "On the Monopoly board we've gone back to the Old Kent Road."

"You're losing me," he said, "and anyway, I thought overall control is very much your department."

"Exactly, and I hold my hands up. But no more, mate, no more; we are bringing in the new Clark Bible and it's called Management Accounts."

I went on 'ad nauseam' and I am sure by the glazed look in his eyes he wasn't exactly enthralled by my evangelic sermon on the discovery of the Holy Grail. But, he listened and allowed me to let off steam and finished the evening by saying he had every faith in what I was about to instigate. This made me realise that I wasn't the man for the job to sell the introduction of management accounts to the team. Instead, I persuaded John Costin to take on the mantle in return for a case of Scotch. Sadly John was an alcoholic and like all those great people who let the servant become the master, he subsequently lost everything he held dear in life to the point of becoming destitute. I lost contact with him for several years, but was pleased to hear that, through Alcoholics Anonymous, he eventually rebuilt his life and was reunited with his family. There was a five-year gap when he must have endured his own personal hell.

He was not at that point then, thankfully, and conducted the weekend seminar with all our key players at the Lyttleton Arms in Hagley. By the end, they were as convinced as me to the value they would bring to the business. Management accounts became like subscribing to your favourite magazine which you couldn't wait to peruse from cover to cover. It was the missing piece in the jigsaw and, once more, we moved forward. They became a subconscious form of belt and braces, a back-bone if you like. I would pour over them at night; everything had a column and everything correlated. They are, common sense - a bit like the housekeeping book my mother kept. The devil is in the detail, analysing and scrutinising the content.

I cannot emphasise enough to anyone who is growing a business: introduce MA's and make them your best friend. That way lies success; ignore what they are telling you at your peril. Why, with management accounts, you could run your business from the moon if needs be.

The loyal and highly capable Eleanor Rigby (Neale) prepared them and my main function, once they were prepared, was to interpret them. They ensured efficiency and profitability. Order was once again restored to the house of Douglas Clark. The days of rumpy-pumpy in the back of a customer's car had long since gone; these were the days and nights of moving up into the premier league of business. There could be no distractions from the mission. Now that we had the service-only franchise and an ever-growing national reputation, I had to consider my own reputation as well. I ran an honest little empire. I know that, down the road at Longbridge, the stories of corruption were and still are legendary. I do not intend to dwell on that or name names. That would be spiteful and unnecessary. Suffice to say that, had I lost a contract with them for reasons along those lines, then I would have enjoyed a far larger sum by selling the story to the News of the World than the contract would have been worth. Gladly, it never happened and I can, hand on heart, say that every contract we obtained from them was honestly brokered.

III

One of the things that management accounts threw up was the takings tally at our College Service Station branch in Bromsgrove. It seemed that the till takings didn't equate to what was going out at the pumps. Not by a huge amount, but it was a constant drip. I suspected foul play and paid them an unexpected visit. We had a lady working for us there who was always very pleasant, in fact, ready for a laugh. But it was on the days she worked that the pattern showed the discrepancies.

"How's business?" I inquired of her.

"Been a bit slow today, a bit like me," she tried to joke.

I didn't laugh, but looked her straight in the eyes. I knew then and there she had become a thief. "Let's hope you get a rush later on then, it is market day," I said, as reassuringly as I could.

As soon as I left I went straight to the police and told them of my suspicions. They decided to set her a trap by way of installing a camera and filming what she was up to. For a week there was nothing, but I was still convinced she was a bad apple. I may have frightened her off by my visit, but then the next day, I had a phone call from the police to say they had something to show me.

On viewing the footage it showed her as bold as brass putting a bundle of notes into her shoe and leaving with it still concealed. I took no immediate action and sure enough, two days later she did the same thing. It was time for confrontation. She broke down and admitted she had been stealing from us for nearly ten years to the tune of about twenty grand. She burst into floods of tears, the mascara running down her face like a black river. She sobbed, "I had only meant to do it the once when I was desperate for money and then it just became a habit."

I felt sorry for her; it had become an addiction just like drugs, gambling or alcohol.

"Please don't prosecute me," she begged. "They'll send me to prison and my children will never forgive me for the disgrace I've brought on the family"

"Can you pay me back?" I asked her.

"Not all of it, but a lot. I've got it saved," she replied quietly. "I haven't spent it on holidays or anything - it was for a rainy day."

"Well, the storm clouds have broken luv," I told her. "Give me what you have today and I want the rest in weekly payments, pound by pound and penny by penny."

"Yes I will, I promise, and thank you Mr. Clark," the relief evident in her voice. "And you are of course fired," I told her. I then escorted her off the premises and down to the bank where she withdrew all the cash she had stored away. Straight after that I obtained a court order to make the payments official. She was as good as her word, which I knew she would be. She didn't have to confess to the long period of theft or the amount; we could only prove the two occasions and surmise the rest. I actually pitied her, but letting her off a single penny was neither in my nature nor in her interests. By taking the money back from her on a regular basis, I am sure cured her addiction. I am neither a saint nor a Samaritan; some people will tell you I am mean. Maybe so, but I play by my own rules and only treat others in business and in life as I wish to be treated myself.

There were numerous actual and attempted thefts, it goes with the territory of a cash business, I suppose. We were never approached for protection money or anything like it, not that I would have paid it anyway, as you've probably guessed. In fact, I'd sooner be in a coffin than give in to that nonsense. I know many a dealer that has though, particularly up north.

We were ram-raided on one occasion; that was at the Cross Keys. I got called out in the middle of the night to find an abandoned Austin 1100 inside the shop. Utter chaos. They had also done Little Chef next door and tied up the cashier. The next day, much to the amusement of one of our longest serving employees, Jean Coleman the cashier at Cross Keys and Shaw Taylor the presenter of ATV's Police Five, turned up with a TV crew to do a re-enactment. It was the nearest Jean got to being a film star.

IV

As I mentioned earlier, Lloyds were our bankers and at the time they were quite heavily into local sponsorship. Whilst the likes of Barclays were sponsoring bigger fish such as the Royal Shakespeare Company, Lloyds looked to have a presence at much more of a community level.

Maurice Beasley, the senior manager at Halesowen, approached me regarding the Halesowen Carnival which they were sponsoring, asking if I would like to get involved by providing a car to take the star to the opening ceremony. Well, I did have stored away a lovely little royal blue, open-topped, Austin 7 Chummy, which I had swapped for a Mini some years before. It was in a sorry and neglected state when I got it, but it had over a period of time, been restored to a fantastic condition by Doug Burbridge, a trimmer in the design department at Austin Rover. Although I paid him, he had mostly done it because he wanted to and took such enjoyment and a tremendous pride in his work. It almost looked like it was smiling and gleamed like a Rolls Royce.

I met with the carnival committee and they loved the idea of using it. So, come the big day, I drove the wonderfully charismatic Gail Tillsley from 'Coronation Street', at the head of the Carnival Procession through the throngs of well-wishers that lined the pavements of Halesowen to the opening ceremony. I felt incredibly regal and enjoyed giving the royal wave which Gail taught me in between fits of laughter.

Following on behind us, before the floats, was a little Sinclair C5 which I also provided; this created quite a degree of hilarity. The C5 was destined never to become anything other than a vehicle of curiosity and still remains so today and those, like mine, are collector's items. There were only 17,000 of them sold. Clive Sinclair is a very clever man, we owe the calculator and possibly the computer to him, but his foray into the motoring world was both a historical and hysterical non-starter.

It was at about this time that I was awarded an honour which may not seem much to you, but meant the world to me. I was asked to become President of the Chaddesley Corbett Football Club. I accepted with grace and thanks; to think: little Dougie Clark, one of the poorest kids in the village, would receive this ultimate accolade. I filled the president's role for many years, attending the matches as often as I could and when the time came to hand on the mantle, I was made life-time president. Wow!

17 – Pay A Ten-Pound Fine Or Take A Chance

I

Christmas 1985 is a Yuletide I will never forget. It was a time of celebration and as usual we were laying on a splendid party for all the staff and their partners. Malcolm and I went to Makro, the wholesalers, to get the booze for the party and some fancy bottles of spirits for our special customers and suppliers. We were in a bright yellow Ford transit 35 hundredweight van and it was filled to the gunnels. We were both happy and were planning the party as we travelled the return journey.

I was driving and approaching the traffic island at Halesowen, which has several lanes and exits and can be confusing if you're not used to it. I was quite used to it, but a motor cyclist approaching from my right obviously wasn't and swerved in a manoeuvre to get himself into the right lane. This in turn caused me to brake to avoid him. No harm was done, the bike went on its way and so did we.

On the other side of the traffic island is a fairly steep hill which is the back road through Romsley to the M5. As we went up it a police panda car came screaming past us and flashed its left indicator.

"What's he up to?" asked Malc.

"Beats me," I replied, "maybe he's late for his Christmas dinner."

There was a lay-by about fifty yards ahead and we noticed he had pulled in there.

"That's odd, no other cars about," I said, not really giving it a second thought.

We carried on for about a mile to a cross-roads where there was another police car blocking the road.

"What the bloody hell?" I said to Malc.

"Must have been a robbery," he replied.

Just as we pulled in, the police car from the lay-by came screaming up behind us, sandwiching us in like they had caught the Great Train Robbers.

An irate sergeant got out and strode across to us. I was amused to see that he had creased his hat to make him appear like an American cop. There was nothing amusing about the way he spoke though. He was absolutely incensed.

"Right!" He exploded, "I'm booking you for dangerous driving and failing to stop when instructed to do so by an officer of the law."

"Hang on a minute, Officer," I replied, as courteously as I could. "I dispute both of those accusations."

"Dispute what you like sunshine," he scowled. "you're booked! Give us your license now."

"I'll show it at the station, when I report you," I told him.

He issued me with a notice to produce my documents and a note reporting my alleged misdemeanors. I tried to get out of the car to talk to him, but he slammed the door on my outstretched leg and stormed off still furious, only to return seconds later with a breathalyser in his hand. I blew in the bag and it was negative. He didn't comment, just made a sharp exit once more.

I was furious for two reasons: one, that my leg hurt like hell and two, that he had been such a jumped-up officious bastard telling a whole bunch of porky pies.

"Right Malc," I exploded, "I'm not having this, we're going to the local nick to report him."

"Too bloody true," said Malc who was as wound-up as me.

So the fugitive twosome set off to Halesowen police station and asked to see the officer on duty. Here we waited and waited and, despite repeated requests, no officer came to talk to us. I was told: "They were all busy with a bomb scare," and, "wouldn't you rather come back another time."

At one point I saw the sergeant who had booked me smirking away with a couple of his colleagues and downing mugs of tea.

"They certainly don't look like they're up to their ears in a bomb scare to me," I told the desk clerk, a remark which he chose to ignore. Eventually, after over two hours of waiting, a female inspector came out to us. "I understand you wish to make a complaint against an officer," she said in the manner of a schoolteacher addressing an errant student.

"Yes, I most certainly do," I replied.

"Would you take a piece of advice," she told me, suddenly becoming my best mate. "Be sure this is really what you want to do. My advice is that you just go home and wait for your day in court."

"I believe I am totally within my rights to make a complaint and that's exactly what I intend to do," I told her.

She sighed and switched on the recording machine into which I gave my statement. I spoke, word for word, the truth of the matter.

The case duly went to magistrates court, my statement was not read out or referred to - seems it had mysteriously gotten lost. I was found guilty on both charges, given points on my license and fined £200. I left the courtroom absolutely livid.

Now, I suppose most people would have left it there, swallowed the bitter pill and cursed about the injustice over a pint of beer. Not me! I vowed not to leave a stone unturned in righting this wrong and was straight on the phone to my solicitor, Brian Hopkinson of Pinsent & Co.

"I want to take out a civil action against the police," I told him.

"It'll be expensive," was the reply.

"I don't care how much it costs," I replied, "get me the best brief there is and let's go for them." Well, the upshot of this part of the story is that we did. Several months later, the case went to crown court. The officer was subpoenaed to appear and on cross-examination was proven to be a liar. The judge also reprimanded the police for covering up for each other and recommended an internal investigation. This apparently took place and it was discovered that two supporting officers admitted they had been asked to change their statements. The sergeant was demoted to a beat bobby; personally, I would have sent him down. The points were deducted from my license, my fine refunded and I was awarded substantial damages.

My faith in the British legal system was restored, but I remain sceptical to this day as to the merits of magistrates courts. My advice, to anyone who suffers the same kind of miscarriage of justice as I did, is to be tenacious and pursue it to the end. Don't let the buggers get away with it.

II

This was the time when, in my game of Monopoly, I looked at the board and realised that, in company terms, we were spreading ourselves too thinly. I am sure you all know the game and the strategies that can be used. It's not only about buying up all the properties you can, but more about collecting sites and building: first houses and then hotels on them. You just have to wait till someone lands on one and then it's the beginning of the end. I loved the game as a child and to play the real life adult version gave me the ultimate buzz. I wanted to buy more land and properties; therein lay the future but, in order to do that, I realised some things had to go. We were no longer reliant on petrol sales as a major source of income. The margins were getting tighter and tighter and it wasn't the most efficient way of maximising profit. The supermarkets were fast becoming the major providers of choice. They would cut prices to the bone to get customers who, once there, would go on to do their grocery shopping. There was far more wealth in servicing and repairs and so this was to be the focus for the future. With this in mind, it was time to say goodbye to the Cross Keys at Hagley. This was our only really large-scale, petrol-only operation and so I transferred it at an acceptable price.

It was time to disband the Treble-S club too. In reality, it had reached the end of its cycle; all the players had moved on to other things and our meetings were non-existent. What had started out as an innovation, every garage had now cottoned onto and Shell, like the other big companies, moved to take the shops entirely under their own wing. I didn't blame them, nor did I feel any sadness; it had been the right move at the right time and the time had come to move on again.

Robin Hunter and our SAS pension scheme became the prime consideration in every move I made. The scope of possibilities seemed endless. Robin interpreted the small print and took advantage of every detail that was both legal and advantageous, giving a strong 'thumbs down' to any grey area.

One of the main advantages was that we didn't get clobbered for capital gains tax every time we sold something, as the profits remained in the trust. The downside was that we couldn't take any money out to spend personally, or purchase residential properties or be a trading company of any sort, but that was of scant concern during the 'Monopoly years'. It was all about expansion with footholds of concrete, not sand. We ploughed money in and the fund escalated and the business expanded on an almost daily basis. As managing trustee, the mechanics of the structure started to occupy more and more of my time. I didn't mind though; I was on a new mission and my thirst for financial knowledge knew no limits. My message to any would-be entrepreneurs reading this is that you will never find anything better to invest in than yourself.

III

I was keen that we should be seen as excellent practitioners in every aspect of our business. As well as Personnel Manager my strong right-arm Stephanie took up the mantle of training. In addition to spearheading the 'Clark Care' indoctrination, she joined us up with Bourneville Technical College where we tailored a special NVQ (National Vocational Qualification), not only for our own staff, but for anyone wanting to come into the motor business.

There were many government training schemes around at the time which a business could incorporate into its workplace. These included the ISO 8000 and the coveted 'Investors in People' of which we were, thanks to Stephanie, the first car service company to be awarded the prestigious plaque. By the mid 1980's our borrowings were now in the region of three million pounds, mostly from the trust. But I slept at night in the knowledge that everything was tied up neatly and efficiently. Belt and braces!

IV

By 1986 Clark's were the biggest Rover Warranty account in the whole of the country. Our turnover on this part of the business alone was in excess of one million pounds a month.

It wasn't enough though and I still wanted the ultimate prize of becoming a Rover Dealership. It made logical sense to me, as time and time again, customers came and asked if they could buy their car through us. I continued to ask Rover, but just hit the same old brick wall. So I went around it by the back door - and not too subtly either. I wanted it to get back to the big wigs at Rover that Doug Clark could shift their cars. So, when a customer asked if they could buy their new car through me I would make a phone call to Dave Onions at West Heath Motors and get a price off him for the vehicle to be traded in. It became an unwritten agreement that the price he gave me over the phone would include fifty quid for us. Then I would phone up and order the new car for the customer through one of the Clark-friendly dealerships, usually Lex of Stourbridge, Colliers of Yardley or Parkside in Coventry. Again, the on-the-road price would include a fifty pound commission. Nearly always these deals were for Rover employees or their relatives and took into consideration their 25% discount. Everyone was happy: the dealership who had sold a car with no work on their part, West Heath Motors who knew I would only pass on good second-hand ones and the customer, who was buying his car through the company that would be looking after it. A hundred pounds was a nice little earner for a couple of phone calls, so I was happy too.

This was such a farcical situation that I was actually selling over 400 cars a year - and all without a showroom.

One memorable day I had a phone call from Ian Bryant of the old-established family Rover Dealership and service garage in Bromsgrove requesting a meeting.

"You're far better than us at this entire servicing lark," he told me. "I also know you're selling cars without a franchise."

"Is this some sort of veiled threat?" I asked him.

"Not at all, old chap," he replied. "Just thought that if you stopped doing the backhanders and put the business our way then we would leave all the grease monkey bit to you."

I saw red and turned him down flat. "I don't need a franchise to sell cars mate," I told him, "and, if I ever get one, you'd better watch out 'cause you'll be out of business. Now, if you don't mind, I've wasted enough time with you already. I'd best be getting back to the oil can."

I made it my business to see that Bryant's suffered at every turn. Their attitude to customers was that of laziness and contempt. Not surprisingly, they went bust within the year. Although I may just have played a small role in that downfall, ultimately, like the fall of Rome, the decay came from within. They were once a great company, but rested on their laurels. Business is an ever-changing feast and you have to change with it or, better still, be one step ahead.

In the meantime, I bought the unused Midland Red Bus Depot in Bromsgrove from the bus company and mothballed it in readiness for the next part of the Clark Meccano set. It was up for sale at an asking price of £285,000 and had been empty for two years. I offered them £225,000 and payment within two weeks and they bit my hand off. As luck would have it, I didn't have to part with the money for nine months, as they couldn't locate all the relevant paperwork. Meantime, I had taken possession and had the old building razed to the ground before anyone could object.

Next to the garage there was house with a huge garden. I knocked on the door one day soon after purchasing the garage and asked them if they wanted to sell. Mrs. Lacey, the nice lady that lived there, was quite a sharp cookie. She ran Strand DIY, a very successful forerunner of the B&Q's of this world. It was a little DIY supermarket that stocked everything and anything for home improvement. They had no plans to expand outside Bromsgrove though and were content enough with the business and income as it was.

She told me that she didn't really want to sell, but a developer had already offered them £400,000, which was way above the market price at the time. It was worth every penny of that to me though and so, thinking on my feet I said: "How about if I match that and you continue to live here rent free for a year while you find the house you want?"

She smiled and shook my hand on the deal. We remained friends for many years.

Twelve months later I ran a bulldozer through the garden, but the council were now wise to my reputation for demolition and slapped a preservation order on the house, which remains to this day. It is no longer a private house though, but the best Indian restaurant for miles - The Mint Lounge - if you are ever in the area, do give it a try; say Doug Clark recommended you via this book. You won't be disappointed. So I had the property I wanted on the board. It was time to shake the dice again and move onto the next stage of the game.

18 – Ship Ahoy

I

I have always loved boats and have never missed the Boat Show at Earls Court. It was the one day each year I marked in the calendar for a treat.

The first craft of any substance that I bought was in 1982. I saw this advert for a Butler 40, it was berthed in Chichester and I decided to go and see it. I never really expected to buy it, but I could dream.

The Butler 40 was made by a company called Halmatic, based in Guernsey; it is classed as a fishing boat. Although it was listed as second-hand it looked, to all intents and purposes, brand new. I drooled over the hand-built vessel, with its resplendent blue hull and white superstructure. It had two pristine 150hp turbo Sabre diesel engines.

"You could go round the world twice in this and it wouldn't even bother it," I said to Jan who had come with me for a day out.

Although it was in mint condition there were still some things left unfinished and oddly there were unpacked suitcases on board. "The owner left in a bit of a hurry," I thought to myself. It turned out that I wasn't far wrong. The owner of Stamp One, which would have been more aptly named Stampede, was all set to leave the country for a new life in Spain when he had been arrested by the Chichester Coast Guard before he managed to get out of the marina. His intention was to do a runner with the boat without paying for it. Hill Samuel, the finance house, had it impounded.

They wanted a quick sale and asked me to make an offer. I knew I couldn't afford it and said, before I did, that I wanted my brother Malcolm to come and look at it with me. I didn't really expect to come back, but rather, make a call from a distance saying no. I dreamt about owning it that night. There I was at the helm of this wonderful craft bobbing up and down on an aquamarine sea illuminated by a star studded sky.

However, after that dream I did indeed go back with Malc and we took it out for a test run. It was fantastic except, on the way back, I got the engine stuck in gear and crashed into the mooring dock, half demolishing it. Luckily no-one saw and we managed to repair it before my boating skills were discovered. Then I made Hill Samuel an offer, when pressed by them to do so. It was for half the asking price and to my delight and amazement they accepted it.

I had it finished off and completely overhauled, whilst negotiating a mooring in Brixham amongst the fishing boats.

II

It was one hell of a journey to undertake from Chichester down to Brixham and so I put a crew of friends together who had trained on the Sir Winston Churchill, sailing boat. With me on that epic voyage were Dave Dryhurst, Terry Saunders, Nick Strong and Ken Gibson. The first mishap was that we had to go past the Needles at the Isle of White and pull in at Weymouth with generator trouble. We were warned not to go out to sea again as there was a severe weather warning, but I ignored that. On the turn from Portland Bill we ran straight into a force seven gale. The sea was like the Malvern Hills, giant waves battered us. All the rest except Dave and me were throwing up and hanging on for dear life in alternative movements. Dave was below decks with the rest of the crew; they were so ill he was the only man capable of attempting to steer from the lower helm position. I was stuck up on the bridge and if I had attempted to try and get down the bridge ladder then I would have been overboard for sure. So I just clung on to the upper wheel, more to stay upright than anything else. I have never been so drenched in all my life. When eventually I was reunited with Dave, he told me I looked like I'd been through a car wash.

If you have seen the film A Perfect Storm then you will get the picture - this one was ours. How on earth we survived it I'll never know. But we did! The Olympic Yachtsman, Barry James, was not so lucky. He was thrown overboard from his craft and died in that storm.

Having survived, my crew including the captain were all so ill that I had to drop them off in Poole whilst Dave and I soldiered on alone. We steered by compass, charts and landmarks such as church spires on the coast line. The next thing to happen was that, whilst I grabbed a few hours nap and Dave was at the helm, he managed to take us completely in the wrong direction.

But make it we eventually did and I felt like Christopher Columbus, as I saw the three church spires and the cliff face of Berry Head that meant we had reached Brixham Harbour. After that inaugural and epic trip I took every opportunity to go down and play big boys' games with it.

III

I changed the name to - what else - Badger's Moon and regularly sailed to Dartmouth amongst other places. Over time I took my Day Skipper's exam with the Royal Yachting Association and became an accomplished seaman with a qualification in VHF radio. It made me realise how foolhardy I had been making that initial journey.

Once on a trip to the Torquay Boat Show I was about to enter the marina when the steering failed to respond as it should. What had happened was one of the propellers had just worked loose and fallen off. In fact, when a marine survey had been carried out, the propeller had been removed and not refitted properly. It was an accident waiting to happen.

I called the harbour master by radio to let him know of the emergency and he told me to "Just do the best you can to moor up".

That was easier said than done and, in a manoeuvre that took over an hour and watched by an enthusiastic audience of over a hundred sightseers, I managed to get close enough to a fishing boat to perform an Errol Flynn flying leap onto its deck, grab the rope of my vessel and tie it onto the anchor chain of the other. What followed was like a Mr. Bean sketch, as I had left Badger's Moon in gear, with Jan and Julia on board. It was doing its best to pull the poor fishing boat out of the water and elope with it to the open sea.

"Put it into neutral," I yelled. But my crew didn't understand, they thought boats were merely for sunbathing on.

I tried demonstrating with my hands, but still no response, so desperate times called for desperate measures. I crawled like Captain Bluebeard along the chain and back on board Badger's Moon, swiftly putting it into neutral and out of danger.

The onlookers burst into spontaneous applause and, taken with the moment, I bowed back to them.

I rang the insurance company who sent out a diver to recover the propeller. He didn't find the holding nut though and I had to have a new one cut before we could move again. As this was naturally the subject of an insurance claim because of the cock-up by the surveyors, we were put up in a very nice hotel until all was finally rectified.

On another infamous occasion I lost the dingy off the back of the boat, but didn't realise it. That is, until I heard on the radio that the coast guard had found the empty dingy and assumed the occupants had been 'lost overboard'. There were helicopters combing the area for any signs of survival. Sheepishly, I rang Tony Rigg the Harbour Master at Brixham and asked him to get it for me, as I was too embarrassed. That cost me a tenner, a few pints and a lot of piss-taking.

Over the next four years we had some great family fun on board Badger's Moon. I also had some good times on it on my own and when I needed solitude to plan, I would take off and work out solutions and strategies alone in the cabin without fear of being interrupted.

IV

In 1986 I felt it was time for a change of craft. I advertised Badger's Moon for sale and sold it to a Scotsman of all people for three times what I had paid for it.

I loaned the money I got for the boat to the company and took the interest for the time being. I wasn't in a rush to get a new boat, as I just didn't have the time to make use of it in that hectic period of expansion.

I also realised that what I wanted to buy in the future was the Rolls Royce of the sea – a Hatteras. They were introduced to me by Malcolm Verey who I met in 1986 at the Boat Show. He worked for Boat Showrooms of London, they were huge dealers of the very best and biggest boats and had the Hatteras franchise throughout Europe and as far as Egypt, where President Nassar's family were some of his personal clients.

Malcolm had a Hatteras 48 on display at the show that year and I spent most of the day on it. It was my dream. Hatterases are classed as luxury sports fishing boats and they make them up to 110 feet long. Tiger Woods the golfer has one, amongst other celebrities from sport and screen.

It was out of my league, but gave me another incentive to succeed, not that I needed one but it's always good to have an incentive. I would often say to my sales team: "Write down what your dream purchase would be this year, whether a house, a car or whatever lights your fuse. Refer to it as an incentive to make those sales; be determined to get it and you will.

Malcolm Verey became a close friend and we attended many social functions together. I guess I was on his list as a long-term purchaser. It was also Malcolm Verey who introduced me to the Dorset Yacht Company. They were agents for 'Boston Whalers', which were a range of speedboats.

V

When I say I didn't have a boat at all, I did in fact purchase a small eleven-foot speedboat, a Boston Whaler, which I bought for fun, though rarely used. I had quite an experience in that though; once, whilst bouncing around in it at Brixham, I spotted the pilot boat going out to one of the big ships, which were not allowed within two miles of the harbour.

I followed it out in my tiny, but none-the-less powerful craft and watched as the pilot boat scythed through the water causing an enormous wake. Filled with devilment I decided to cross the wake at full speed. This launched my boat fifteen feet into the air in a stunt that would have made James Bond proud. The engine came completely off its mounting and flew over my head and into the boat, still whirling away till I managed to shut it down!

My mate from the saddlery days, Terry Bird, rocked with laughter as he watched the shenanigans from the comfort of his own 23 foot Blue Bird speed-boat that he kept in Brixham. He was still laughing as he towed my battered boat back into the harbour. I may have been older and wiser than when I raced the bikes, but I never lost my love of thrills and speed. This was one of those 'got to do it' moments and I did it.

The engine was returned to Perrys of Paignton who were the Mercury Engine dealers for the west coast. I didn't tell them about the stunt and they replaced it full of apologies, saying that they had "Never had one break before."

Afterwards, I sold the Boston Whaler too and determined just to wait for my Hatteras moment, which I knew would one day come.

You will recall, in an earlier chapter, how Tony Bird and I went into a short-lived business together on horsey things in The House of the Cavalier. Well, whilst I stuck to the motor trade, he stuck to saddlery. By this time he and his wife, Anne, had built a huge and highly respected company called originally Cottage Craft and then, as it grew in size and stature: Cottage Industries. They were pioneers in the development of nylon products in the saddlery industry, making head collars and girths that were sold around the world. It was interna-tionally respected and Harrods had a special department devoted to his goods. They were even used by the royal family. I helped introduce Tony to Malta, where he set up a subsidiary manufacturing company under the auspices of the Maltese government, not long before selling out to a British public company.

Jan became very friendly with both Tony and Anne, starting to spend a lot of time out there with them whilst I, for the most part, stayed in England.

I must say that Tony was a good business mentor to me, his knowledge of business academia was second to none and I learned much from him.

19 – Advance To Mayfair

I

I guess by now you have realised that I am persistent if nothing else. I had constantly pushed for a car dealership with Austin Rover to the point of becoming a worn-out record. With the demise of Bryant's there was now an obvious opening in the Bromsgrove area and I managed to secure a meeting with Peter Johnson who was the then sales director at Rover and who had the major say in franchising. (Peter later became CEO at Marshalls of Cambridge, the premier motor and aeroplane company).

"You really don't give up, do you Douglas," Peter said looking over his glasses.

"And you know it makes sense, Mr. Johnson," I said to him. "Clark's has an unrivalled reputation for servicing Rover cars, we have quadrupled our turnover and we'll do the same for new car sales."

"From what I hear you're already selling quite a few." He told me, a wise grin spreading across his face.

"I'm sure I don't know what you're referring to." I feigned innocence.

"If I were to recommend you for a franchise, I couldn't let you have a showroom at Rednal, it's too close to our other franchisees - you do understand that?" He asked.

"I do indeed," I told him, "that's why I've already got the land in Broms-grove to build the biggest and the best showrooms you've ever seen; just give me the chance," I implored.

He agreed to think about it seriously, talk to the board and get back to me within the week. Peter was as good as his word and five days later I was in his office again.

"Right," he told me, "no beating about the bush, Douglas. If you will sell your Tessall garage to Evans-Halshaw then you can have your franchise in Bromsgrove. I know it's asking you to give up a big chunk of your servicing work and you may want time to think if that is what you really want."

"I won't beat around the bush either," I told him. "The answer is: yes!"

It was a deal made in heaven; I would make a handsome profit on the sale of Tessall Garage and get my opening in Bromsgrove. Plus, I would be get-ting Austin Rover to loan me the building money - a deal on top of a deal, what could be sweeter? I felt just like the kid who found the golden ticket for the Willie Wonka Chocolate Factory must have felt, punching the air and leaping around like a mad man as soon as I got into the car park. In fact, I doubled my money on Tessall, moving it on for half a million. Though, in fairness, we had spent some money refurbishing it.

I was straight on the phone to our architect, Mike Chapman. "This has to be the best showroom ever, Mike," I told him. "I want no expense spared."

And, indeed we didn't! It was a totally unique multi-sided design and was to be fitted out like a palace. The marble for the floor was chosen and cut in Malta to the same external shape, to compliment the building, and shipped over. Though, therein resides another story. It was delayed four weeks by Her Maj-esty's Customs and Excise, whilst they went through the container with a fine tooth comb. The scrutiny was like something out of The French Connection, so I am told. They were convinced there was a mighty stash of cocaine concealed somewhere. Eventually, they conceded they were wrong and released it. Despite that delay, the building still came in on schedule.

It was a wonderful construction, glistening aluminium, tinted glass and impressive marble on the floor. State-of-the-art lighting and air conditioning complimented the elegance of the octagonal design.

For the crowning glory, we had a clock tower with a weather vane on the highest exterior point. Instead of the traditional cockerel however, we had the Clark Care logo made out of brass. I was hoisted up on a crane to fit it with cameras flashing away to record the moment. We made a great deal of coverage of that in the local papers. The grand opening was exactly that. Truly grand! A dressed salmon and champagne buffet greeted the host of dignitaries in attendance. This included the sales director of Austin Rover, John Parkinson, who cut the ribbon, radio and TV people and crews, most of the local council, a host of notables from Austin Rover and our most cherished customers.

It was an instant success. On the first Saturday we were open we sold fifty-eight new cars and in our first year we achieved sales of over eleven hundred.

'Experience the difference' the huge sign said outside and indeed they did. Buying your car from us meant you got it serviced in our state-of-the-art workshops and were treated like royalty. I moved my office from Rednal to Bromsgrove, along with my key staff. Again I positioned myself so that I could see who was coming in and out of the building - old habits die hard.

Tony Foden moved to Bromsgrove as the service manager and instilled in his staff all that was wonderful about 'Clark Care'. Adrian Smith became our sales manager there and led a team of smiling and knowledgeable professionals.

Once again, we had pulled off a minor miracle. Even I, at that point though, didn't dream that it would be only a matter of time before we became the biggest Austin Rover dealer in the world.

Christmas 1989 brought to an end one wonderful year for Clark's. There were so many employees now that to throw the festive bash we wanted, and to include everyone, I hired the exhibition hall at Longbridge for the purpose. It gave me a great thrill that our employees drove right into the heart of the Rover factory to celebrate. It was decked out traditionally with holly and mistletoe. There were crackers and streamers, a great band, magnificent food and as much drink as anyone wanted. We partied until the early hours and then the chosen few came back to Badgers Cottage to carry on until dawn. I think I smoked my final cigar at about seven in the morning. Indeed a night and a year to remember.

"You know, Doug?" I heard a voice saying to me in the background. It was Jan, "Listening to you tonight, the speech you gave and everything. I realised how much you've changed. You've become an actor."

"The Laurence Olivier of the motor industry, that's me," I smiled at her.

"No, more the Michael Caine," she replied, somewhat ironically. "You're more of an 'Alfie' than a 'Richard the Turd."

I presumed the reference was to my philandering nature; I didn't rise to the bait, but took it literally, responding: "The company's grown so much and I have to deal with people from all walks of life, every day's different. It's like appearing on a different stage every day. You have to know your act and perform it to your best ability. There's no room for stage fright, even though I do get it from time to time." I turned round to look at her, but she had gone and I realised I had been talking to myself for the past few minutes.

II

So, life that was good became better as far as the business was concerned. We were making profits, big profits. There wasn't a part of the company that was not contributing. We were beating targets by healthy margins and costs were contained within stringent budgets. It was time for a little healthy diversion.

This came in the form of speed once again. Malc and I built two replica Lotus 7's. We called them 'Clark Caterhams'. The name came through a company called Caterham Sports Cars. This was owned by Graham Nearn who was the racing car driver Colin Chapman's partner until the latter died in around 1982.

We had started in a small way, collecting classic cars - the Austin Chummy being one of the first. So, the Lotus 7's were to be built using as much modern technology as possible. We went down to meet Graham who was really enthusiastic and as amiable a guy as you might expect. It helped that he shared our passion for speed. The upshot of the visit was that we bought two long-cockpit Caterham 7's with the Di-Dion rear suspension. If you haven't a clue what I'm referring to then substitute the word chassis. We also got some body parts and came back as excited as the day we made our first trolley racer from bits scavenged at the tip.

It would have been easy to have the staff put the cars together, but we wanted to experience the thrill of doing them ourselves. So, after-hours at Rednal, I hung up the business suit, donned the overalls and smelt the oil. We lovingly put those cars together with pride and laughter. The only thing we didn't do ourselves was the trim, this was a Doug Burbridge job once again and a splendid job he made of it too. The engines were BDR race-tuned Cosworths; with those beauties inside, our cars were capable of going from 0-60 in under four seconds. "Sex on wheels," I purred to Malc and he just purred along with me.

Of course, we had to race them and the first opportunity for that was the Bugatti Owners Driving Club Hill Climb meet. Our machines caused quite a sensation, as we were amongst real enthusiasts and they'd never seen anything quite like our hand-built Lotus 7's.

We did our first run and were only fractions of a second behind the series leader in his racing car version of the 'Lotus 7'. We were in road-going cars, complete with sandwiches and coffee flasks.

Immediately after the race, the scrutineers (judging panel) notified us that they had received a complaint that our cars were technically in breach of the class.

So having been thrown out of that class we were re-categorised at the same meeting to take part in the single-seater racing car class. This proved to be a no-hoper, we were out-gunned at every turn. It is a bit like putting a Ferrari Testerossa into a formula one race.

With my insatiable thirst for knowledge I took racing driving lessons, which really elevated me into another league. I thought I knew all about driving skills till I went on that course, then I came to realise that what I had done up until now was based on pure instinct. Not a bad fault, if you can call it that, but it's a bit like giving an artist a box of chalks then showing him how to use oils and canvas. I ended the course by winning, via their points system, the 'Driver of the Year' award.

So, having given up on the hill climbs, we decided to switch to the driving school events organized by the Bugatti owners club at Prescott in Cheltenham, where the event is still held today. Here we ended up as joint winners and enjoyed a massive champagne celebration.

"Top of the world, Malc!" I said and all he could do in response was grin from ear to ear.

"Get that down you," I laughed, pouring him a generous measure into the winner's cut glass tankard.

III

The next year I was the outright top driver against all comers. It was not an event without its thrills though; I went into a spin and only avoided a major pile-up by a miracle manoeuvre that I still don't know to this day how I pulled off.

I now had the bug for racing again big time and started competing on a more regular basis. I was in a major race at Donnington Park in Leicestershire and finished just one second behind the winner - only to be disqualified as the judges said my MG V6 Sports was really a racing car and not a saloon class entry.

I took Jan along to the driving school and bought her a Porsche to practice in. She never really took to racing, but loved the experience of it all and it gave her a lot to talk about with friends. Her passion was horse riding and that was true of my daughter Julia too. Julia had the education I never had and she mixed with the cream of the county. She started off at Chaddesley Village School, at my request, then on to private school: firstly Whitford Hall in Bromsgrove then on to Dodderhill Girls College.

It was in the late eighties when Julia started dating boys. I vetted them all very carefully and any that I didn't approve of were made to wait outside the gates at the end of the drive. She used to find this quite hilarious, as did her mother.

IV

In 1986, BL (the parent group) changed its name to The Rover Group. The British Government insisted on the selling-off of the truck and bus side of the business, so that the focus could be purely on car production. It was not enough however and two years later, in 1988, the government sold the entire company to British Aerospace. This was a good move and the company, back under private ownership, enjoyed a period of renaissance. New disciplines and investment were introduced and Rover competed with its foreign rivals on a more level playing field.

We had already worked with British Aerospace successfully for much of the decade, preparing their fleet cars, so our foot was already well in the door.

I found myself listened to by the new regime with a new respect and, along with this, came the opportunity to travel to international conferences and seminars as a participant.

This came with a life-style change that was quite dramatic. Winning the sales franchise and the change of ownership of the principal opened more doors than just financial ones. These were doors to society; I was courted and feted by politicians, council officers and bigwigs from the motor industry. Jan and I were whisked off to exotic places like the Caribbean and South Africa for 'seminars'.

One fantastic junket was on the Wind Spirit, a small luxury cruiser, with two hundred staff to look after the one hundred guests on board, of which we were two. By day we would anchor at the most fabulous white sand beaches and by night dine on endless-course banquets comprising the most exotic foods, whilst being entertained by every form of music from string quartets to reggae.

"Who would have thought little Dougie Clark from Chaddesley Corbett would end up doing this?" I said to Jan as we gazed out over the ocean late one night.

"Oh, I think I did," she told me. "I think I knew it all along. You've worked for it, Doug, but you're very fortunate too."

No more words were spoken between us, we were just lost in our own private thoughts, as the sea gently lapped against our cabin wall and the stars provided a backdrop that no photograph could capture.

V

Even with the lure of the new lifestyle, I'm proud to say I didn't take my eye off the ball when it came to business expansion. If anything, it started to accelerate.

As always with me, I didn't rest on my laurels with just the franchise at Bromsgrove. I was immediately on the lookout for new opportunities. The first came in the town of Kidderminster where there was no Austin Rover Dealership.

I learnt that Mr. Bottner, a corporate Nissan dealer with quite a large property portfolio, had built a large AFG Nissan showroom in Kidderminster, but couldn't open it. I'm not sure entirely what happened, but Nissan took back the concession to sell their cars from him and a few other sites up and down the country in a major dispute. Nissan was getting into bed with Renault to form one enormous corporation.

I went along to see Bob Harrison, Sales Director, Austin Rover, and proposed that I negotiate for the site and open a huge Austin Rover Dealership there. "After all," I told him, "the nearest you've got is Stourbridge, a different market and you can see what we've done with Bromsgrove. Think Kidderminster and think Austin Rover."

He conceded my point, but it took eight months to get the go-ahead. In the meantime, I had made Mr. Bottner an 'offer he couldn't refuse', as they say. I owned the site and was ready to rock.

Come the start of 1990, we opened Kidderminster for business and so ended the monopoly years and the time of the premier league commenced. It was to be a period of high drama in more ways than one.

20 – Back To School

I

One picture is worth a thousand words the old adage goes and how true is that! Along with the franchise to sell Austin Rover cars came a substantial package of dealer benefits and requirements. This included the insistence that we spend thirty grand on advertising in the local press. Now we knew our market and our customers, so I believed that was to be money not terribly well spent.

The experience of public relations I had gained through our involvement with Lloyds and Shell had taught me that one article in the press, particularly with a photo, did far more good than an advertising campaign. Customers would see me and say: "Saw you in the 'Messenger' last week, Doug." No one ever said: "I've come in response to your advert".

I had a plan, which I wanted to put to Rover, but I needed to do it from a position of strength. That was to invest the thirty grand into providing equipment and services to local schools, from infant through senior schools. We would provide transport for their sports teams, pottery kilns and other special equipment for the classrooms. I would talk to the students at assembly about careers in the motor industry, what qualifications they should go in for and where to find the opportunities. I felt that the kids would go home and tell their parents about Clark's and what we were doing. That, I figured, would encourage the Dads to buy their new motors from us.

I met up with Russ Clayton, a Bromsgrove District Councillor I had met a couple of times at functions and put the suggestion to him. Not unnaturally, he thought it a great idea and so with the blessing of the council, I put the plan to Rover.

They were wary at first. "No other dealer turns down press advertising," I was told.

"It's not that I'm against advertising," I responded, not wanting to appear arrogant, "but Clark's know their market: it's local, it's loyal and the best way to capitalise on that is to be giving as well as taking."

They agreed, after consideration, to give me the opportunity to use the money in the way I suggested for two years. After that, it would revert back to scheduled advertising.

I called a meeting of the board and told them what we were going to do. There wasn't an objection; not even a murmur of protest. Most of them had kids at school and knew what difference thirty grand a year would make to the activities of the kids.

II

So began the period when I would get up on the stage at schools and, after receiving a round of applause from the kids, would launch into a speech about everything and anything, but most particularly, the motor industry. I loved it, the kids were great, they asked intelligent questions and laughed at my attempts at humour.

I was asked to judge competitions and present prizes at sports days. We were forever in the papers, which meant the name Clark's was continually in the public eye. It was a halcyon period and, just as I had guessed it would, it reflected in sales. To tell the truth though, it wouldn't have mattered if that hadn't happened. The PR exercise turned into a special relationship and I felt proud of what 'Clark's in Schools' achieved. Some of the kids came to work for us in a variety of capacities. We even went as far as to do a tie-up with Bournville College to introduce special extramural courses.

21 – The Premier League

I

The decade ended with a series of disasters including the Kegworth Air crash where a British Midland Boeing 737 came down approaching East Midlands Airport, leaving forty seven dead; Hillsborough, one of the biggest tragedies in football, claimed the lives of ninety six Liverpool supporters when the stadium collapsed; fifty one people died when the Marchioness pleasure boat on the River Thames collided with a barge and in the Purley Station rail crash five died and over one hundred were injured.

On a happier note, the Iron Curtain and the Cold War both came to an end. This started with Hungary dismantling 150 miles of barbed wire fencing along the border with Austria, swiftly followed by the Germans tearing down the Berlin Wall. All over the Eastern Bloc communist governments tumbled and democracy began to replace them. The decade ended in a historic meeting, off the coast of Malta, between U.S. President George Bush and Soviet leader Mikhail Gorbachev announcing that the so-called Cold War between their nations was at an end.

The first satellite television service, Sky, was launched in Europe. A massive diplomatic row with Iran occurred following the publication of Salman Rushdie's novel The Satanic Verses. The Ayatollah Khomeini broke off diplomatic relations with the UK and put a three million pound bounty on the writer's head. Ironically, it was the Ayatollah who was to die later in the same year.

An environmental disaster occurred when the Exxon Valdez spilt eleven million gallons of oil, in Alaska's Prince William Sound, after running aground.

The Prime Minister, Margaret Thatcher, introduced what was to prove the most unpopular tax ever: the poll tax. In China, the 'Tiananmen Square Massacre' took place both in Beijing and elsewhere. The student demonstration was watched live on television, as they made their bid for democracy.

We lost the great Spanish Artist, Salvador Dali famous for his 'melting clocks' in 1989, along with the actresses Bette Davis and Lucille Ball, the legendary Sir Laurence Olivier and the naturalist and explorer Sir Peter Scott. The only two births of note were the footballer Theo Walcott and the country and western singer Taylor Swift.

II

The decade ended for me however, as it had begun, with a frenzy of buying on what I now referred to as 'The Monopoly Board'. I bought from the post office, by tender, a two and a half acre site at the far end of Bromsgrove. It was a lucky strike. I was in Malta with Jan for a long weekend away when the thought came to me that I had perhaps put in too low a tender. I rang Malc and asked him to put a new one in at the eleventh hour and before the bidding closed. We increased the bid by twenty grand and that just squeezed ahead of the other interested parties.

The post office had plans to build a large sorting office and depot which hadn't materialised for reasons best known to themselves. It was good news for me though, as it already had a planning application granted for a retail development. I had plans to put a sort of 'Motoring Village' there. Drive-in tyre centres, spearheaded by Kwik-Fit, were springing up all over the place. Well, I planned to build a Mr. Clutch, Mr. Brake, Mr. Exhaust and a Mr. Bunn the bread man if there was a demand for it.

However, events overtook the plans and within a year, I was approached by the council and asked if I would sell a major part of the land to Safeways, the supermarket chain, who were keen to come to town. Well, I quadrupled my money on that one and got the council to agree to sell me a three acre site just down the road at the recently closed Garringtons factory - the car parts manufacturer. They had used the land as a shooting range. My idea was to build an industrial park there. It amazed me why they hadn't thought of it, as it might just have saved them from the liquidator.

Part Five 1990-2000

22 – Money Changes Everything

I

Rover was back in private hands in 1990, having been acquired by British Aerospace. Initially, in the 90's, it started to return to prosperity, the partnership with Honda proving to be a turning point for the company. Rover steadily rebuilt its tarnished image to the point where, once again, Rover-branded cars were seen as upmarket alternatives to Fords, Vauxhalls and even BMWs.

The Rover Group's first significant new car launch was the Rover 200; it was a three or five-door hatchback instead of a four-door saloon. It offered a new range of 16-valve K-Series petrol engines as well as a Peugeot 1.8 diesel and a turbo diesel. Sales were stronger than for its successors and its launch coincided with a winding-down in production of the similarly-sized Maestro. Coupe and Cabriolet versions of the 200 were also developed and were good sellers. It never achieved the sales or following of the ever-popular Ford Escort though. The 200 was swiftly followed by the 400 range. The 400 was essentially a four-door version of the 200 hatchback, but was slightly longer and offered a trunk. It was aimed as a competitor to the Ford Sierra and Vauxhall Cavalier.

If only Rover had continued, nurtured and gone into full partnership with or even been sold to Honda, things might have been very different. Although there was a sense of jubilation in the industry when, in 1994, British Aerospace sold the Rover Group to BMW, I'm afraid I didn't see it like that. I can remember clearly saying to Malcolm, when we heard the news, that the Germans would strip out the best and move on.

He didn't agree, but sadly they ended up doing exactly what I predicted they would do - but all of that's for later.

II

Timing has been everything in my life: sometimes I engineered it, sometimes I was just damned lucky. In 1990 we lost the British Aerospace contract, not surprising really, as they now owned Rover and had all the facilities on tap to prepare their own cars and to continue the high standards we had set. That left me with the dilemma of what to do with Britannia Works. I was just about to resign myself to the fact that all it was good for for the time being, was storage when the phone went and, hey presto, the new Austin Rover wanted to buy the twelve acres at the Groveley Lane corner of the West Works. This included our state-of-the-art autocentre. I protested a little, but not much, at this sad loss and in my mind had already shifted the equipment in the autocentre across to Britannia before the end of the phone call. So I was fortunate enough to kill two birds with one stone and make a handsome profit to boot. In real terms, this meant that, having bought it for a hundred and twenty grand, I was now selling it back for a little over 1.6 million.

III

Our business was now really turning from car sales and servicing into something very different. It was almost a fully-fledged property and land development company, running in tandem with our core motor business. It was a new game for me and all the wheeling and dealing I had done in the past, where I had learned my own set of life skills, were in full flow. I still got the same head-rush though as I did when I was starting out. That never changed, you had to want to do it; in fact, you had to let the adrenalin pump through the veins without showing any emotion. I call it the poker game of business life.

Then there is commitment. I discovered what my 'eureka' moment was, like Archimedes jumping out of his bath when he discovered his revelation in volume measurement, when it came to deal-making. During negotiations you reach a certain point, let's call it a window of opportunity, when the time is right to commit. Miss it and the deal is lost. So, the skill is to recognise the moment and go for it. You can always get out of it later should everything not stack up, but that window will never open again.

So let me refresh your memory and paint the picture of the start of the 90's portfolio. We had three major car sales centres, all with unique and customer-friendly showrooms and exemplary service and parts facilities. Those were at Bromsgrove, Kidderminster and, Rednal - where it all began some thirty odd years earlier.

Our newly launched autocentre housed in the Britannia works was split into a 'paint and panel shop' and a 'refinish' shop. We used the move to bring in even more cutting-edge technology and equipment than we had enjoyed across the road. It was a joy to behold, the ultimate in repair centres and the envy of our competitors. Malcolm was still the specialist in this field and just as I had developed my specific areas of skills, so had he. There wasn't a thing he didn't know about car repairs and everything that came out of the autocentre gleamed like a showroom model.

The only real petrol and shop business we had left in the portfolio was at Lickey, the Lynwood Service Station. I had bought the old butchers shop which adjoined it a couple of decades before we actually acquired the petrol station. I also bought up, at different times, the off-license next door and the land behind it all. I had just sat on it until the pieces of the land jigsaw were in place and I could do something substantial with it. This was not to build another big garage, it was too close to Rednal for that. I looked around at what were successful businesses and jotted ideas down on my bedside note pad. But it was to be a few years until I came up with a blueprint.

There was a whole new ethos developing; no longer was I just building premises to use, I was building a property portfolio that could be rented and leased out to other companies. I was, in essence, building a company of far greater worth and complexity than I could ever have contemplated - but all the time sticking to the adage of 'belt and braces'. I cannot emphasise that enough. Never take a step forward before you have checked and double checked that where you are stepping to is concrete and not sand. Then reinforce the concrete.

Naturally, virtually all the new properties were bought by and contained within the pension fund which was now converted into a SIPP (Self Investment Pension Plan).

Never was this more true than with the development of the ex-Garringtons site. I decided there to make a momentous decision. That was to build a business park. Again, I designed it myself in conjunction with my structural engineer, John Fisher. We then presented how we wanted it to look to the architects for them to draw up the definitive plans. It was to comprise twenty two units and to contain a conference centre and training facility for the entire Clark Group. I wanted it to stand out as a monument to design amongst business parks.

Once planning was granted, the building crew worked long hours and a seven-day week. It took just twelve months to build and when The Silver Birches Business Park opened for business in 1991 it was nigh on fully leased and I had six hundred grand a year committed in rent. It had an international flavour to it too and we proudly flew, at the entrance, the flags of all the countries that had companies based there.

We kept two units back for Clark use: one became a central depot for the preparation of all new and used vehicles and the other was our valeting department.

The flagship of the park was the conference and training centre, which was, for the most part, kept for our own needs although we did allow it be hired occasionally. It comprised a large meeting room with all the facilities conducive to constructive thinking. When I chaired the first meeting there I smiled to myself, "I wonder what my Dad and Uncle Jess would say about this?"

Then came the royal icing on an already rich cake. A new development was planned next to Silver Birches; this was to be a hi-tech business park. The only trouble was that they had no access to get to it. At a hastily called meeting, out of the kindness of my heart, I let them have permission to build an access road at the very reasonable cost of one million pounds. The site was worthless to them without it so they had no choice but to agree. Now isn't that a lesson in 'belt and braces'? Make your plan and plan your move before you make it, then check to make sure you haven't forgotten anything. I'm so glad they didn't! Whilst Rednal remained the group headquarters, the only business we had that struggled to find a permanent identity was the Marlbrook site. Even that was about to change and set me off on the next journey, but there were some personal problems to come first.

23 – All's Not Well On The Home Front

I

I was up by five and out of Badgers Cottage by six and at my desk twenty minutes later. I attended to the paperwork in this quiet period. By the time we opened for business I had said "Good morning" to everyone, gone through what was happening that day with Eleanor Rigby and then went off on my rounds of meetings amidst the Clark Empire. I did that six days a week, week in, week out and loved every waking minute. I would come home late, most times make myself something for supper, write notes then grab a few hours sleep before starting over.

I didn't see much of Jan; we were living separate lives. She was spending a lot of time in Malta and had developed quite a circle of friends out there.

One night I came home and Jan was back from Malta earlier than I had in my diary. She poured us both a drink and said that she wanted to talk to me. She was cold, calm and very definitely collected.

"Doug, we've grown apart," she started.

"It won't be forever," I told her. "You know how much I've got going on at the moment."

"There always was, always is and there always will be," she sighed. "I suppose I knew that when I married you, but I can't go on living like this. We're strangers, leading separate lives, who just meet up occasionally."

I couldn't deny any of what she said and I was thinking that this perhaps was the exit I had secretly wanted for a long time, but hadn't had either the opportunity or the nerve to mention. I had fantasised about being a free agent again. In honesty, any love and passion that we had shared in the formative years had long since disappeared. Oh, don't get me wrong. I hadn't thrown myself into work just to escape a loveless marriage. I would have done it whoever I was with and a less tolerant woman than Jan would have given up a long time before this.

We talked and talked, we even laughed a little, but we both knew that this was the final act of the play. Jan wanted to move permanently out to Malta and, although I made the platitudes, I really said little to dissuade her from the notion.

She went back to Malta and as time went on we agreed to have an amicable divorce. However, that was not to be once the solicitors got involved. Matrimonial lawyers seem to make a sport out of divorce rather than a vocation. The dialogue became increasingly hostile and the transaction messy in the extreme. At the end of the day it all comes down to money. It's a job I couldn't do, digging your hands into the stuff of people's souls; I don't know how they sleep at night. The joke that springs to mind is 'What do you call a plane crash that was filled with divorce lawyers and no survivors? Answer: A good start!'

Friends took sides as I suppose they always do and life outside of business was a lonely affair, so I spent even more time at it.

II

I gained a new addition to Badgers Cottage though, he just walked in and adopted me and is still a squatter to this day. He's Pepper the cat and a more feral feline you won't ever meet. He has extremely long claws and has scared off many a fox, killed many a rabbit and, sadly, many a duck in his time. Although he is now getting on in years, he still retains the look of a sleek, coal black, green-eyed panther.

So wrapped up was I in business and divorce proceedings, that one morning when everything was churning round in my mind, I committed what, upon reflection, was a hysterical faux pas!

It was Monday morning and I always attached the wheelie bin to the back of my Land Rover Discovery and took it to the top of the drive in readiness for the council dust cart. Well, I reached the top of the drive when my mind went into overdrive and I just carried on to Bromsgrove ignoring the protestations, gestures and flashing lights of other motorists. Little wonder that one poor lady I overtook, who had flashed and gestured and held her hand down on her horn, became so incensed when I gave her the finger! I was oblivious to the fact that the bin was bouncing along behind me at sixty miles an hour.

On reaching Bromsgrove I turned onto the forecourt in readiness to reverse into my parking spot when all the office staff came running out blocking my way. At first I was angry, then embarrassed and finally broke into fits of laughter which was a wonderful leveller and put every problem into perspective. I had a call within minutes from The Sun who wanted to photograph a re-enactment. Life was going to be fun again!

I also went back to grass track speedway as a form of mental and physical release from the divorce pressures at this time. Malc didn't rejoin me in the grass tracking this time round, he now had a new passion – flying - and had got himself a Piper Cherokee. He asked me to take up flying too but I declined, telling him: "I prefer my wheels to be on the ground and not in the air." I entered the pre-1975 class where the requirement was simply that your engine had to be no later than 1975. What you did with the rest of the bike was open season. I had Jawa speedway engines that ran on methanol and had two replica Hagon frames made for them. These were designed by Alf Hagon himself who held the Santa Pod sprint record for nigh on a decade. My bike was put together by Roger Taylor, a mechanical genius. His son, Mark, followed in his father's footsteps as a whizz motorbike mechanic and, in fact, still works at Rednal to this day. Mark also won the British 350 grass track championship in 1998.

I dressed in the outfit I had retained from the sixties: red leathers with white stars. Only difference was, I now had to lie down to zip them up.

I raced against the Welsh champion, Cyril Jones, and beat him despite him trying to ride me off the track. I also came off it once at full pelt, was thrown twenty feet into the air and landed facing the oncoming pack. It had happened before so instinct told me not to try and run, but face it out and curl up into a ball as best I could. I figured that way they could see and avoid me, to run would add confusion. They roared past me on either side, but I emerged unscathed, if a little relieved and wet between the legs.

This near miss was a bit of a wake-up call; I wasn't the mad cap I had been any longer. So my flurry of racing was short-lived and I hung my boots up for good shortly after.

III

Everything I had was tied up in some way with the company and my dilemma was that I needed to raise cash for the divorce settlement without upsetting the company's financial apple cart. I had always preached to Malcolm that the company was not there to be used as a personal bank, so there had to be another way without raiding the coffers.

It so happened that, at that particular point, our bank borrowings were in excess of three million. This was covered by the property portfolio, which was worth several times that figure, but it wasn't ready cash on deposit - just collateral against the O/D.

What I did in fact, through the good offices of Grant Thornton, was to sell my entire beloved classic car collection to the company. They were to be used for events, displays and showroom attractions. It wasn't a happy course to take, but it was the right one. Over the next twelve years I bought them back one by one and still retain the collection to this day.

From the night Jan went to Malta for good to the time we got divorced was almost exactly two years, that was in 1992. My daughter Julia continued to live with me after Jan had gone; this was for us a happy time and we shared a unique bond. I didn't show any pain, nor did I show elation. I never discussed the details of the divorce proceedings with her nor encouraged her to take sides. All things run their course and when the papers actually came through, Jan and I helped her buy her own home together.

With Julia gone, the realisation finally sunk in that I was indeed a free man. Free to pursue whatever hedonistic pleasures life could provide – and I did.

24 – Tokyo Calling

I

We were doing OK with Rover and had the sales and after-care off to a fine art for them, but there was no denying that the Japanese were now making huge inroads into the British market and this had a knock-on effect to us. With the factory down the road and all the employees' deals, we retained a competitive edge over any other Rover dealer, but when it came to non-employee customers, who had no discount incentive, then there was no denying we were losing out to the overseas invasion. Foreign cars breathed reliability and every list of best-value cars in the motor magazines had the Japanese and the Germans at the top of the tree. 'Made in Japan' meant something very different these days from some of the goods we sold back in the Treble-S shops. From televisions to computers and from machine tools to motor cars, they were getting it right. It was with this thought in mind that I welcomed first a phone call from Toyota, swiftly followed within a week by one from Honda. Both were very interested in offering us franchises at Bromsgrove. I was in a bit of a dilemma; obviously I couldn't take both and so, after some careful thought and negotiation, I persuaded Honda that they would be better served by me building a dealership centre for them at Marlbrook and letting Toyota have Bromsgrove.

Whilst the buildings were being constructed, the circus came to town - in that I put up very smart white tents which we traded from. It looked like Camelot; you could be forgiven for thinking that knights in shining armour on white chargers would appear any minute.

It couldn't have worked out better, as Honda pulled out of their partnership with Rover at almost the same time as they opened with us at Marlbrook. Mike Wollacot, who had been with us for ten years on the Rover sales side, was made up to dealer principal and there was never a better man for the job. Marlbrook was transformed from a mundane building into a sparkling glass emporium. So began our first car sales diversification away from Rover.

So importantly did the Honda organisation view the dealership that they sent their MD from Swindon up to perform the opening ceremony, which was in May 1995. The public reaction was swift: the combination of Clark's Motor Group and Honda had cars flying out of the door and we doubled our forecast in the first month, exceeded our quotas of vehicles and revised our expectations rapidly upwards. The Japanese quickly upped their game to meet our requests and demands; whatever we asked for, we got. It was a pleasure doing business with them.

I was reunited with the UK Honda chairman a few months later when I was invited to a special dinner and it seems that I was highly valued, as I was actually seated next to the world chairman himself, from Japan. Whether it was the heat in the room or my scintillating conversation, I will never know, but during the speeches, I felt this weight increasing on my left shoulder. He had fallen asleep on me. The CEO of the all-new Honda facility in Swindon signalled to me to 'please let him be'. I did as requested, but that meant I really couldn't move for the next ten minutes. This caused great mirth on the table amongst the other guests, but the chairman awoke as if nothing had happened and joined in the ensuing applause.

There was a fabulous cabaret that night too, a young comedian who would go on to become a household name, Mr. Jack Dee. This was the time of the first fire in the newly-opened Channel Tunnel and Jack brought the house down when he did his impression of this great Anglo-French rabbit warren under the sea, by rolling up a menu and blowing smoke through it.

"Maybe it's what they do in Japan, take a power nap. Your shoulder was probably more comfortable than those capsules they sleep in those funny pod hotels." Malcolm laughed when I told him the story later.

"He did tell me that it's not unusual in Japan for the chairman to take a day occasionally and wash the cars of his fellow directors, even employees. It's a sort of level-mind thing, a sign of humility despite your rank," I told him. There was silence for about thirty seconds as he just looked at me then we both burst out laughing. "No!" I told him, "In your dreams, laddie!"

At the same time as we were making inroads into the Japanese manufacturers, another opportunity arose. I was invited to attend a board meeting at Ryland's, the big BMW and VW dealership in Birmingham. They talked about me becoming their property development director. I soon discovered there was much more to this suggestion than met the eye; it was, in reality, an acquisition meeting. Ryland's wanted to acquire us. I was flattered, but not interested. For all the fancy titles and platitudes I wasn't ready to let go of my own business nor share it with anyone else but Malcolm. So I bid a polite farewell and left the building.

II

We opened the Toyota showroom in Bromsgrove the year after, in 1996, with a blaze of publicity. It was a brand new hexagonal construction - this time looking like an Imax theatre from the outside. It was erected on the land I had bought next to our existing octagonal building, making the whole site one of the first multi-franchise dealerships in the country. Trevor Taylor the CEO of Toyota UK performed the opening ceremony. He was an ex CEO of Rover. I'd had some dealings with him and found him to be fair with a reputation as a forward-thinking operator albeit with hands which must have been tied, more than his liking in his Rover life. Now, with the freedom to take Toyota his own way, he was gaining a formidable name as a high-achiever in the motor industry. I was delighted to be reunited with him and he, in turn, was delighted by the stunning premises we had built for Toyota.

All was going along swimmingly when I was presented with another dilemma. Honda wanted to close Marlbrook and open in Halesowen. This was despite the fact that Marlbrook was only twelve months old and doing great business. Their thinking was to open in Worcester instead with an even bigger centre for which they had already lined up the dealership. In my limited negotiation with Japanese companies I had quickly learned that it was as much about 'face' as business. I had perhaps paid a little too much attention to Toyota and they wanted to be the centre of things once more. So I knew I had to deliver on Halesowen and quickly.

The solution came through a tiny franchise Honda already had in Halesowen with a small company called 5-Star Motors. I had actually had my eye on that business for some time, as it was a very old-fashioned operation that was crying out for innovation to bring it into the modern world of motor retailing. So I proposed to Honda that Clark's should take this on and expand it.

Being Japanese, Honda didn't want to get rid of the incumbent dealer, so they asked me to do the deed instead. It was owned by a nice old-timer, Will Hawks. He didn't present too much of a problem and was glad of a bit of pension money. I settled with Will Hawks for two hundred grand and took on all liabilities. In return, he gave me a lease on the premises and relinquished what was a water-tight contract with Honda.

I ran the business as it was for eighteen months whilst investigating the possibility of buying up the nearby properties. This consisted of a ramshackle petrol filling station owned by Sid Griffiths of Lye. Sid had a major Vauxhall dealership in Halesowen and the petrol station was a bit of a left-over dinosaur to him and so he was keen enough to do a deal with me. He was a wily and shrewd character though. We knew each other through a love of bike racing; he was the sponsor of the Yamaha teams in the Isle of Man TT races.

"What are you up to Clarkie?" He laughed when I put the proposition to him.

"Oh you know me, bit of this, bit of that, bit of speculation," I replied, not giving anything away.

"You've got something big up your sleeve - I can tell. But, whatever it is, it suits me to sell; no money in petrol these days," he conceded.

The other property I wanted was an adjoining nightclub called 'In Excess". Well, I say night club; it was, in fact, one of the very first sex clubs in the country. For one brief moment I was tempted to buy it and just run it for a few months myself to enjoy a little of the action. However, I resisted and prepared to put a bulldozer through it as soon as the ink was dry on the paper. Glad I didn't pursue the original idea too, judging by the dreadful state of the beds and mattresses we took out of there. They may have looked like love nests when they were dimly lit in exotic red lights, but in the cold light of day, ugh!

III

So that was that! We were ready to rock except for one small, but aggravating detail that I hadn't expected. We had a squatter move in to part of the old night club premises - an Indian taxi firm which tapped into the water and electricity supplies and proceeded to run their business from the basement where they had bunkered themselves. Squatter's rights, being what they were, meant I couldn't just chuck them out, lest I incur the wrath of both the council and the press. So, more subtle action was needed. Let's just say a deal was struck to the satisfaction of both parties.

Everyone was happy; Toyota had their prestige showroom in Bromsgrove and Honda had their fabulous premises in Marlbrook (for the time being with the knowledge that Halesowen was 'on the way' and the current little operation was being managed by us). Honour was served; both companies were delighted that Clark's brought the same after-care and attention to their vehicles as we had to Rover. We promoted some key people and trained up and brought in others who were very soon well and truly 'Clarked'.

IV

Obtaining planning permission had become a fine art with me. It seemed I was dealing with several councils at once: Bromsgrove District, Birmingham, Dudley and Wyre Forest. All had their own challenges and ways of working. The one thing they all had in common was people with egos.

Mike Chapman was my main negotiator at most of the meetings. I loaded the gun and Mike fired the bullets. He was better at that than me.

Although I talk of egos, I would like to give praise to David Hunt of Bromsgrove District Council. If only council officers could all have been like him - proactive and forward-thinking. He encouraged industry and commerce, knowing they would bring jobs and prosperity to the community. Sadly, many others in positions of elected power seemed blessed with a lethal combination of jealousy and an inability to recognise commercial opportunities. A few people from my past were amongst those who gave me a hard time: including Sam, one of George Smart's sons and also his wife. Oh and let's not forget 'The Demon'- Richard Deeming. His father was the 'Grocer Jack' I referred to in the early chapters, a truly lovely man. Richard and I never hit it off and I suppose it was ironic that when Richard rose to the dizzy heights of 'Chairman of the Council', I would find myself in many a run-in with him. Nothing that could be described as breach of office, merely 'unnecessary resistance', shall we say. A good instance of that was the umpteen times I applied for permission to turn the off-license at Lickey into part of the garage. Still, persistence won out in the end. Likewise, with all the small pieces of development we continued to undertake at Rednal. Any objection they could raise - they did, be it: size, access, colour or some other nonsense. Then the compliments would fly when all the work was done and they would bask in the reflected glory.

To put it into perspective: short of hospitals, Clark's were one of the area's biggest employers; we sponsored local charities and football teams. I often used to think that the councils didn't really deserve us, but then, would it have been different elsewhere? Not really, was the answer as I was soon to discover. Let's face it: it's only the elected people that cause the problems not the people who work in the offices. Who votes in a local election anyway? What training do councillors have? I think they should have to take exams and get qualified. Where else but on a council can a numbskull be put in charge of massive finances? Now, I think that can apply to national government as well as to local government, but let's not go there.

It took three years to obtain planning permission for the Halesowen project and just six months to demolish everything and build our finest showroom and servicing base to-date. Honda Halesowen opened right on the Millennium.

Those were the years of diversity that took me through the most sensational period of change in my entire business and personal life. I felt I had been very much an innovator in every aspect of business, including being one of the very first employers to bring in a no smoking policy. It went off without a hitch and the council were intrigued as to why, as they were finding a lot of resistance in other industries. I showed them the very nice facilities I had specially built for smokers outside. Worked a treat! Now, though, I believe it's all gone way too far, with the anti-smoking lobby trying to ban even those last bastions of nicotine indulgence.

25 – The Bright Side Of Life

I

Someone walked into my life one afternoon in 1996, in Bromsgrove. Her name was Leigh, Leigh Toogood, and she certainly was. Too good to be true that was, indeed it was.

Leigh was working as an advertising representative for a local magazine entitled Business Report. Despite the rather naff name it was quite a hallowed journal with highly respected editorial and in-depth company profiles. It was owned and published by two pretty smart cookies, John Teece and Andy Skinner.

I say Leigh walked into my life, which is an understatement, as it was more of a head-on collision. She was just twenty five years old, stunningly beautiful, curvaceous in all the right places like an egg timer. She had sparkling, wicked eyes that promised much and told nothing, long dark hair that shone like a beacon and a smile to make you return it. To cap it all, she had a vivacious, instantly warming personality.

Ten seconds and I was hooked. My jaw dropped and for one of the few times I was rendered speechless. When I did eventually speak, I must have appeared a gibbering idiot.

I hung onto her every word and gesture, as she appeared not to notice my state of discomposure, but just pitched the virtues of an advertorial feature on Clark's. I agreed to do it; in fact, I would have agreed to anything at that point. Were it a job interview I would have said: "And you can spell CAT. How clever Miss Toogood; now, how much would you like?" However, some way into her pitch, I did recover sufficiently to insist that she got our suppliers to support the feature with ads and not us.

In the days that followed, Leigh was constantly on my mind. I would ring her as often as seemed plausible to inquire how the feature was coming on. Not that I was interested, it was just to hear that silky voice.

When the ad was finally completed, she rang and invited me to have lunch with her at Rossini's in Droitwich to show me the proof. It was a memorable lunch; the food was good, but the company even better. We seemed to enjoy each other's company with the age gap not mattering in the least. I was a love-sick teenager all over again.

When it came to coffees, with the waiter awaiting our order, I asked, whilst gazing into those sensuous eyes, "Would you come back to Badgers Cottage for coffee?"

I suppose I expected a polite refusal, but instead I got an enthusiastic: "Yes please!"

She followed me back to the cottage in her own car; we drank brandies and a pot of coffee whilst talking about everything, anything and nothing. Leigh was a good listener and an excellent conversationalist. Eventually, there came a lull where talking ceased and we looked at each other. I plucked up the courage and seized the moment to ask, "Do you mind if I kiss you?"

"Why, Mr. Clark," she responded huskily, playfully and I'm sure truthfully, "I've never been asked that before" – and we did!

II

Then followed what I can only describe as six years of ecstasy and I mean that in every sense of the word. I thought I knew it all, but she taught me more, much more. I was hopelessly in love with her. We were as one, partners in crime and purveyors of passion. She rolled away the years to my youth and took me to places I never thought I would ever go. Leigh was and remains a unique human being. Though we are no longer together, I will never forget those crazy times we spent in absolute hedonism, if not always harmony.

After the first encounter at Badger's Cottage, I rang and asked if she would act as chauffeur for me to a corporate clay pigeon shoot I had been invited to down in Wiltshire. It was one of those days I would normally politely refuse, preferring to work, but it seemed a glorious excuse to see her again. Well, she did indeed agree to drive me, but then proceeded to get so drunk at the after-shoot dinner that I had to drive her back and tuck her up snugly at the cottage.

I soon discovered that Leigh was a wild child with all the territory that goes with it. She was well into drugs of all sorts and colours and had an insatiable thirst for alcohol at all times of the day and night. She carried me along with some of it, then I got a wake-up call realising that what I deemed fun at first was in fact a major problem with her. It was disrupting my tidy business lifestyle and I couldn't allow that to happen. Neither did I want, nor could I bring myself to contemplate, finishing with this siren who had turned my life upside down. So I made it a mission to try and tame the hell-raising side of Leigh to a tolerable level and to solve the problems that seemed to be causing her somewhat catastrophic private life. She became a permanent fixture ensconced in the cottage; this in turn brought about confrontations with my daughter who, although she had moved out, now looked upon Leigh as one major threat.

I managed to tame the lioness, but it took time and patience and I was never really sure what I would come home to. We fought, we argued and we made love - often all three! She thought she was in charge of the relationship and I thought I was. Neither of us was really, but upon reflection, who cared?

Leigh soon showed any competitor who was in charge though. I remember, not long after we had been together in earnest, she bought us tickets to see one of my all-time heroes: Hank Marvin of The Shadows fame. This was at Southampton where we stayed in a nice hotel. Whilst I was showering in the bathroom, she took the opportunity to ring another woman she knew I had been seeing. As I walked back into the bedroom, wrapped in a bath towel, I heard her conversation. "Hello, I'm Leigh," she purred "and I'm just about to make mad passionate love with Dougie Clark."

This chapter had to be told as Leigh was such an important part of my life. I will continue my chronicles about Leigh as events in this decade and the next progress, but suffice to say for now, we travelled the world and went to heaven and hell together.

26 – Big Boys' Toys

I

I still met up with Malcolm Verey fairly frequently and always at my annual pilgrimage to the boat show. By the early 90's he was the main dealer for Hatteras outside of America, where they are made. His clients included Arab princes and heads of state all over the Middle East.

I took Tony Bird with me one year to the Southampton Boat Show, when he had just sold out his company for a huge sum and was therefore cash rich. Tony had his heart set on buying a Guernsey-built, Aquastar 38, a lovely boat, but not in the same league as the Hatteras; he had his cheque book burning a hole in his pocket with him to do it too. Then fate intervened: Aquastar broke their long-standing appointment time in a manner that Tony felt was rather rude. I didn't tell him what my game plan was, but rather just took him onto the Hatteras stand and let Malcolm and the boat do the talking.

The upshot was that Tony ordered a £240,000 forty-foot Hatteras there and then. Malcolm was delighted that I had brought him the business and took us out to a superb French restaurant in Southampton. This in itself turned into quite a party and we were joined by a bevy of female revellers. It was a good night.

Despite nursing severe headaches the next day the elation continued. Tony had something to show and play with for his lifetime's work. He had a big boy's toy. And I wanted one too, more than ever.

II

When the boat was completed, Tony named it Cottage Craft after the company he and his wife had founded. The boat eventually found its way to Malta where Tony moved to.

Knowing that my pal now was the proud possessor of the object of my own desire, I wanted one more than ever, but couldn't afford as much as Tony had paid. However, I knew Malcolm had a forty-footer Sports Fisher specially built for the Earls Court boat show, which he hadn't yet sold. I was sorely tempted to make him an offer for it. It was difficult though, as I didn't want him to think I was expecting a huge payoff for bringing him Tony as a client and I didn't want to abuse the friendship either. I told Tony of my dilemma. "Why not let me ask him for you?" He asked. "If he's hot to trot then you get what you want at a price you can afford. If not, neither of you will be embarrassed".

Malcolm wanted 230 grand - that was a 20 grand discount because it was being walked all over by potential buyers at the show. A phone call and a few gin and tonics later, a smiling Tony came back to me with the news.

"How does a 150 sound?" He smiled.

"Bloody hell, you are the world's greatest negotiator," I told him. "I bow my head in reverence to the master."

"Ah, but there is a condition," he told me.

"What's the catch?" I asked.

"Malcolm insists that you work for him at the boat show, on your boat, figures he'll get good value that way."

I laughed my head off and duly did as requested. I loved it, showing people over my new toy. I'm sure that I got him at least six positive leads as well.

I had budgeted 175 grand for it, that being around 25% discount and as much as I could have hoped for. So I spent the 25 grand difference on having the very latest radar system and hi-tech navigational equipment installed on her.

III

I wanted to take my boat to Malta too, so I arranged after the show to travel with her, alongside a police escort all the way up to Liverpool docks from where I had her shipped on to Malta.

I named her Tuna Moon and moored up next to Tony in the harbour. We were the two kings of the sea.

Sadly my friendship with Tony was about to go through a sticky period as, within a year of buying my boat, the divorce proceedings with Jan started up. As Jan was out there permanently, I suppose it was not unnatural that Tony's wife, Anne, should take her side. Jan spent a lot of time on Tony's boat and I felt like most men feel when this happens, a little betrayed.

Tony bought another Hatteras, this time a huge 70-footer; he paid 600 grand for that one. He called it Miss Comino, the name of a small island between Gozo and Malta.

He and Anne invited Jan to live on the new boat where she really lived the high life, mixing with the rich and infamous of Maltese society.

I took exception to this and moved my boat away to a small marina, as far away as I could get.

For a few years I gave all three of them a wide berth. If they happened to be in the same bar or restaurant out there as me, I would leave. However, time heals all wounds and though it took quite a period to mend mine, Tony and I are again the best of mates. I owe him far more than to fester any more over that dark period and I would rather reflect on all the help and advice he gave me prior and since.

I believe Jan had plenty of suitors during the period after our divorce too. I used to get the reports back; she was mixing with the party crowd. It annoyed me at the time, but now I just say good luck to her.

IV

A couple of years went by and Leigh had entered my life. Immediately after the divorce I had thrown my all into work. I suppose I'm not alone in this; divorced men go either of two ways: they either get on with life with a new urgency of something to prove to themselves and others or they mope around, bemoaning the hand of cards life has dealt them. I did the former and, when Leigh came along, I was ready to live my personal life as well as business to excess. She was a real boy's toy and I was about to up the stakes and get another one - not another Leigh - I defy anyone to handle that. No, another toy!

I still saw Malcolm Verey from time to time and knew that he had a million-pound 58-foot Hatteras in his stock which had remained unsold for nigh on three years. The current owner had suffered a heart attack just a month after taking delivery and, sadly for him, was never going to be able to use his dream again. A plan hatched in my mind; I discussed this with Malc and, as always, he readily agreed. The company was going through a bit of a purple patch, cash wise, and I suggested we should try and buy the boat from Malcolm Verey at a knock-down price and use it for corporate hospitality.

"We'll call it Sea Rover," I enthused, "and have it decked out in the Rover burgundy. What do you think?"

"I think you've already made your mind up, Doug," he smiled, "Go get 'em".

"And," I smiled back, "I thought you might like to buy Tuna Moon - bargain price, and just one careful owner."

Malcolm beamed and I knew he was hooked. Tuna Moon remains his pride and joy to this day and still shines like a new pin.

As I was a Hatteras-owning client now, I had no problem in bargaining with Malcolm Verey this time. Incredibly, I got that million-pound boat for three hundred and fifty grand. I told our accountants, Grant Thornton, what I had done, but only after I had done it. They wrung their hands in frustration at my cavalier attitude and said that it should go on the books as a benefit-in-kind. I protested and insisted it went on as a corporate expense.

Well I can tell you that, in addition to doing corporate charters from Southampton to the Isle of White once a month, Sea Rover was the setting for many all-out, full-on orgies. I won't mention names, apart from mine, but a few people reading this will no doubt say, "Happy days!"

Leigh and I got down most weekends too. It was a halcyon period in my life. I felt like I was twenty-one, not fifty-five.

V

Just when everything in my garden was truly wonderful, the Inland Revenue kicked in and would not allow the corporate expense arrangement to continue. The accountants said: "We told you so!" I decided to buy it out of the company myself and sail off on a new voyage of discovery - in more ways than one. I had a crew of three: Captain Ian McGilvery, John Dews, an experienced sailor and a good friend (whose father used to own Smokey Joe's, the famous coffee shop you will recall from earlier in the book) and Leigh, who was going through a particularly wild phase. She had mood swings between angel and vixen. When she was angelic you could forgive her everything; when she was a vixen she was my worst nightmare.

Just before entering the Mediterranean for the big run to Malta, we berthed over for the night in Gibraltar. The customs officers were particularly intense and asked for firearms declarations. Leigh all but corpsed and I had no alternative but to declare my twelve-bore shotgun which I'd brought for a bit of deck shooting. Well, they broke it down, bound it with industrial cling film and sealed it with gaffer tape, then put official government stickers all over it and finally made me store it in the deep freeze. I had to notify them exactly one hour before we set sail and they once again came aboard to remove the official seals.

On the open sea there are no lay-bys. You have to keep going till you reach port, which means, although steering on autopilot, you had to keep watch in shifts. Mine and Leigh's was either severe rumpy-pumpy on the bridge or physically fighting. In one particular attack she ripped off my glasses and stamped them underfoot. I don't normally swear, but I came out with a torrent on that occasion. She thought it hilarious and laughed her head off whilst I scrabbled around on the deck picking up the pieces. The lenses remained intact, but it took the captain the rest of the night to painstakingly repair them with wire and glue.

She had kicked off once before on this trip, just as we were leaving our first port of call, Bayona in Northern Spain, by shouting to the coastguard that my boat was full of drugs. I was not amused. It's a bit like announcing you have a bomb on a plane. Luckily their English wasn't too good and I managed to pass the incident off as a language misinterpretation. A protesting Leigh was locked in a cabin below till we were safely out to sea again.

Just after that we hit a major storm which somewhat took precedence over our lovers' tiffs and tribulations.

We saw some wonderful sights on that adventure including whales, sea turtles and even a submarine. The most hairy incident though was as we approached Portugal. I was on watch with Leigh and, on glancing at the radar, noticed with some alarm that the screen was absolutely full of ships. It was like we were approaching the Spanish Armada. Somehow I had managed to get on the wrong side of the shipping lane. There was no turning back and everyone else was asleep below decks. To cross the shipping lane was going to require all my nautical skills, as there were some huge tankers in that lane which would have turned us into matchwood in a hot second. Several times I tried to get through and each time was thwarted at the last minute. It was just too dangerous; the best way to describe it is that it's like trying to get across Hyde Park corner in the rush hour. Eventually, I spotted just the tiniest gap between two tankers and went flat out for it with horns blazing and lights flashing. The vast ship seemed like a huge mountain coming towards us, but I just scraped through the ever-closing passage by the skin of my teeth.

We made it to Malta on time, got a temporary mooring and celebrated in style that night. It had been one hell of an adventure and it seemed we had been at sea for months not weeks.

Later, I got a permanent mooring next to the famous Black Pearl, the ship that was specially built for Clark Gable.

Although Sea Rover was a boat the like of which I never dreamed I would own, it was not to be my final toy, but that is for much later. There were stormy waters to go through before we reach that.

27 – Reading The Signs

I

I had a few other memorable trips with Leigh in the middle part of the nineties; one in particular was to Hong Kong where I was invited to attend a special dinner at the Hotel Shangri-La hosted by Honda. It was an amazing trip, but started off by us arriving at Heathrow Airport a day early by mistake. It shows the Japanese do have a sense of humour though, as they presented me with an international alarm clock at the dinner, engraved with the date.

I loved watching the excitement on Leigh's face when the dragon dance was performed, it was a truly awesome spectacle and she was enchanted by it, seeming almost childlike and I loved that momentary innocence.

You can tell a lot about women when they are asleep too, almost read their minds. Leigh was a conundrum though, angelically tranquil whilst at slumber and sometimes seemingly possessed upon waking. We also went to the West Indies, Canada and to every major capital in Europe.

II

Those were the halcyon times, but despite the fun, I believe the 90's were the last great stand of the entrepreneur as I know the word. As the decade went on, more red tape and legislation, ever changing technology and just plain margin erosion limited the opportunities that previously had been there for the taking. I'm not saying they weren't there or aren't still, but the days of starting businesses in your garage or on your kitchen table were nigh on extinct. Everything had huge set-up costs and no sooner than you were up and running were you facing a mountain of taxes and paperwork with heinous penalties for lateness or default. In a way, the labour government was hoisted by its own petard. Whereas Margaret Thatcher had beaten the biggest threat to business growth stability by taming the unions, governments of the 90's invented hurdles to opportunity on every corner. A university degree was fast becoming a necessity on the CV of a road sweeper whilst gumption and common sense were smiled on condescendingly. Language was being bastardised in the pursuit of political correctness and equal opportunities were very much unequal. Everything had to be done in accordance with an ever-increasing book of legislation, almost to the point where you couldn't fire and hire, promote or demote according to achievement and suitability.

By 1994 Clark's had achieved the accolade of being the largest independent Rover dealership in the Midlands. That still gives me satisfaction today. If only Rover had applied the Clark principals to their own business; if only British Aerospace had sold to Honda; if only I'd had the opportunity to help run Rover. So many 'ifs'!

Please forgive that reflection, I make it because we are approaching the countdown to the final chapters of the demise of what once promised to be the greatest motor company in the world.

As it was, although we were the biggest dealership by volume of Rover cars, it was no longer the major part of our business. Toyota and Honda sales were far in excess and so much more hassle-free in terms of after-care and delivery.

III

So, having gone down the road of diversification, I embraced it. When we opened the huge Honda dealership in Halesowen I agreed with them that we would close Marlbrook. My plan here was to make this into a sports car specialist dealership. I entered into talks with Lotus, but they came to nothing and I ended up doing a deal with TVR. My logic being that here was a small but enthusiastic and loyal target market.

I poached a great sports car salesman, Paul Carvell from P.J. Evans, where he was their Aston Martin specialist. Paul did a good job and exceeded his numbers, but I had underestimated the problems associated with the brand. TVR insisted on making every piece of equipment themselves, a commendable, but naive approach to manufacturing. It meant they could not take advantage of communal research and development; paddling your own canoe also meant being constantly plagued with failure rather than showered with success. It soon became clear that TVR was the least profitable of all our dealerships as the cars were off the road as often as they were on.

I tried various avenues to address matters, but eventually the only sensible thing seemed to be to sell the business on, which I did a few years later, but in the interim, we persisted. Paul Carvell did an amazing job under the circumstances. TVR changed ownership a few times, always it seemed on the brink of going bust. Nowadays, it is Russian-owned, but as far as I know, the manufacturing problems still persist.

IV

The diversification continued; I entered into negotiations with VW for a dealership. Our marriage came in the form of a magnificent complex in Stourbridge. It took me two and a half years to acquire four separate pieces of land to build this showpiece. Planning was difficult to get to with hard and protracted negotiations with Dudley Council. They wanted changes and I kept saying no. Then I would go away and present the same information in a slightly different way. By playing to their egos I eventually got what I wanted and work finally commenced. My experience with Bromsgrove Council stood me in good stead and I had learned the art of patience, as galling as that was.

By now, the building division had the materials required to meet the specifications off to a fine art. Granite for the floors, large plates of shatter proof glass for the windows and walls, block paving and portal frames encasing everything. The shape always altered to suit the creativity of the design and reflect individuality. Low maintenance, great fire protection, high security, sleek and chic monuments to enterprise and endurability - most of which still stand today. Quite a few other dealerships have since followed my lead; I don't mind that, it's nice to be regarded as a pioneer.

All along, I had this vision of a huge goldfish tank for the VW site, rectangular in shape and, from the outside, it would resemble a see-through shopping mall. Once inside, the customer would be transported into a transparent world of comfort and class without it being overly opulent.

The cars would be displayed to best advantage and kept in pristine condition, smelling of leather polish and with gleaming bonnets you could see your face in. My mission was to make Stourbridge VW break all barriers in customer care and satisfaction.

A gallery was the 'pièce de résistance' of the design. Here you could look down at everything that was happening within. I wanted to create the feel of an upmarket department store within a car dealership and I believe that was achieved in spades.

I took on VW-trained staff alongside our own in the workshops; this was a perfect fit, German-trained engineers with a Clark mentality. As with all Clark centres, the customer was encouraged to come and see for himself where his car was being worked on. I kid you not; you could eat your lunch off the floor in our workshops.

V

The conference centre at Silver Birches was in constant use for staff induction training and meetings. Such was the demand for it externally, by Bromsgrove Council and Lloyds amongst others, that the diary used for internal meetings was strictly time tabled and adhered to. I kept a small office there, which I used regularly for one-to-one meetings with the managers.

With all the units on the business park now rented out, the whole area was one of thriving prosperity. The international flags flew proudly at the entrance.

I was in control of my business empire and now the 'belt and braces' principal was applied to every aspect of the Clark corporation.

Unfortunately, I couldn't legislate how other people ran theirs and down the road at Longbridge it was about to be 'all change' once again!

28 – For Whom The Bell Tolls

I

In 1998 my daughter, Julia, was married at Saint Cassian's in Chaddesley Corbett to Christopher Duggan. It was the proudest day of my life and she looked absolutely stunning. The church was bedecked with wonderful displays of flowers and even the lytch gate entrance was entwined with white roses. We had a suite at Brockencote Hall for her to get ready in - ironic that I once used to clean the cars there and was now hiring it. As bride and father, Julia and I shared a chauffeur-driven Rolls Royce to the church and the bridesmaids travelled in a powder blue Daimler.

The only downside was that Julia had banned Leigh from being at the wedding at all, so she hid across the road at the Talbot and watched the procession arrive and leave, then made her way discreetly home to Badgers Cottage.

Meanwhile, we enjoyed a lavish reception at The Granary Restaurant and I presented Julia with a wedding gift, which was a fully restored eighteenth century governess cart. I hired a horse and driver to collect Julia and Chris, her husband, from the church and take them to the grounds of Brockencote Hall for the photography session. This was the end of an era and the start of a new one.

On my napkin at the reception, I finally came up with a plan for developing the land by Lynwood Service Station at Lickey. It wasn't a Eureka moment, just a bit of logic. I was thinking of grandchildren and so was born Lynwood Way. This was, I decided, to be a small commercial development to include a day care nursery. It wasn't a mad diversion either; I already had a willing tenant in the wings, Tony Richards. Tony already had two very successful day care nurseries in Redditch and Alvechurch and had built a respected brand name 'Rhymes'. I also planned to build a medical center and four quality flats on the same site. Planning permission was quickly sought and eventually granted. I soon had the construction team at work whilst the garage business continued as usual.

On completion, Tony took on the day nursery as promised, the flats were quickly let, but the medical centre, despite good marketing, sat empty with no takers. That seemed a shame as there was certainly a local need for one. I suppose the error in my calculations was that doctors like to purchase property, not rent it; it's often part of their pension planning. I waited for the best part of eighteen months for it to go as a medical centre. Then, as the millennium approached, Tony asked me about renting it for a second nursery, which seemed logical so I agreed.

II

I started this decade of the book with a taste of things to come when British Aerospace sold Rover to BMW. I told you of my premonition of foreboding when all around me were saying that this was the best thing for Longbridge since sliced bread. So the question is: why did BMW buy Rover? I can only tell you that bringing Germany to Longbridge was the start of a very difficult period for us and the beginning of the end for the car company we had all grown up with, worshipped and assumed would be there forever. Longbridge was, after all, to the local community what the Houses of Parliament are to London, the Statue of Liberty is to New York and the Eiffel Tower is to Paris.

Let's face it, BMW was and remains a class act. They have always been known for their leading technology and reliability as well as good looks. The fact that they sold out Rover within five years of buying it must surely beg the question: did they ever intend to keep it or was it just a Trojan horse?

Despite their upmarket image, BMW only had a small market, outside their domestic one, into which they sold their cars. So they had stood still whilst their competitors, particularly the Japanese, were becoming global players on a grand scale. BMW was also described derogatively as: 'making only one saloon in three different sizes'. If they weren't to be left well and truly behind, they had to expand their market and their product range without damaging their upmarket brand image. What better way to do that than to conduct 'The Longbridge Experiment'.

BMW was already talking to Rover - it was common knowledge that they were to be engaged by British Aerospace to supply diesel engines to the Rover Group for the new Range Rover. The Range Rover was selling well in continental Europe and they were actually on course to overtake BMW's own 4 x 4 sales in Germany. So, when BMW looked at Rover as a target, I think they were eyeing up the goodies, perhaps through rose-coloured spectacles, but certainly with a game-plan and an exit route. Nothing wrong in that, I've always planned an exit route for every aspect of our business, in case the need arose, but have never gone into a deal with that specifically in mind.

There was no protracted due diligence carried out in preparing for the buyout. In fact, the deal was completed in just ten days. British Aerospace wanted out, BMW wanted in; lawyers worked through the nights on the paperwork, the announcement was made and the eagle landed.

Honda was not happy, in fact they were seething. They had been Rover's partner for over a decade and had every right to be miffed at the snub. As far as I am aware, they weren't even offered the chance to make a counter bid.

Now here's a massive example of what happens if you don't apply the belt and braces principal every time - no one considered that Rover cars were dependent on Honda for their engineering and the ramifications that would present if they said "Nien!" Well, they did very swiftly throw Teddy out of the pram and stopped cooperating over-night. They sold their 20% holding in Rover because they were left with little alternative and simply walked away to paddle their own canoe. I believe this was exactly what BMW wanted to happen and they hoped that the disruption would set back Honda's European plans by a few years or they would retreat to the east completely. In this they failed dismally and, instead, set the seeds for the destruction of Longbridge.

I don't believe BMW had the slightest intention of keeping Rover. In the next five years they developed cars which were never launched, planned the Cowley exodus from day one and earmarked the mini as a BMW brand for the future.

I have no axe to grind with them personally, as under BMW, Rover's dealership base was drastically cut, working to our advantage as we were the largest and most respected. Our relationship with them was always good, if frustrating through lack of new product. The MGF was already substantially developed when BMW purchased Rover and they continued with it. Only the Rover 75 was launched under BMW, in the five years they owned it, and this was delayed and delayed with one excuse after another. When it finally arrived, it proved a poor second to the BMW 3 series and, along with the other dealers,

I felt cheated by this. To cap it all, at the motor show in their final year, BMW actually announced they were contemplating selling Longbridge. Great marketing that was! Also, with so much choice out there, no wonder sales declined. Did they just buy MG Rover and Land Rover to take the Honda technology? Was this just one more part of the master plan dreamed up in Munich?

BMW's excuse was that they were dripping money at Rover. "We invested millions," they said and, when they eventually broke it up and sold it at the end of the decade, they publicly appealed for sympathy saying that: "Enough was enough!" Privately, they did very nicely.

They purchased the whole group for £800,000,000; then sold Land Rover alone for £1,800,000,000. That is a £1bn profit. The vast majority of the investment in plant went to Cowley, which BMW retained. BMW invested in a new engine facility (Hams Hall). BMW retained that plant. BMW retained the Longbridge Engine & Transmissions facility, thereby forcing Rover to buy components from BMW to be able to continue making cars. The same goes for the Swindon panel pressing plant. BMW made money out of Rover car sales, even if Rover itself was taking a loss. Eventually, they sold these facilities to Phoenix, but it was for a fair value and not included in the infamous £10, which I will come on to later. For now, it's time to get off the soapbox and back to what was happening with us in that period.

III

One fabulous thing came out of the BMW period as far as I was concerned. Another diversion - one which fed both my love of developing new projects and my passion for two wheels - we started selling motorbikes at Rednal. A BMW franchise, to be precise, and the only real one of prestige outside of their Park Lane showroom.

This came about through an introduction by Clive Bannister who we called 'Minister of Fun' at Rover. His real title was Head of Corporate Events and Well Being. He organised hospitality events and bought the fine art for the boardroom. He actually managed to get the number plate 'RILEY'; I'd love to know what happened to that. Clive was an extrovert and a lovable character who would do anything he could to help the dealers. He also had a direct link to the then CEO, Dr. Hasselkuss, who was quite gregarious in his own right. It so happened that the good doctor had been in charge of BMW motorcycles in Germany and was very approachable on the subject of us selling them at Rednal.

I did my research thoroughly and realised that, unlike car dealerships, there weren't really any corporate standards. In fact, it was all a bit of a hotch-potch and bikes were sold to enthusiasts who were used to seeing them bunched handle-to-handle in tight lines in badly lit sales centres. So I decided that we would sell our bikes in the same way that we did cars, by displaying them to their best advantage - gleaming and accessible on podiums within a carefully designed showroom.

Dr. Hasselkuss performed the opening ceremony himself and I recall we presented him with a Royal Worcester bone china dinner service to mark the occasion.

Whereas the car showrooms attracted very much a local audience or client base, the motor bikes pulled people in from up to a hundred miles away. In fact, some made a day out of it. It was a good and, as it turned out, a shrewd move. We became one of the biggest sellers of BMW bikes in the country. Car sales of Rovers, meanwhile, were fast declining.

IV

The banks' early warning system was jittery about our association with Rover from about two years into the new BMW regime. Although we were exceeding sales figures at the Toyota, Honda and VW outlets, we were under performing on Rover. I was summoned to a bank meeting. They as good as told me that they wanted us to get out of Rover altogether.

I was incensed. Rover had been our start and our backbone. "But we're still selling 1,200 cars a year!" I exploded, "You want us to walk away from that?" There followed a shrug of the shoulders and we agreed to disagree.

"If you don't take what we are saying seriously then we will have to review our position on your overdraft facility," I was told.

Our gross borrowings were now in excess of five million; if the plug was pulled overnight on that then Clark's could collapse like a house of cards. Whilst we had substantial money tied up in property, it was not easily accessible and so the threat to our existence was a real one. I left the meeting fuming and worried in equal measures. It truly was a case of handing you an umbrella when the sun is shining and leaving you to drown when it's about to pour down. We had no cash flow problems; it was only the bank that wanted to create them. The poetic justice of 2005 was only eight years away and I, for one, think they got their just deserts with the boot on the other foot.

V

The next problem was one that still makes me fume with anger to this very day. You must have got the message I have been preaching throughout this biography that goes right back to when we first serviced cars in the Rednal bus shelter: that standards of service to the customer are everything. It had always been our leading competitive edge over rivals, praised by manufacturers, competitors and customers alike. So what happened next very nearly destroyed that carefully nurtured reputation.

Somewhere in the ever-growing 'jobsworth' department of Trading Standards, some prat in a white collar thought it a good idea to set us up for a fall, by booking a doctored car in for service, at our business in Kidderminster. Eight small faults were deliberately put into the vehicle. Our technician missed two of them! A small bulb not working on the dashboard was not spotted and a perished wiper blade not replaced. Yes, the technician should have found the faults and fixed them, but did it really warrant an exposure in the papers and tarnish to a hitherto unblemished reputation?

We were fined ten grand by Trading Standards and lost our MOT franchise for 6 months. This meant we lost it, by default, to all our six MOT centres, as we were classed as fraudulent criminals. As livid as I was with the technician for the shoddy work, I was madder at a government which seemed bent on introducing measures to destroy business rather than encourage it. In essence, this was their version of a suicide bomber.

Customers rang to console us, letters appeared in the papers extolling our virtues, but the damage was severe - it cost thousands in lost revenue and put a question mark against our integrity. In forty-five years of trading, never had this ever happened before. There had been small problems from time to time, but with hand on heart, they were always rectified. Clark's' law means the customer is, was and always will be king.

I even went to court to try and get the decision overturned, but to no avail. We had been effectively nobbled by people who knew nothing about the motor industry. For the sake of a bulb and a blade they put good people out of work.

I longed for the days of old, before all this employment legislation and industrial tribunals. When you could promote and give pay increases to good workers and staff and dismiss those that didn't pass muster, without ending up defending your actions for days on end in a courtroom reminiscent of the French Revolution.

I was starting not to enjoy business for the very first time in my life.

VI

It seemed we were suddenly beset with problems. In Brussels, a piece of legislation had been passed, the enormity of which had escaped the whole of the car dealership business, namely: 'block exemption'. It was, like most legislation, intended to bring about fairness. In this case it was supposed to end manufacturer-monopoly by allowing dealers to sell whatever brand of cars they liked. What it did was to introduce panic into the market whereby some manufacturers took steps to have their own wholly-owned showrooms. Other manufacturers pressured dealers such as ourselves (which, because of their size, were subject to the block exemption) to sell out to smaller dealers to whom the rules did not apply.

Mercedes terminated all dealerships, but gave the franchisees two years notice, more than enough time to sort their lives out. VW, on the other hand, who we were heavily in bed with now, took the attitude that they no longer wanted entrepreneurs, but companies over which they had total control. They set the rules and the margins and if you didn't achieve the targets you weren't entitled to your discounts. To explain: they put together criteria which included customer care, audit of sales, service and repairs. Failing in any one of those meant you didn't get your 'hold back'. This was a monthly figure relating to discounts and bonuses and it was very much in their interest for you to fail. Honda and even Rover swiftly followed suit. Where there was once respect there was now disdain. Where our workers were once treated as friends by the manufacturers, they were now expendable slaves. They ruled with an iron rod and they all wanted me to sell. I was to them a dinosaur left over from a bygone age. There was no room for the Doug Clark's of this world in the new order, even if I was, to the press, still the voice of the motor industry. I was flattered that my opinion was sought on all things and they knew I would give an honest answer, which did little to improve my relationship with the manufacturers.

The time had come to do just that. Sell out the franchises, transfer the staff and move on. The motor dealership business was changing rapidly and would never be the same again. It needed someone at the helm who understood what was required to survive and thrive within the new rules. It wasn't me!

It made total economic sense to retain the land and properties, but in my mind, I was now planning a complete personal exit from the motor industry. A momentous step, but it was time to let someone else take up the reins. So the words 'management buyout' formed the note I wrote on my bedside pad one morning.

29 – Let It Be

I

If I were to put a management buyout in place I would need a young top dog to orchestrate it. Yes, I had some great managers within the company - friends and colleagues that I wished to see get part of the action; but no, I didn't have anyone capable of leading a buyout, their skills were of a different sort - they were Clarked. By design, they were part of the whole and could only see their part within it. Not a criticism, a reality.

So I searched high and low throughout the land, as they say in story books, and found who I believed to be the ideal candidate. He was in a senior position at a huge car dealer group and was introduced to me by quite an eminent member of the trade. Other people talked him up to me and he talked himself up too at the interview. He grabbed the opportunity - and what an opportunity it was. To take control as CEO of the entire Clark organisation, to do the deals and to put in place a financial structure that would see him, and whoever he selected to join him, as the new owners. I relinquished day-to-day responsibility and concentrated my chairman's role solely on the property side of things.

We paid him a salary in excess of £160K a year in recognition of the importance of the position and, true to my word, I did not interfere, but gave him his head. I felt a sense of relief that, at last, it was someone else's job to take the tough decisions and to make their vision a reality. I truly believed that he would let me retire a rich man. I relaxed, planned to travel more and let the new CEO get on with doing what he was employed to do.

So the decade and indeed the century drew towards its close, bringing with it a state of serenity. I contemplated the good, the bad and the ugly in both my business and my personal life and thought of how it had all changed. It didn't seem long since it was all about selling fuel, sweets, cigarettes and servicing. Now we had closed all our petrol operations bar Lickey. The supermarkets dominated the market with massive petrol volume and so could afford to take the tiny margins. It was impossible to compete with that. Gone too was U-can-Hire, no call for it once the manufacturers started providing loan cars. We had some fantastic showrooms, but were being forced to surrender some of them thanks to Brussels and misguided legislation. On the bright side, the Silver Birches Business Park had a waiting list of tenants. I had lost Jan and gained Leigh and, along with her, more adventures than most men experience in a lifetime. The solutions were there; I knew what had to be done and I had put in place just the man to do it - a new broom for a new Millennium. The widget maker had to move with the times and provide widgets that suited the looming new century.

I was, after all, approaching the big six-o. Where had the time gone? It seemed just five minutes since I was a rep selling tyres and had that fateful first encounter with Uncle Jess.

II

Away from Clark's, the world breathed a sigh of relief when the prediction that computers would not shift from the two digit '99' to 2000 and bring with it business chaos, never happened. America On Line (AOL) sold out to Time Warner for 162 billion dollars, one of the biggest corporate sales in history. The infamous Doctor Harold Shipman was found guilty of murdering many of his patients. The pop icon and actress Madonna married the film producer Guy Richie at a castle in Scotland. Microsoft launched the state-of-the-art software Windows 2000. Vladimir Putin was elected President of Russia and George W Bush, President of the USA. The Long Kesh Prison in Northern Ireland, home to many an IRA member, was finally closed and another notorious building, The Millennium Dome, opened to a blaze of glory and closed within the year as a massive white elephant.

The Academy Award went to American Beauty and the record 'Smooth' by Santana won the Grammy. On TV we watched Friends and at the cinema the big movies of the year were Gladiator, Chocolat, Trainspotting and Crouching Tiger, Hidden Dragon.

We lost the actor Oliver Reed whilst filming Gladiator. He was perhaps more famous for his off-screen antics than his screen work. It is said he once drank 160 pints of beer in one day.

Amongst other actors who died that year were: Sir John Gielgud, Walter Matthau and Sir Alec Guinness. We also said goodbye to the singer/songwriter, Kirsty McColl; the comedian, Victor Borge; the cartoonist and creator of Peanuts, Charles Schulz, the film director who enjoyed the company of some of the world's most beautiful women including Bridget Bardot and Jane Fonda, Frenchman Roger Vadim; 'Mr. Football', Sir Stanley Mathews; Lee Petty, the American racing car driver; Dame Barbara Cartland the romantic novelist; Sir Robin Day, the political broadcaster, and Reggie Kray, the East End gangster.

On the birth front it's worth noting that the billionth living person in India was born.

III

Millennium night came and Leigh and I went to a party at her father's house in Lichfield and saw the new century in with about forty friends and relatives. I played the guitar and sang Beatles numbers to them until the early hours. I celebrated the Millennium along with the rest of the world and counted my blessings that I was still there to celebrate it and could look forward to reaping the fruits of my labours in the precious years yet to come. Everything in the garden of Douglas Clark was truly rosy; for once I was finishing a decade with no storm clouds gathering on the horizon, or great challenges ahead for that matter, and with the comfort of having passed the baton on to a business champion for the new Millennium. No, I would play the recognised chairman's role, motivate the troops, ask the right questions at board meetings, but most of all, be noted for my absence, as I indulged myself in a wind-down to exiting the business entirely.

If only I had known then what the new decade really had in store, I wouldn't have slept as soundly as I did that night. They say there is calm before the storm and this was the perfect calm before the perfect storm.

Part Six - 2000 to 2010

30 – You Can't Judge A Book

I

Although I fully intended to keep hands-off, there was something I had started myself that I needed to see through. That was a new dealership for a new Millennium. I had been working on bringing in KIA, the new Korean manufacturer who was making fast inroads into the small car market. I had met with them at the 1999 motor show and been very impressed with their keenness and intention to give far longer warranties on their cars than any other manufacturer. This was a unique selling point in my book. Today they offer an incredible seven year or 100,000 mile warranty on their very low-priced 4x4's. The franchise was for Rednal and from the time we started selling them in early 2000 they proved to be quite a winner, almost outselling Rover, which in fairness, wasn't so difficult at the start of 2000.

It was also at that fateful 1999 motor show that BMW announced that it was putting Rover up for sale. What a time and place to do it. At the same time as they were actually launching the long-delayed Rover 75, they were putting up a 'for sale' sign on the company. Who on earth was going to buy a new Rover when there was no stability to the company? In comparison with KIA, there wasn't going to be a warranty with a new Rover that was worth the paper it was written on.

We national dealers started ringing round each other and alliances were formed. This initiative was spearheaded by the main dealer from Oxford, Richard Eades, who was also our national representative for the dealer network and was therefore already negotiating with Rover. He called a meeting where we decided to take matters into our own hands and to put forward a proposal to buy and run the company ourselves. We each put in equal nominal amounts to give us some money to cover the initial legal costs. It came as little comfort to realise that we were, at that time, the largest Rover dealer in the world. But it was right that we should join the rest of the pack in the bid to own the company whose cars we sold. Sadly, it was to prove a pipedream. Who knows what would have happened had the bid been successful, but it was rejected before the ink was dry on our signatures and our deposit duly returned.

The reason for the abrupt rebuttal was that BMW had agreed to a deal, in principle, with the investment company, Alchemy. However, this was to break down at the eleventh hour. BMW and Alchemy issued brief statements referring to 'conditions of contract' as the reason for the breakdown in their negotiations on 28th April 2000. Alchemy would not agree to the costs of redundancy coupled with the threat of legal action, not only by the Rover trade unions, but also from legal representation, engaged by Rover management, over possible breaches in employment legislation.

Who could blame them? Alchemy was facing potential liabilities estimated at over 100 million pounds for failure to consult managers and employees respectively. This would have been in addition to the cost of funding redundancy at several hundred million pounds more.

Twelve days later, on 9th May 2000, the immediate future of the Longbridge car plant was secured when the Phoenix consortium headed up by John Towers, bought Rover from BMW for just a nominal ten pounds. During negotiations with BMW, the Phoenix consortium received the backing of trade unions, employees and dealers as well as implicit support from the government due to their intention of maintaining Rover as a mass producer of vehicles in the long term. There was much press hysteria and locally a huge sigh of relief was breathed, as jobs were thought to be safeguarded. Rover was vital to the West Midlands economy. At that time, vehicle manufacture at Rover and Land Rover supported up to 50,000 jobs, or 8% of all manufacturing jobs in the region.

Both Phoenix and Stephen Byers, the Trade and Industry Secretary, said that, "While the rescue plan was viable in the short and medium term, Longbridge's long-term future would require Phoenix to link up with a worldwide producer for the purposes of product development and platform-sharing." If only they had stayed with Honda, none of this would have happened. As it was, BMW took the prized Mini with them to Cowley and gave Phoenix the Rover 75 for Longbridge. Not the best deal in the world, I'd say; however, the trade unions at Rover warmly welcomed the successful conclusion. Stephen Byers and local MP, Richard Burden, were credited with behind-the-scenes activities in bringing Phoenix and BMW together.

What it meant to us was: business as usual. We could reassure customers that warranties would be honoured and that manufacture was improving under the new regime.

II

I knew that there would be no more big construction projects needed and so I started the wind-down of the building division, just keeping a skeleton crew for group maintenance. It was the end of an era and it grieved me to do it; I loved the buzz of planning a new building and seeing those plans come to fruition, but it had to be done.

Malta called more and more and Leigh and I started spending a lot of time over there. We went to other places too, including Paris and Rome; all over Europe in fact - wining, dining and viewing lots of the beautiful places and buildings I had always intended to visit, but never had the time to indulge in till now.

I kept in contact with my CEO to make sure everything was proceeding in accordance with his task of preparing for the big buy-out and I got all the right answers back.

Christmas 2000 was a happy time and I fully believed that when the New Year came it would bring with it the lifetime achievement reward for one Douglas Clark - in the form of a generous pension. My mind was full of pleasant daydreams of how I would occupy my days in the pursuit of a lifestyle bereft of big business.

III

2001 continued in much the same relaxed vein as its predecessor, and if anything, I had my eye off the ball even more. The word from the ranch was that the management buy out continued a pace, due diligence was about to be done and I was told the banks were ready to provide the necessary funding.

It was whilst on a vacation with Leigh to my cousin's house in Canada in the latter part of the year that I scanned the latest management accounts that had been faxed to me for reference. The scan quickly turned to scrutiny when I realised the figures did not stack up and rather than taking the company forwards, the new structure was in danger of bringing about chaos and ruin. Rome wasn't built in a day and neither was Clark's, but there was a clear and present danger that we could follow Rome's destiny and fall apart in maybe not a day, but double-quick time. The position was serious in the extreme, in fact nigh on critical. No way would any bank sanction funding for a management buyout, I had been led well and truly up the garden path and I wanted answers.

I cut short the trip, having made some decisions overnight, flew home the next morning, spat feathers and spilt blood. My CEO told me that I was perhaps reading too much into the figures. "Management accounts never lie," I told him.

I was like a dog with a bone and wouldn't let go, putting daily pressure on him to provide more depth and justification to his widely optimistic forecasts. I knew, legislation being what it was, I needed solid proof that he was failing in his duties as CEO to the point where I could get rid of him, if necessary, without having to spend weeks in a tribunal justifying my actions to strangers, whilst I should be heading up a turn-round. The first thing to do was to call a board meeting with all the key players present and request an explanation from him.

IV

All this activity meant that I was getting very little quality time to spend with Leigh. I thought the best solution to this was to encourage her to start her own small business. She was becoming a changed woman, more in control of her life than at any time since I had known her. She was beginning to have aspirations outside of our relationship; she took on work for charity companies as a part-time fund raiser and clearly enjoyed the challenge.

My sixtieth birthday was fast approaching and Leigh wanted me to have a major party to celebrate it. I thought, "Why not?" I had always planned to have a once-in-a-lifetime bash on reaching sixty. We had been through such a turbulent period business-wise that a little celebration would serve as a 'thank you' to everyone involved in the company turn-round and be a chance to show the outside world that, contrary to rumour, Clark's was in the best of health.

31 – Sixty And Still Standing

I

The idea of one big once-in-a-lifetime bash really appealed to me. After all, I was supposed to be retired at sixty and here I was, working harder than I had ever done, so why not indeed.

Leigh took everything under her wing and planned the big day with all the care and precision of a military manoeuvre; nothing was to be left to chance, every detail organised and unique.

The only thing I insisted on was the venue, it had to be at the Chateau Impney, which was not only the most famous local landmark in the vicinity, but also held so many personal memories for me. It was there that I had sold the most expensive tyres in my portfolio to the then owner, Eric Pillon, for his Rolls Royce. It was there that I had played some wonderful gigs with the band and it was at the Chateau I had some amazing encounters, with a bevy of beautiful ladies, over the years. Currently, it was owned by Zak Steven Ragutz, a Yugoslav by birth who had been a successful entrepreneur in Malta, until being kicked out by Prime Minister Mintoff. Dom Mintoff had been infamous for his nationalisation of companies and property that were never his to take, save by his own decree. Zak Ragutz was a pleasant and wily chap who I liked the more for doing a good deal with me on the price for the day, which included a 50% discount on all the rooms for everyone staying over and the honeymoon suite thrown in for me and Leigh.

The guest list included my brothers and sisters along with other relatives. I thought it might well be the last time we would gather together, as in fairness, with the exception of Noel and Malcolm, we had little contact.

From the world of business, I invited, amongst others: from MG Rover, Tony Jennings the plant director, Pat Hemmens the Finance Director and good old Ken Smith who had recently retired, but was the former director of service who had helped us greatly; Stan Thomas the regional director of Shell, and of course, Slade Arthur and Paul Johnson from Motaparts were included along with Dave Fletcher the construction engineer and many other people who had been such an important part of my business history.

Other invitees included: Estelle Fletcher, who was no relation to Dave, but the widow of Jimmy Fletcher, the owner of the Copper Coin Amusement Arcade at Rednal, who had known me from the day I joined Uncle Jess; J.J Davis, a builder who did some amazing work on the re-designs of all the Shell forecourts; my mate Terry Bird; Paul Wakelin the guitar dealer; all my old band; all the key members of staff; my ex wife's Mom and Dad, Olive and Jim, of whom I was very fond; my next door neighbours Bryan and Sue Powell and Frank Verlic (who's claim to fame is that he deserted from the French Foreign Legion decades ago and for all intents and purposes, is still on the run); Leigh's family and my daughter Julia and her husband Chris. Along with their respective partners the guest list was in excess of 200.

Leigh worked everything out to the finest detail, down to the invitations made by Tony Richmond which were in the form of a number plate 'DOUG 60'. The place settings were all themed and gifts for my guests consisted of paperweights, engraved with a caricature of me playing the guitar, for the men and handmade chocolates in a beautiful presentation box with my signature on it for the ladies.

Royston Evans of Startime Promotions, who was the original agent that took The Suedes to the 2 I's coffee bar all those years ago was employed to provide the entertainment for the evening. There was also a master of ceremonies and a team of six male runners in DJ's and bow ties, employed by Leigh, to do her bidding on the evening, ensuring everything ran like clockwork. Her organisational skills astounded me; this was a new person, so very much in control and so creative.

II

So the big day arrived, I was all 'Versaced up' by Leigh in a grey silk jacket and black silk collarless shirt with gold buttons. Leigh looked stunning in a long black silk dress with a silver grey wrap. We felt and looked like film stars, as we stood at the top of the steps to greet the guests with a glass of champagne, as the magical hour of seven o'clock arrived.

The grounds were all floodlit and my classic car collection was used to form an archway on the approach to the car park. Amongst the meet-and-greet ensemble were stilt walkers and other circus performers creating a carnival atmosphere.

For me, the best bit of Leigh's creative genius was that she had got my grass track racing bike on display in the reception area and on it was a mannequin dressed up in my racing leathers. This caused quite a sensation and many an irreverent comment.

Strolling musicians played, close-up magicians performed and photographers snapped away during the reception and we sat down to a five-course feast at eight thirty.

There was a top table where Leigh sat on my right and Julia on my left, all hostilities between them were put aside for this occasion and they both concentrated on making my special night unforgettable.

A Beatles tribute band played during the meal and 'Gary Allcock's All Stars' twenty-one piece big band played after we had eaten. It was an all-round tremendous experience and I could not have asked for more.

At the end of the meal I gave a speech mentioning everyone I could think of who had helped me over the years. As I drew to a close I put on a very grave face and said that I was going to use this occasion to make a very special announcement. Out of the corner of my eye I saw that Julia looked startled. Everyone thought I was going to announce that Leigh and I were getting married - except Leigh of course, as I had already cleared this little bit of mischief with her in advance.

"Ladies and Gentlemen," I said, "today is a very special day for me in more ways than one." I paused for silence and you could have heard a pin drop. "I have a very important announcement to make about someone very special. Today, Eleanor Rigby will have worked for me for twenty-five golden years." Much laughter and applause greeted this and I invited Eleanor to come up and receive a Longines watch from me. She was overwhelmed and it added a wonderful spice to the proceedings. I received a standing ovation and felt both proud and humbled at the same time.

So we partied on and on and the evening would not have been complete without a set from me and my old band, The Citizens, except we now called ourselves 'The Senior Citizens'. That was perhaps my favourite part.

Eventually, Leigh and I turned in at about three a.m., leaving the hard-core revellers, still revelling. When we got into the suite, Leigh told me it was not over yet and proudly gave me her present. It was unbelievably what I wanted most in the world - a Gibson Chet Atkins Country Gentleman Guitar. How she had saved up for that I will never know. It was a wonderful, thoughtful gift which I played away on for over an hour, all thoughts of tiredness disappearing. Today, that guitar is kept in Malta in the safe hands of a great guitarist and friend Joe Grech.

I received so many generous gifts that evening, two complete van loads in fact, which I spent a whole day opening back at Badgers Cottage. They ranged from paintings, cut glass and engraved silver through concert tickets for Cliff Richard. There was even a solid oak bench engraved with my name on it. Such thoughtful gifts; I was overwhelmed, but nothing compared to that Chet Atkins guitar Leigh gave me.

It was indeed the party of a lifetime, a reunion of friends, a celebration of business life and of 'coming of age'. It's where I coined a new catchphrase: "I'm only a pensioner!" This has stood me in good stead since and gets me a healthy discount all over the world, whenever I say it.

Come the morning, just when I thought it was all over, I was delighted to find that, unknown to me, Yvonne Evans, Group Human Resource Manager, had arranged a staff party the next day for all the people that hadn't been to the Chateau the night before. Yvonne and her sister, Barbie, prepared masses of food and had it delivered to every site. I was then escorted to them all and celebrated many times over. It was the best working day I can recall.

32 – Pistols At Dawn

I

It was March and the euphoria of my birthday bash was fast becoming a distant memory. Back indeed to the harsh reality of turning the Clark empire fortunes around. It was all a bit like playing poker, just sitting in there waiting for one good hand to go all in.

In the weeks leading up to the board meeting I made a complete review of where we were heading and the company strategy needed to deal with it. The situation was actually worse than I had first thought. A fact which Grant Thornton concurred with, they suggested I had Eric Williams accompany me to the meeting. Eric used to work for the Inland Revenue and was a bit of a game-keeper turned poacher.

There was little pleasantry at that meeting on the 22nd March and I went straight for the jugular addressing my comments ostensibly to the board and directly to my CEO.

"In the trading period to the end of February you have managed to lose £327,358," I announced. "Overheads have gone up by nearly 33%. It is my view as chairman that there are key issues that have not been managed by the board, and in particular, by my chief executive officer whose role it is to control such matters and with whom the buck must ultimately stop."

I paused and he dropped his eyes away from me, not issuing a hint of a challenge.

I continued: "In particular, I believe control over overhead costs has been lost, the superb computer system I installed has been totally under-utilised for budgetary control, forecast measurement is non-existent, you might as well have stuck your finger in the air".

I wasn't angry, but I was passionate and went on to chastise the lack of communication and accountability at all levels. At the end of my address there was silence. Both the CEO and his assistant looked like rabbits caught in headlights.

It was time to hand over to Eric Williams. Where I had outlined my concerns he added another layer of finger pointing supported by hard facts.

I finished by giving everyone a copy of my written statement and asking Eric on behalf of Grant Thornton to write up the minutes.

The statement basically asked for completely revised budgets for every department to be put together by the CEO immediately.

Within days his resignation was on my desk. At a face to face meeting he intimated that he was considering going for constructive dismissal. This incensed me, but I kept my calm and told him that was his prerogative. I heard no more from him after that.

So my thoughts of an easy drift into an early pension and retirement were washed away like the ebb tide. It was 'roll your sleeves up' time once again. Daunting yes, necessary yes, exciting? You bet it was.

II

"As you are all aware, our CEO has resigned with immediate effect. I shall be once again taking on that role along with my duties as chairman," I started. "The motor industry may have changed, the challenges are different, but the principals of good old 'belt and braces' management still apply and will ultimately be our salvation," I told the meeting I had called. In attendance was every senior manager and dealer principal in the group. I had even broken my own golden rule by pulling them all out for a meeting in the working day so they knew it was serious.

"I want dealer principals back selling," I told them. "You need to be out full-time on the floor, leading by example not stuck in your offices. Anyone who steps foot into one of our showrooms doesn't leave without committing - do I make myself clear?"

I was so fired up that it didn't register with me that this was not going down well. I was insulting their managerial status, reducing them to the level of their sales force and they didn't like it one bit. "The same goes for the parts managers; you'll no longer leave any of the buying and selling to your staff. You'll physically do it yourself instead and cut some numbers. I want you to scrutinise every invoice, drive harder purchasing bargains, move stock and increase your bottom line. We're a business not a charity, a fact some of you seem to have forgotten." This was greeted by silence; my message was still being misinterpreted as just a mindless rant so I changed tack. "Everyone, please listen to me! We've all had it too good for too long and we've grown complacent. Believe me, we'll never see the good times again unless we pull together as a team and tackle every inch, every item and every penny of our business. I'm on a crusade to turn things around and I need you up there charging with me. The party is over, the gravy train has stopped running; am I getting through now?"

Realisation dawned at last; the penny had well and truly dropped that this great company, of which they all controlled some part, was indeed in grave danger of ceasing to exist. As I looked at the sea of faces, I could see most of them were with me, but some were already planning their exit routes, having made a mental choice to abandon what they perceived to be Doug Clark's sinking ship. They didn't want demotion or to be part of a rescue plan and who could really blame them? There were, after all, employment, life and relatively risk-free opportunities outside of Clark's. I knew that this feeling would be even more apparent when the managers spread the word down to the workforce. I didn't want a mass exodus, but rather to use it as an opportunity to make us leaner and meaner. The majority of managers though were not only loyal to the core, but shared my pride and passion; they were quite simply not prepared to see it all end in tears. I had steered them well in the past and they believed I would do so again. They left that meeting on a mission and immediately set about planning and implementing their individual cost-saving measures.

I followed this up with a confidential strategy memo detailing everyone's new role. Adrian Smith became Operations Director as well as retaining his deputy MD ship, in essence my deputy; Melanie Radford, the Group Management Accountant, but working alongside Paul Long, the Group IT manager, to implement the financial performance reporting system. In addition, I made Paul Group Parts Controller. Malc's role as a director with particular responsibility for the Accident Repair Centre remained unchanged. This was my new tight management team; they would head up the charge back to profitability.

No stone was to be left unturned in any department. We held many a meeting outside of hours and talked through events on a daily basis, often till the early hours of the morning.

The managers actually asked their staff if anyone wanted voluntary redundancy. Ironically, one of those who was first with his hand up to go was David Hughes, son of Aunty Ivy who used to live at The Barracks before it got knocked down. David had come to me in the 90's asking for a job when he had taken redundancy from Rover in that early shakeout. I had given him a position in after-sales administration. I can't remember what extra responsibilities he was asked to take on, nothing too onerous but enough to get him to walk. I never saw him again. I single him out because he was family; many others with no similar ties walked away at the same time.

Overall, I implemented in the following weeks a complete company restructure with water-tight management control. Without causing any panic in the workplace or a drop in standards, the total workforce was cut back by some 5%; both direct and indirect costs were attacked and trimmed back to the bare bones. I knew that, rather than the bank funding a management buyout, a day of reckoning would be coming sooner rather than later and I had already begun work on a new business plan in readiness for my D-Day.

I seconded Yvonne Evans from human resources to work alongside Malc in the Accident and Repair Centre. She had a directive from me to carry out a complete assessment on the staffing levels and the systems being used. It wasn't that I didn't trust my brother to carry this out, but implementation was his forte not planning, so even he was subject to my all-embracing scrutiny.

It soon became evident that in the eighteen odd months I had given up the helm the biggest contributor to the Clark demise was the 'big company' attitude that had crept in like ivy around a tree, almost choking the life out of the group. Previously, every department took pride in being an individual profit centre; this had been replaced with a false concept that the whole was now much bigger than the sum of the parts. Everything was A-OK because some other department or person would make up for any shortfall your department incurred; there was an underlying malaise of 'manyana'. I had to drum it in that this was now totally unacceptable; everyone had to contribute to the bottom line and I made it my business to make it common knowledge who was contributing what. "Villains and Heroes, a game for all employees; winners get to keep their jobs," I told them and added: "In good old-fashioned terms, ladies and gentlemen, when the going gets tough, the tough get going."

Decisions had to be taken, hard ones. The balance was finite, get it right and we could still be in clover. Get it wrong and Clark's would become another statistic in the corporate graveyard and my epitaph would read 'Here lies wee Dougie Clark, he led the race only to fall at the last bend; RIP'.

III

On one of my many sojourns to Malta I had met an amazing systems man Harry Hombach; Harry was an enigmatic German who had a boat berthed next to mine. He regaled and impressed me with his father's background of having rewritten the software system for BMW in North America and long before computer technology had elevated the task to an art form; he was an original systems boffin. Harry then learned the trade from his Dad, adding his own touch as a master of computer skills. He also enjoyed a double talent, being an excellent marketier and a pioneer of both websites and their use as a marketing tool. In short, Harry possessed all the talents we were lacking and I wanted him as part of my restructuring team. I rang him and offered what I considered to be a very attractive deal. He was interested, but reticent to accept, not relishing the idea of leaving the warmth and comfort of Malta for the unpredictability and living costs of Britain. So I got on a plane and went to talk to him, face to face, to make him appreciate just how much I wanted him on board. This show of seriousness on my part indeed impressed him. I appealed to him that I needed him by my side and in no time at all he agreed to come on board.

By the time he arrived in England he was fired up and ready to go, hitting the deck running from day one. Harry is the sort of guy that may be reluctant at the outset, but once committed, becomes evangelistic in his zeal. His Germanic personality was direct and abrupt. He asked awkward questions, ruffling feathers initially, causing a little resentment amongst the managers. This extended even further down the line to some of the employees who referred to him as 'Heinrich' rather than Harry, after the SS boss 'Heinrich Himmler'. It was certainly not an easy job and we both appreciated that he wasn't there to be liked. However, he became accepted as part of the team and whilst his popularity didn't increase, he gained respect throughout the company.

Harry reviewed our administration procedures and fine-tuned all the computer systems, linking them together to produce definitive corporate information at the touch of a button. He set up our first website, which was a signal to the outside world that Clark's was once again trail blazing when it came to marketing. He made us look better and bigger than we actually were at that time and I had no objection to that.

"You have two types of managers, Douglas," he told me the night he presented his initial evaluations - "those that can't and those that won't - take responsibility, that is."

"That's a bit harsh, Harry," I responded. "Are you saying I have no good people at all?"

He tutted at me in exasperation, "I am only talking about the failures, the misfits. The good people we will use more and the deadwood must be rooted out and removed. Those that are simply not up to what has to be done should be demoted. It's as simple as that."

Simple to him it may have been, but I was dealing with people I had known for a long time. I had brought him in to do a job and knew if I didn't accept his plan there was every chance he would lose patience, and worse still, face. He would give up and hot-foot it back to Malta.

So I went along with his findings; it wasn't easy. I had to balance saving the company and protecting the livelihoods of many by sacrificing the few. In the aftermath of those days of the long knives, I am sure there are many people who still curse my name today. That, however, bothers me not one jot; I did what had to be done and make no apology for my actions. In the world where death is the hunter there is no time for regret or doubt - only decisions. Job done! We were going to regain control and advance at battle pace - Heinrich lined up Rommel's Panzers and I fired the shells.

IV

Typically, Malc's department was the first to turn around. In no time at all it was not only making, but exceeding its revised profit contributions. Yvonne liked and respected Harry, learning much from him; in fact, they fed ideas off each other. Malcolm put them into practise, retaining the respect of his team as their manager. That's not to say it was right first time, Harry didn't have a magic wand, merely a systematic mind and if the system didn't work, he would simply refine it or introduce another one until a winning formula was reached. The accident and repair centre became a sort of guinea pig and Malc swiftly learnt to manage constant change.

Tradition became a thing of the past; change was rapid and daily in every aspect of the business. We were buzzing again and I was more fired up than I had been at any time in my working life. There were simply not enough hours in the day, every one of the waking ones was spent planning and implementing in equal measures; it was a seven day week. Synergy was being restored; the sum of the parts was once more becoming greater than the whole.

Although no one was actually admitting it, the country was in the throes of a recession, one that had sneaked in rather than arriving like a tornado. The motor industry is a pretty good barometer for general economic forecasting. Car sales were down nationally and industries, that twelve months ago were thriving, were soon merely surviving. The measures we had taken and were continuing to take were indeed in the nick of time. Our profit was coming from parts, repairs and servicing, not from new car sales. There seemed little point in opening all four MG Rover dealerships on Sundays and so I kept just one going, varying it each week. Any potential Sunday customers were redirected via notices in the windows; it was a little like a chemists' rota.

Incremental expenses like health and safety, environmental issues and employment legislation all were costs that impacted on the bottom line. Some were necessary, but many were merely a legislative protection racket. Wherever possible, these were attacked without running foul of the law. Again Harry scoured the small print for cost-saving loopholes. Although Clark's was the least affected of all MG Rover dealers, it was obvious from the correspondence that our bank was now in a state of high alert. They appeared totally blinkered, refusing to consider the local picture and our unique position as supplier to the Longbridge workforce and their families. They just quoted the national statistics for the sale of MG Rover cars, which were dire.

Realising our big meeting with the bank was yet to be scheduled (always choose the battleground), I introduced Harry to them in the interim. In initial discussions he kept off the subject of MG Rover, but used the block exemption statistics to our advantage, playing on the national strengths of Toyota, Honda and VW. He was an immediate hit and they found in him a kindred spirit with whom they could do business and this staved off setting a date for the big meeting, until all our business plans were complete.

V

Once completed, my next mission was to appease the bank. Not an easy task, the twitchiness about MG Rover was now at fever pitch and the request for a meeting was turning to demand. It was set for one week hence, the last week in March 2003, and was to be held at Rednal.

Harry was well ensconced now and bringing him on board had proved a good business decision. He spearheaded the business plan for the meeting and I formulated our team. It was to be Melanie Radford the Management Accountant, Yvonne Evans Head of Human Resources, Adrian Smith the Deputy MD, Harry, Malcolm and myself.

The bank matched us in numbers at the meeting which commenced at 11am sharp and continued through a sandwich lunch to 3pm. We presented what I know to this day was a superbly constructed, balanced and logical plan for the future.

My great bank chum and advisor, Grant Warren, who had stood us in good stead over the years, had been side-moved on our account and in his place a tough, hard nosed, soulless heavyweight called Tom McCartney brought in as supremo. I found him emotionless, a stickler for financial protocol, unbending, inflexible - a man who seemed intent on single-handedly shutting down the motor trade from his opening comments. Nevertheless, I took the stone-wall start on the chin and responded by saying that I intended to prove that Clark's was worthy of continued bank support through our new business plan and the report on the prudent measures already introduced in the first quarter of the year. The team then proceeded to make a superb presentation. The figures and predictions were realistic and justified by economic fact and forecast. There was no bullshit in there, no pie in the sky, jam tomorrow stuff, it was solid and I was confident we would deliver everything that was promised and predicted.

McCartney was immovable throughout, looking at me as if I had got Aids. It was obvious he just wanted to close us down and get the bank's money out as soon as possible. He wouldn't accept our plan or any part of it; he wouldn't even give any credit or credence to the progress we had made since I had taken up the reins either. Grant was in the meeting and weighed in as much as he could on our side, but was shot down at every turn by McCartney. I would liken his methods at that fateful meeting as akin to those taken by his near namesake in America, Senator McCarthy, and his infamous witch hunt. The regional manager from Lloyds TSB was also there; he didn't say much, other than make asides about music to me. He was clearly embarrassed and knew that McCartney had an immovable agenda before entering the meeting, which he and Grant were being forced to go along with.

Then we got to what they wanted, which was to close and retrench. McCartney had done his research too; he presented the MG Rover national facts and told us he wanted far less exposure. I was told, and had little alternative but to agree, to letting Honda go at Halesowen, as they knew there was a keen buyer for it. There were all sorts of other suggestions, but in essence, he insisted I recapitalise the business by raising cash from selling assets and not from bank investment. I was told quite bluntly by McCartney that the bank was going to reduce its exposure with immediate effect. The overdraft facility was to be drastically reduced and the rates put up. Currently, we had a three and a half million pounds loan, plus three quarters of a million OD facility; this might sound a lot, but in the scale of a turnover of sixty million it was really very little. He took some comfort in the property portfolio, but not much. Why not? I couldn't fathom that, after all, they were good solid tangible assets, even if they were mostly owned by the pension fund. I'm sure that if McCartney could have got his hands on the fund he would have raided it there and then, but it was watertight and out of his grasp.

I was angry, but didn't show it; we barely touched palms as we shook hands on his exit. He had rubbished our plans, ignored our history and pushed me too far. In my mind I was already preparing to move banks. Such a tragedy really - that one man could end what had been a glorious partnership for many years. McCartney was no financial wizard, not even a man for the times, at least that was my opinion.

The very next day McCartney wrote stating that the bank was going to introduce a new scale of charges for managing every aspect of our account. It was outrageous on top of everything else. I refused point blank to accept this and called his bluff whilst opening negotiations with other banks.

VI

To cap off what had been a very bad week, I was in a meeting with Tesco about selling land to them when I had a phone call to say the garage where my car collection was being housed had caught fire. What had happened was that a mechanic, doing some work on a Mercedes 300SL, was draining the petrol tank when a spark from somewhere caused it to explode. This introduced a rapid domino effect setting everything ablaze. The fire could be seen from four miles away and as well as the fire engines, TV cameras were swiftly on the doorstep too. Most of the cars were wheeled out and saved, but when the fire was eventually put out, there was a great pool of molten alloy on the floor from the wheels of the Mercedes and everything was black with soot. Thankfully, no-one was hurt. All in all, there was nigh on half a million pounds worth of damage done; it could have been much worse, but mercifully most vehicles still inside were salvageable. A lengthy restoration process was undertaken and still continues today.

VII

The following Monday, I instructed agents to sell off part of 'Silver Birches' as I knew this was highly sought after and would go quickly. It did - to an investment company for 3.8 million, which went straight into the pension fund. Some of the cash came swiftly out again to pay off the bank OD and so I swiftly told them to stuff it.

Within weeks, I had moved our account to HSBC. What a difference: our new manager, Patrick Florence, was a switched-on enthusiastic go-getter who spent a day going round every branch with me, asking all the right questions and putting forward some pretty good suggestions. Where McCartney was the executioner, Patrick was the bringer of light, our 'Lady of the Lamp'. Far from closing down our business, Patrick Florence in true 'Florence Nightingale' form, wanted us to expand.

VIII

April came and with it the end of another episode in my life; Leigh and I agreed to part. It happened as it had started at Badgers Cottage. She was a changed person and I was happy for her. Gone was the boozy, druggie, any-thing-for-a-laugh party girl, and in her place, a woman with big ambitions. We had started making plans for her to open a restaurant in Bromsgrove but her heart wasn't in it and to be honest, I had cold feet on this venture too. We had named it 'Pumpkins Pantry' and it had been kitted out and was ready to go save almost only for the tablecloths and cutlery. Leigh said she "Wanted to make her own way and not take handouts from me" and I admired her all the more for this.

It was a sad and emotional time and we shed tears; it had been a life-changing period for us both. We still loved each other, we respected each other and we were grateful for what we had brought to each other, but it was time we moved on. I wouldn't say that the end of our relationship was a bi-product of the company restructures; it hadn't helped, but this split had been coming for some time and was an inevitable conclusion. Leigh knew, that as soon as it was possible, I wanted to move my base to Malta and carry on seeing the world from there, whilst she was at the point where merely being my companion didn't light her fire any more.

Leigh married a gentleman named Duncan. Together, they bought 'The Bluebell' in Henley in Arden, a pub that had seen better times. Leigh built it up, along with her new husband, into a very successful restaurant whilst, almost simultaneously, using her artistic and organisational flair to create an interior design company. We have remained and still do remain great friends. Duncan is a great guy, mild mannered and engaging; they make a perfect couple.

Pumpkins Pantry is now The Mint Lounge, the Indian Restaurant I men-tioned earlier.

33 – Rovers Retreat

I

Eighteen months after the dark period began, the light was shining again. Having looked metaphorically into the barrel of a shotgun close to my forehead, we were now making money again and the gun was safely back in the display cabinet. The restructure had worked, the relationship with HSBC solid and happy, and I was in the final throes of applying my belt and braces principals into every aspect of the company. My intention to exit had not changed, even though the philanthropic route of a management buyout had proved to be an abortive fantasy; there were still other ways to achieve the same objective. I may have spearheaded the turn round and enjoyed the challenge, in a perverse way, but it hadn't revived my love affair with the car industry.

Whilst Phoenix taking over Rover had helped stop the rot, sales still were not a patch on where they used to be. I knew that Ford, Chrysler and Vauxhall were all losing market share, to not only the Japanese manufacturers, but also to good old reliable VW and in the upmarket stakes, Audi. I wanted to reduce our exposure by reducing Rover from three to two dealerships (in Rednal and Kidderminster) and replacing Bromsgrove with VW. Sometimes though, you have to go backwards to go forwards.

As luck would have it, an opportunity in Redditch came up; an existing dealership operated by Startin's was unofficially up for grabs. I was made aware of this fact by Bob Neville, one key player in the Phoenix team whom I regarded very highly. I figured, by acquiring a Rover Dealership there, I would have a pincer movement covering Kidderminster, Bromsgrove, Rednal and then Redditch. The four points of the compass - which I could then rationalise into two, and replace the others with VW or other manufacturers that were actually selling cars. As far as Rover was concerned this is exactly what they should have been doing, rationalising. I was, in fact, doing their job for them.

I actually paid 500 grand for the business and a further one million for the property, all through the trust fund. There was a coppice of trees on the site, which I swiftly had cut down to expand the whole sales area. However, I had hardly got plans into operational mode when I had an approach for the site. This was from Sir Peter Vardey, the son of Reg Vardey the high-profile, Newcastle-based motor dealer. I sold it to him for 1.8 million. After writing down the goodwill, it meant an 800k profit, with no capital gains, as it went straight into the pension fund. Sir Peter put a new VW franchise on the site and did very well with it too. Events started to move very rapidly now. We still weren't doing too well with Honda in Halesowen and they wanted us to sell the dealership to Nick Whale, a dealer I was not too fond of. Ironically, he was at the Ryland meeting too, back in the nineties, along with his brother; Nick now had his own company.

I may as well mention my dust-up with Nick now and get it off my chest. I was all set and had shaken hands on a deal to sell the Halesowen Honda business to his company. I had negotiated the deal with his managing director and his management accountant. This was in the presence of my deputy MD, Adrian Smith, and representatives from Honda. In fairness, we had never maximised the potential for Honda there and so it was not unreasonable that someone else should be given a chance. I had stated this fact and wished them all the best and made ready to leave when Nick came into the room unannounced and tried to renegotiate the deal his MD had agreed. He wanted to pay less for the parts. I refused point blank, kept my calm and apologised to the meeting and swore never to do business with him again. Whilst Nick Whale bought the dealership, Honda bought the land and property. I took every opportunity to embarrass Nick, with Honda, that I could engineer from that point on. So, when I say that later, the TVR dealership at Marlbrook was sold to Nick Whale, I kept my vow. I sold it to Droitwich garage who in turn sold it immediately on to Nick. He then took on a Lotus franchise, giving up TVR, then moved on to Ferrari, Maserati and Lamborghini. Personally, as we approached the biggest recession the world has ever seen, I didn't envy his position.

II

Three years after they took over the manufacturing side of Rover at Longbridge, Phoenix started to look at the dealerships in line with the block exemption treaty. They started buying up some key dealerships and I knew it would only be a matter of time before they approached us. They were livid, that having introduced me to Redditch, I had sold it on so swiftly - and to become a VW dealership to boot.

I told Phoenix, that rather than regretting my decision to forego a Rover dealership in Redditch, I was ready to sell Bromsgrove to Tesco who had approached me for the land. I was also ready to close Kidderminster and just keep Rednal. They swiftly agreed to buy out all our dealerships and the accident and repair centre. This was, in every case, the 'business only'; we retained the property and rented the premises back to them.

The deal was that they would take on all our 268 Rover people; there were to be no redundancies. I talked to all the managers and key members of staff and pointed out that this was for their future rather than our profit. It was the end of another era for us all. I meant every word. It was the final curtain for Clark's Motor Services and MG Rover. That left a lump in my throat, a big one. In essence, I had effectively removed Clark's from the motor sales and servicing business with MG Rover entirely. However, the numbers were such that retirement was once again possible and an exit route in place and that sweetened the pill. We agreed to accept payment in five annual sums starting from the date of signature on the agreement.

The final deal was signed off as a formality at The Roundhouse Conference Centre at MG Rover. All the top directors and executives from Phoenix were there and so were my team. Hands were shaken, papers signed and then we went back and made virtually the same presentation to all our staff, followed by a 'question and answer' session.

I took all twenty senior managers out to a celebratory dinner at Jaipur Cottage in Clent; there was also a party for the whole company at the DDSS club in Bromsgrove. It was decked out with bridges of balloons and the Senior Citizens played. The feasting and dancing went on till gone midnight and it was a truly memorable way to celebrate the last night of our long Rover journey and adventure.

I had engaged the international accountancy firm, Grant Thornton, in 2003 to review the company status, with a view to a restructure of the company, based on the diversed operations that had developed within the group. The two accountants working on the document were Eric Williams and Katheryn Godfree. What they produced was worth its weight in gold as a route to divestment.

Wherever possible, this was to be done through a new company: 'Doumal Investments', which may sound like a Middle East investment house, the sort which buy premier league football teams but is in fact just a play on Douglas and Malcolm, the Fabulous Clark Brothers.

Another very important event happened in 2002 too; my grandson Thomas was born on the 23rd April and I became a very proud grandad.

III

My mission now was to off-load everything, the final act of the chairman. I even got out of BMW motorbikes at Rednal, selling that to Daniel Morgan, and formed a special 'slip road' limited company called Exit Autos to do this deal. Doumal Investments retained the ownership of the land and applied for and got planning permission for 46 flats - a belt and braces move.

Meanwhile, amidst all the euphoria of selling the Rover dealership, things were not going too well with Toyota. They were making it very clear that they didn't really want us running Bromsgrove anymore, but wished to put in Westlands in our place. This was an operation headed by a guy called Nick Wyczenski who already ran Toyota in Stourbridge and was more of a company man who would play strictly by Toyota rules. There would be far less danger of him exhibiting any entrepreneurial flair-ups than there was with Doug Clark. Nevertheless, I wasn't too happy with this plan and felt slighted. I put forward a counter-proposal to them that not only should we keep Bromsgrove, but also start up a Worcester dealership under their 'open points' policy. So fired up was I over this that I found a site in Worcester, then took a team of eight down to Toyota headquarters and gave them a major presentation. They were appreciative and friendly, but it was a non-starter. Although they didn't say no then and there, it came as no surprise that I got a negative phone call within a week.

I looked at getting Toyota out all together and bringing in VW. My talks with the latter did not get very far; they weren't really interested in Bromsgrove. I should really have known better than to try and change German strategy. They plan well in advance and have little or no room for deviation. So I let Bromsgrove go to Westlands. It seemed we were destined to become wealthy landowners and landlords and no longer car dealers. This was all part of the exit plan, but the game had to be played to maximise the winnings.

The relationship with Toyota was to take on a new dimension. Whilst I was in Canada (at the same time as I had spotted the management accounts discrepancies) I had seen an innovation which I believed would do well if cloned in the UK. This was a 'Motor Village' where customers could come to view new and used cars from major manufacturers in one location. There were even restaurants and visitor attractions so they could make a day of it. It wasn't housed out of town either, but right in the heart of a business district - so attracted both business and domestic consumers.

It was with this thought in mind that I took a flyer on buying another eleven acres in Bromsgrove, adjacent to the two I had bought eighteen months previously. This was a newly named area 'Bunstford Gate' and was from a development company with planning permission for retail and office premises near to Morrison's Supermarket. I decided to call the Motor Village 'Bunstford Park'. It was perhaps a strange and risky concept to bring a Motor Village to Bromsgrove when we were trying to off-load everything else, but as I said: to maximise, you just have to keep rolling that dice. I employed the excavating skills of George Pardoe who was, incidentally, a cousin of my cousin Kevin Clark in Canada, if that makes sense. Anyway, George's job was literally to move mountains. Along with his two sons, Colin and David, George was brilliant at anything that involved excavation. I got them to level and set out the whole layout of the Motor Village, so that I had something to show potential buyers - and a magnificent job they made of it too.

When I let Toyota give Bromsgrove to Westlands it was on a gentleman's agreement that they would take a site at the newly named Bunstford Park, if I got it off the ground. Well, they were as good as their word and became our first occupants when we opened for business in 2006. This was the coup I wanted, I had the most financially successful motor company in the world showing faith in the Motor Village venture. They vacated Bromsgrove and relocated to Bunstford Park, they bought the freehold and built their own showroom; I didn't want to start getting embroiled in that side of things again.

Since Toyota left Bromsgrove, the premises has become a very successful operation for kids entertainment known as Imagination Street, probably more successful than the motor trade today.

IV

In Kidderminster we relinquished the Honda dealership to Worcester Car Sales, but remained the service agents. We were, however, dealers there for KIA. Malcolm took over as the KIA Dealer Principal. When we sold the Accident and Repair Centre to Phoenix Venture Holdings, he was certainly not going to go with it. He ran Kidderminster until 2005 when we sold this final dealership, again to Worcester Car Sales. Martin Stannard, their main man, became the Dealer Principal. In 2008 they bought the whole site and changed to SEAT which is VW under another name. A topsy-turvy world of changing loyalties in this auto industry, as I'm sure you've noticed. It has its own language too, for instance: we never have price cuts only market realignments.

Stourbridge, where we had opened our biggest, most fantastic premises in 2000 for VW, was sold to Sir Peter Vardey in 2003. He arrived at Rednal by chauffeur-driven Rolls Royce, every inch the tycoon, and proceeded to dominate the conversation by telling me how to suck eggs. This amused me, but I gently, but surely let him know that if there was no mutual respect there would be no deal. He may have thought he was dealing with a country hick, but soon found how ill-founded an assumption that was. Sir Peter went silent for almost a minute and when he spoke again his whole approach changed. We did business and not only did he buy Stourbridge but I sold him Redditch as well, as previously mentioned.

V

Lynwood Service Station at Lickey where attended-service petrol sales remained as a bastion to our former days, endured until we eventually sold it in 2004 to Stateside Products. The Lynwood Way Centre, however, remained in the portfolio.

Silver Birches was sold, except for two units and the conference centre.

That was what happened to the Clark Empire, but there would be one more twist of fate before the fat lady would sing and the final curtain fell.

34 – Off To Elba

I

During the restructure I got very close to Yvonne, she was a top player in the team and this meant I had to meet with her frequently. She always was an extremely attractive lady, a stunner in her youth, with beauty and vivaciousness that she carried with her right up to the present day. She was meticulous in her appearance and I really liked that. There was clearly chemistry between us; she had not long split up with her husband, whilst I had spent the time since Leigh adjusting my own life. Looking back, it was, I suppose, inevitable that two lonely people 'thrown together' would end up 'getting together'.

It happened: where else but at Badgers Cottage when I invited her over for dinner. Steaks sizzled on the barbeque and passion sizzled in our hearts. That night was the start of a wonderful relationship where Yvonne accompanied me on many maritime adventures and beyond. I owe her a personal debt of gratitude for believing in me when many didn't. Yvonne became and has remained my friend, lover, soul mate and partner in the years that followed.

Yvonne joined me as often as she could in Malta and quickly shared my love of the island, its way of life and its people. In 2003 I had applied for and got residency there, having decided that was where I wanted to make my home. I knew, that as the deals progressed, it would make economic sense to close up shop and make the move to live there permanently, sooner rather than later. I wasn't looking to become a tax exile for the sake of avoiding paying it; it's just that I had made my choice of where I wanted to be based in retirement. Up until 2003, I lived on my boat there, moored next to the late Clark Gable's vessel, the 'Black Pearl', on one side and Harry's yacht on the other. Becoming a Maltese resident meant I actually had to own property there and so I bought a modest apartment and part-exchanged the boat. Much of the business could now be conducted by phone, so I only came back as often as was necessary and made the most of my time here when I did. In the future, England was to be a place for holidays rather than work and Badgers Cottage would become a holiday home.

II

When I originally bought Badgers Cottage it came with just two acres of land. Over the years, I acquired the surrounding fields, wherever possible, so that today, the cottage enjoys over one hundred acres of 'back garden'. Part of this expansion occurred in 1978 when I acquired an old disused pond and stream which were fed underground by freshwater springs. I wanted to turn this into a lake, one which would teem with fish and be a haven for wildlife, where I could sit and contemplate. I said this to George Pardoe, who I mentioned before had excavated Bunstford Park for me. George had, in fact, been working with me right back to the 1960's and had thrived in the boom of construction and destruction in the 60's and 70's. George was from Rushock, the adjoining parish to Chaddesley. We were about the same age and I knew of him right from child-hood days. He came from a poor background like me, and although our paths didn't cross until we were grown up, I knew his reputation as the hardest kid in the village. Besides George, tiny Rushock has another famous son in Led Zeppelin drummer, John Bonham, who was buried there. People still come to the local graveyard to put drumsticks on his grave in tribute to one of the wild men of rock who lived a short but sensational life.

George had just finished a three-year contract to widen the M5, which was obviously a lucrative project but now over and he was 'resting'. I asked him to just give me the possibilities - in his opinion.

"I think it'll be quite magnificent," he said almost dreamily for a big tough man. "It'll stand two lakes but'll have to be dammed. I'll do it for you for the price of the fuel, Doug. Don't want paying. Spend so much time destroying bits of nature 'twill be nice to create sommat for a change."

Well, what started out as an idea swiftly turned into reality. I engaged John Fisher, the structural engineer who had worked on Rednal, to design the lakes, based on my vision of them. It was a major project; the earth removed had to be used to build the dam, and in the correct ecological structure, it was to be made from only natural products. Clay at the base, then the marl, topped with earth. Finally, the whole structure was compressed, sealed and waterproofed. The capacity of the lakes was a fraction under four million gallons; couldn't hit the four million though, otherwise it would be classed as a reservoir under the law.

The principal was that when water travels it has to have a destination or an outlet and my lakes would become part of the route to the River Seven. Completed, they looked as if they had always been there, not man-made at all. Whilst I initially stocked them with a few fish, Mother Nature has done the rest. They now teem with wild perch, tench, brown trout, carp and pike. All, for the most part, brought in by birds, I suppose. I don't allow people to fish them, but would rather they are just kept as nature reserves. It's not that I have anything against fishing. Indeed, I have done my share of fly fishing, having been taught by Ralph Cooper's son (sales manager of Lucas Batteries) back in the 70's when we were doing business together. He was a fly fishing champion at the time. It's not something that appeals to me though, nor do I enjoy big game fishing from boats, which brings me full-circle on that subject too.

III

In 2004 I was invited to the Miami Boat Show as a VIP guest of Hatteras. I was actually out there for my birthday in February and spent that amongst the oil sheiks and billionaire guests in attendance. The Hatteras gala dinner was held in a marquee on a floating dock surrounded by multi-million pound boats. This was opulence in the extreme. I sat with Chuck Cameron the after-sales director of Hatteras and the principal guest, the wonderful Liza (with a zee) Minnelli, who charmed the pants off me, unfortunately not literally.

I spent three days at the show and placed an order to reflect my lifetime achievement award, even if it was me that was presenting it to myself - an eighty foot mother of all Hatteras yachts, twin 1550 horse power V12 engines and luxury beyond belief. I knew what it had to be called: Mission Accomplished.

She took sixteen months to build in New Bern, North Carolina, the town where Pepsi Cola was invented back in 1930. On completion, I had T-shirts made with Mission Accomplished emblazoned across them, for everyone who had helped build her. I took them all out to dinner too, before Yvonne and I sailed her off on her maiden voyage to the Bahamas.

IV

Have you noticed that, for every positive action that happens, there seems to be a balancing negative reaction? Ying and Yang? Well, there I was, celebrating completion and collection of my boat in one of the finest restaurants on Grand Bahama when I got a phone call from Bob Neville informing me that Phoenix (and therefore Rover) had gone bust. They were closing all the dealerships with immediate effect and no more cars would be produced; the plant was to shut for the final time in an hour, all the staff sent home and the gates locked. There was no chance of a government bailout this time.

I was horrified; how could this have happened? I thought of all our people, who had been transferred just over a year before, now out of work. Some of them would feel bitterness towards me, I had no doubt. "Dougie Clark sold us up the river," would be the cry. In reality, they had the opportunity to go out and get new jobs and start again. In fact, 75%t of them had new jobs within a fortnight; that said much about being 'Clarked'.

On the other hand, I was past the finishing line and knew that the prize in the form of the remaining four payments (over a million) was lost forever. There was no-one to sue, and even if there was, no money to pay us. It meant too that we had to find new tenants for all the properties or sell the whole portfolio - lock stock and barrel. "And there I was: thinking I had all but retired," I said to Yvonne. "As if!"

"Thank God," I said to Malcolm later that evening, "that we never sold them the premises. They remain our 'oil in the ground.'"

Within the month, I was back in England and just had to drive up and see the locked-up factory that was once proud Longbridge. I thought of Herbert Austin buying the small semi-derelict printing works which stood there originally in 1905 and then forming the Austin Motor Company - producing his first car just one year later, priced at six pounds and ten shillings. What would Lord Austin have thought of what they have done to his legacy? 'From a ghost town back to a ghost town,' I suppose, or something like that.

The Longbridge plant was more than just a car factory; it was the centre of a community - and one that instilled enough pride in its workers for them to call it 'The Austin', after its founder. As I gazed at the weeds now springing up all over the plant, I took my mind back to the fifty year jubilee in 1954 when the company entertained all the employees and their families on one amazing day out. Complete with free fun fairs, entertainment and food, all day and night. I didn't go, but I did ride round the perimeter on my bike wishing like a lot of other kids that I was inside at the party rather than outside looking in. 'When giants walked the earth,' I thought to myself.

In July 2005 the Chinese car corporation, Nanjing Automotive, bought MG Rover for a pittance. Three years later, very low volume production of MG sports cars began again there. For the most part, Longbridge was razed to the ground and ironically, 'like a Phoenix rising from the ashes', new industry and houses have started to be built. Another era has begun.

35 – Belt and Braces

Music of the future
And music of the past.

Music - John Miles

I

My relationship with Malcolm entered a new phase: that of working together to close down a business, as opposed to running one. As the asset sales piled up, he and I had equal amounts of cash out and we shared an equal amount of the work in tidying up all the loose ends.

I applied the same principles to selling up as I had to starting up - belt and braces all the way. Wherever possible, we were our own sales agents and I had a fall-back in reserve in case the main buyer pulled out at the last minute. I was content to wait for the right buyers too, and fair prices, whether that was for equipment, furniture or property. I did, and still do the planning whilst Malcolm is now the front runner; he collects rents and does the actual face-to-face bit on sales. I call him the 'Jack Russell'.

There's no doubt our relationship is unique; we seem to have followed the same footsteps. We both divorced, we both love boats and cars and bikes and speed. Actually, Malc also enjoys flying these days, but that's where we differ, there is no way you would get me up with him in a plane.

When we worked together in the business, I suppose our friendship was conditional on that fact. Now our friendship and brotherly love is unconditional - the baby Malc and his big bro. We take time out to travel together and just have some mad fun several times a year.

II

Some of the names I have mentioned that played such an important role in building the company went on to achieve their own personal successes after Clark's. I believe we taught them to be unique and outstanding, after graduating from the Clark University of Business Life.

Mike Wollacott, who was our Honda Dealer Principal at Marlbrook, became Dealer Principal for Droitwich Garage Land Rover. Rob Walkden, who started with us as a petrol pump attendant and became an excellent MG Rover sales executive, is now sales manager of Pendragon Land Rover in Stourbridge. I actually bought a new Range Rover from him in 2008. I did an amazing deal, but Rob wasn't so much interested in the commission, as being determined that I would not buy from anyone, but him.

Graham Taylor, the master of body shop work, is his own master these days. Rob Pinches our top technician, nick-named 'The Professor' picks and chooses which cars he works on, and which customers he works for, at his RPM (Rob Pinches Motors) workshop in Bromsgrove. He is the caretaker of both mine and Malc's cars to this day.

Keith Burrows, Malcolm's number two at the Accident and Repair Centre, is now accident repair manager for Gemini Body Shops. Eleanor Rigby is management accountant for the company that bought Clark's motor cycles (they retain the name) at Rednal. Tony Foden is now with a Jaguar franchise in Worcester. Paul Carvell, an outstanding talent, who was our TVR Dealer Principal, is now a private Aston Martin dealer whose clients include many a rock star. Paul Husband, Dealer Principal at Rednal, went to Evans Halshaw as their senior group manager. These are just a few names who became ambassadors of the Clark's name and all we stood for.

You can't be in business for the length of time that we were and expect everyone that worked with you and for you to be a good guy, but on the whole, I believe we chose and trained well. As with every company, inevitably a group evolves, which can best be described as 'The Hierarchy'. The Clark hierarchy consisted of Adrian and Matt Smith, Paul Long, John Harthill, Paul Jeavons, Phil Jones, Bob Hart and Alan Preece. Like all families, we had our ups and downs, but each and every one of them contributed individually and collectively to making our company great and I would like to go on record as acknowledging that.

There were, some who couldn't cope with life outside of Clark's; they were, I suppose, institutionalised and didn't like life outside the institution and so retired. Maybe I am one of those?

Grant Thornton has instructions to wind up the remaining assets of Clark's when the timing is right. Melanie Radford, who has been with us from the early days, will be the last employee to go. That will leave us where we started, just Malc and me.

III

My dream boat, Mission Accomplished, became my floating home. In 2004, Yvonne and I spent our first Christmas together on it, complete with decorations and a Christmas tree on the fly bridge. I kept some of my guitars on board and twanged away contentedly, often in solitude. It was like living on a floating five-star hotel. We sailed her right down the coast past Cape Canaveral, West Palm Beach and through the Bahamas. We even completed the famous Inter-coastal Waterway. Travelling through cities on a boat puts a whole new perspective on everything. I went to the Bahamas four times in her, fulfilling all of those dreams I had over the years.

Those voyages were not without their moments of adventure either. Once, we were almost capsized by a huge freak wave. Malcolm was up on the fly bridge hanging on for dear life. I switched the auto-pilot off and started manoeuvring it like a sailing boat. We were at a forty-five degree angle. I shouted to the crew to make ready the life raft - it was that serious. "Don't panic, Mr. Mannering!" The famous words from 'Dad's Army' kept running through my head. Eventually, she righted herself, but they were a very hairy few minutes. We ran for cover in the ensuing storm, running the gauntlet of capsized boats all around us, who had not been as lucky.

Another time, not as scary but more amusing, was when I was trying to get into Old Bahama Bay and called the dock master by radio for permission. At the same time, another vessel, called 'Mission Impossible', was also trying to get in. This confused him greatly and he ended up inventing a third non-existent boat called Fishing Impossible and called that in. Eventually, it all became so much of a farce that I had to call him and say "This is Mission Accomplished, we know that Mission Impossible has been calling you as well. But there is no Fishing Impossible, repeat no Fishing Impossible"

It was on a trip down to Palm Beach that I discovered Saint Augustine. It is the oldest city in America, dating back to 1560 when the Spanish settled there. Much of the original architecture has been preserved and it is very much a haven for historians as well as artists and musicians. You won't find more courteous people anywhere in America either. The crime rate is negligible and everyone seems to know everyone else just like in an English village. It is currently having the famous 'Bridge of Lions' rebuilt at a cost in excess of eighty million dollars. Meanwhile, there is a temporary bridge in operation, which is the only access to the marina. It was actually closed at the time and so we were stuck outside for a few days. I berthed and booked myself into the Conch House Marina on Anastasia Island and set off to explore Saint Augustine. It was like an adult fairyland, country rock bands played, art shops abounded and there was just this fabulous feeling of being somewhere magical. On the way back to the boat I noticed a fantastic little development called 'Corona-del-Mar'. It was a block of really nice apartments set in magnificent grounds. There was even a fifty foot dock for every condominium. It had been built two years earlier and there was just one condo left. I looked round it and was astounded by the abundance of wild life. I imagined sitting out on the balcony watching nature at its best. I decided there and then that I had reached the end of my travelling around by boat and wanted to have some roots here on dry land. I put my beloved boat up for sale and set the wheels in motion to buy that condo. Mission Accomplished was indeed - experience accomplished.

There were no takers for eighteen months. America was starting to suffer the early signs of recession and the sub-prime disaster was on everybody's lips. So, whenever I was in Saint Augustine, I stayed on my boat. I didn't go through with buying the apartment, as it seemed I was never going to sell the boat. However I made lots of friends there and this only strengthened my resolve to make Saint Augustine a permanent part of my life. This includes David and Melissa Moorhead who look after all my affairs out there when I am absent and Timmy Masters with whom I have had many escapades. Timmy is a lovable divorced guy who has turned his beach-side house into a big boy's paradise, complete with bar room, billiard room and a big open fire pit right out by the water where moonlight parties are a way of life. Then there's Kevin Parry, a Stucco man who swims every day with his two Labradors and has a passion for fishing. Kevin used my lucky number seven as the main ball on his lottery numbers and won himself a cool two million dollars. Along with his family, I was invited to go with him in a stretched limo to collect his cheque.

Then there are the musicians, particularly guitarists with whom I have studied and jammed: Harley Hallett, Pat Murphy (one-time bass player for the legendary James Brown) and James Wilson - all three of them maestros of the art. I love the clubs in Saint Augustine, like Zhanras, The Prince of Wales, The A1A Ale Company, OC Whites, Stogies Cigar Bar, and best of all, the world-famous Tradewinds. My favourite local bands are The Red River Band, The Matanzas' and Sherry and the Stereophonics. They all play country rock, up-lifting, intelligent and fun funky music. In Saint Augustine I am not known as Doug Clark the car man; it's like I've created a new identity - just plain Dougie the English guy from the boat.

I had all but given up on selling Mission Acomplished and decided instead that I may as well ship her to Malta, via the giant Russian transporter ship Dockwise. As another experience, I planned to make the voyage with her, living with the crew. Then, just as has happened so many times in my life, lady luck struck once more. An American International Diamond Dealer, based in Jacksonville, had seen Mission Accomplished and fallen head over heels for her. He offered me more than I had actually paid for her - in 2008, how amazing was that? He took her for a test run, loved her even more, so we struck a deal and settled in days; the transaction taking place in international waters outside of the American tax zone. The exact latitude and longitude had to be recorded, along with the date and time. I was nervous about doing this, especially with all the current hype about modern-day pirates, so I took along two bodyguards with shooters just in case. However, the transaction was conducted in a perfectly gentlemanly manner. The buyer had a lawyer and a notary with him. The money was transferred electronically into my account and I was telephoned by satellite to confirm it was there. We sailed back into harbour, I shook his hand and exited, suitcase in hand.

Oddly, as the buyer's captain tried to sail out of the berth, the wind kept pushing the boat back in. It was if she didn't really want to leave me. Eventually, they got out and after it had disappeared over the horizon, I got into a hire car and drove down to Palm Beach to meet Yvonne who had flown in to meet me. We then flew on together to the Bahamas for a short celebratory stay at The Pelican Point Hotel in Grand Bahama. That night we dined at the famous West End restaurant next to where Tommy Bahama's house is - the one you see on the adverts and right by John Travolta's superb home where his airstrip, for his Boeing 737, is also the drive to his front door. Before I left Saint Augustine however, I put in a call and bought the condo in Corona-del-Mar.

IV

The previous year I had also bought a house in Calgary, Canada, which I had aptly named 'Hunter's Lodge'. So, with Saint Augustine, I now had a home for all four seasons. I could ski when I wanted, laze away the days in Malta, play my music in Florida and come back to dear old Badgers Cottage; I had, it seemed, planned my retirement as I had planned my business. Malcolm took a similar approach with his home in Worcestershire becoming a holiday home. He bought a house in the Isle of Man and lived on his boat in Malta. In the fullness of time he followed me and has bought a small apartment in Malta and qualified for residency of that country.

I have carried on having work done at Badgers Cottage, which is left in trust. I have erected outbuildings - all tastefully camouflaged by shrubbery - planted trees and made pathways. It has been restored to a traditional working farm. There is still some land I would like to acquire so that I can preserve the whole area for posterity. I have decreed that it must never be built on or even used to rear horses - only cattle, sheep and just hay crops. It's wonderful arable land and would provide an abundance of other crops, but I am paid by the EEC (via another crazy piece of legislation) not to do so. It is almost back to how I remember it was when I was little Dougie Clark, in worn-out trousers and wellies, exploring the fields. Generations to come will, I hope, enjoy them too. That's the best legacy I can leave to the village.

I also want to leave my car collection to a motor museum, somewhere where it can be displayed and enjoyed by anyone who is interested in the history of Rover. It's a pretty comprehensive set of the best cars ever made at Longbridge and elsewhere within the group and I doubt there's a finer one anywhere. To think it all started when I swapped that Austin Clubman back in 1972 for a grandfather clock and that little Austin Chummy. That was with John Nook the Cotswold antique dealer who needed a new vehicle. The refurbishing of the Austin Chummy was really what set me off on the classic car path. It was followed by a V12 roadster e-type Jaguar and an MGTF (that one was from the show jumper Anne Moore's father). Next came another e-type, which used to belong to Jimmy Saville the DJ - the white one which was featured in the Bisto ads. I discovered a very special Austin Healey 3000 - special, because it only had two seats as opposed to the normal 2x2. Then, over the years, I've added all sorts of beauties including a Rolls Royce and several motorbikes. Every bike and vehicle has been lovingly restored and engineered to better than factory condition. Today, the collection stands at twenty seven cars and eleven motorbikes, one of which is a BSA Gold Star, an original BSA works bike that was raced at the Isle of Man TT. Its number plate is ROJ 44 and is featured in the

Giants of Small Heath the tribute book to BSA. My half-brother Noel also has a fine collection of racing bikes and agricultural machinery which would form another nice section in any motor museum. I think housing them is a project I should undertake myself in the near future, to ensure it is done how I would like it, rather than leave it to my executors.

V

Taking me full circle in life was the re-emergence of my guitar playing. In 2005 I sold a car to Pato Banton of UB40 fame. We talked about music and he offered me the use of his recording studio, if I wanted to get my old band together and put down some tracks just for fun. We did - calling ourselves The Senior Citizens this time as opposed to The Citizens of our youth. We actually produced a CD of which I am very proud and have given copies to people all over the world. It plays in my car wherever I am. We even did a few charity gigs together, raising money for the Macmillan Nurses charity. The Senior Citizens don't play anymore now, but I still hanker after joining up with some like-minded pensioners, probably in Saint Augustine. Like the song says: 'Music was my first love – and it will be my last!'

VI

I missed not having a performance car whilst I was staying at my place in Calgary, so I decided to invest in a Porsche Carrera 4 Cabriolet. My thoughts were, that when the time came to hang my boots up in Canada and move on to pastures new, then I would ship the Porsche out to Europe. I had my beautiful machine custom built and finished in, Arctic Silver; I even managed to get the registration number DUGS911 - how fab was that? It was like having another lady in my life, sleek in body and shape, but with a fire under the bonnet that would drive any red blooded man insane. It is a beauty!

Frustratingly, it turned out to be a bit of a white elephant really, as the weather was very restrictive to me, driving it around up there for a big part of the year. There is so much snow - that's why Calgary was an Olympic ski resort. So, instead of looking at my beautiful toy just sitting in my garage like a racehorse in a stable, I decided I would drive it down to my home in Saint Augustine, where I could use it all the year round.

I soon discovered that turning dreams into reality wasn't quite that easy. The car had been registered in Canada in my cousin Kevin's name, as I didn't have a Canadian driving licence. After protracted negotiations, when I discovered the current day obsession, with red tape, is now global and because I proved I had a genuine American driving licence, the registration office in Calgary finally agreed to re-register it in my name. Next problem was: the insurance company would only cover it third party. So I set off to drive my beauty, which was incidentally worth over 150,000 Canadian dollars, on a journey of 5,400 miles through some pretty awesomely rugged terrain on just third party insurance. If any mishap occurred it would be down to me to foot the bill.

Undaunted, in fact quite the opposite, and exhilarated I began what I now refer to as my final big motoring adventure. As I left the driveway of my house in Calgary, I felt like that guy in that 60's movie Vanishing Point if you remember it. It started off as a simple task to deliver the high performance car from one end of America to the other. What ensued was 'one man and a car' against all the natural elements nature could offer, plus the human factor of 'zap happy' state police in a race to get, well, nowhere really - just the buzz of the trip.

With adrenalin flowing in my body like that of a twenty-year old buck, I firstly drove right through the mighty Rocky Mountains. The scenery was wild and desolate in part with ice capped peaks and jagged rock formations millions of years old. This barrenness was punctuated with lush forests and valleys - two extremes. I can well see why it is referred to as 'The Great Divide'. I saw herds of deer, elk and mountain goats, even packs of wolves and coyotes. I kid you not; the howl of a coyote at night is blood curdling and sends shivers down your spine. For the most part, it was an isolated part of the journey, as other vehicles were few and far between.

Finally, I arrived at the majestic beauty of Vancouver Island. There, I caught the ferry to the American mainland and Seattle. The first landmark you see, from quite a long way away, is Mount Baker. It stands like the guardian of the American border.

From Seattle I got onto the A1 Pacific Highway and drove to the West Coast, from Portland right down this gorgeous, entirely coastal route to sunny California. At one point I passed by the raging mountain forest fires, which were prevalent at the time. Although I was in no real danger, I admit it was a tad scary. You have no idea, seeing those fires on television, just how huge they are and how brave are the guys fighting them. They had been burning for months and just when they thought they had them licked, they started up again - from a blazing twig or a change of wind. It makes you realise just how fierce and destructive Mother Nature can be when she wants to be. Sadly though, in the cases of many of these American fires, Mother Nature had more than a little help from insane pyromaniacs.

Upon reaching Los Angeles, I made my way straight to the legendary Route 66, following in the footsteps of the lyrics of the song by the even more legendary Chuck Berry. Amazingly, Mr. Berry was actually appearing the following week in Flagstaff, Arizona, which I was to pass through. Fleetingly, I thought about staying over for a few days and going to his gig, but in the end, decided to stick to my mission. The drive after all was my dream. The original dream was to ride a Harley Davidson motorbike like a cool dude from Easy Rider, but my beautiful Porche and I made a wonderful partnership, so I had no regrets for passing on the Harley. I swear the Porche purred in approval, as we reached the city limit sign and actually started to burn tarmac on the legendary road. I drove all the way up to New Mexico and experienced the most incredibly historic and nostalgic times of the whole adventure. I stayed in a diversity of accommodations, from almost deserted roadhouses like The Bates Motel in Psycho to real rock'n'roll cowboy bars with rooms above - complete with pool tables, juke boxes playing country rock and girls in tight check shirts and cowboy hats. I just basked in a temperature which reached thirty eight degrees at times, soaked in all that culture, smoked the occasional cigar and was one happy man.

At the end of Route 66 I reached Albuquerque and from there drove to Dallas in Texas where there were torrential rains causing flash flooding so bad that cars were aquaplaning, pirouetting and literally floating away like in some bizarre water ballet. It's worth noting that here the speed limit was raised to sixty and no-one was slowing down. I really had to keep my wits about me; it wasn't so much me, but the American drivers who are just not used to driving on wet surfaces. The whole ballet, you could have set to music. In fact I did; I had the Beatles' 'Hey Jude' CD on, which seemed to be pretty apt. Just as the end chorus 'nah nah nah nah nahnanan nah' belted forth, a black Corvette crazily sped passed me, blinding my vision with a tsunami spray. My heart was momentarily in my mouth, 'til I could see again. Five minutes later I encountered the Corvette again. It had been in a massive collision and was split into three pieces strewn across the road. I couldn't stop, not even rubber-neck, as I just had to move with the constant flow of traffic, so I have no idea if the driver survived, though I fear death was the only winner in that pile up. The weather changed once more and the rains disappeared, as I saw the road signs for New Orleans.

I stopped at the first roadhouse for fuel and food, and as I got out, I saw a sign warning me to 'Beware of Rattlesnakes'. "This trip is so off the wall," I said to the barman, as I downed a pint of coke.

"Only in America, Buddy," he chuckled and I had to concur. So, as you can see, I experienced it all on that trip from rock and ice to scorching sun, fire and floods – Dougie against the elements – unbelievable!

On four occasions I was chased by state troopers who took one look at the Porsche and wanted my blood. They never caught me, nor did the police helicopter which followed me through the mountains in another state. I never actually saw it, but heard its drone like an angry swarm of hornets and its shadow cocooned me for a good fifteen minutes whilst they monitored me. Then, unable to find the slightest speeding infringement they got bored and flew off after another victim. Great sport! Actually, I swear by the Garmin satellite navigation system, which gives you a far more accurate reading than the speedometer. This saved me many a time from those overzealous cops, that have zero tolerance to speed and a pair of silver bracelets, waiting to cart you off to the sheriff's office given half a chance.

Another very scary experience was when this huge articulated lorry carrying one enormous white rock boulder, probably weighing in excess of forty tonnes, wandered across the carriageway towards me and nearly crushed me up against the central reservation. I actually had two wheels onto the edge when the driver spotted me. I'm not sure whether he was texting or had fallen asleep, but he pulled back just in time to avoid a collision from which I guess I would have been reduced to the size of a biscuit tin. He gestured an apology, but almost instantaneously it seemed that Blackpool illuminations came on behind me as a convoy of police cars pounced on him. I left him to it!

I drank in some amazing bars too, with real cowboys, rednecks, hillbillies, hookers, dreamers, schemers - you name it! I loved them all in their own way. It was the trip of a lifetime and didn't disappoint. Me and my magic Porsche arrived in Saint Augustine without a scratch on either of us. We thanked each other and I swear if it could talk, my beauty would have said: "Douglas Clark, I was born for this, what an experience, Mein Herr!"

Back in the sanctuary and sanity of my own four walls in Corona-del-Mar, I poured myself a generous glass of Chivas Regal, put my feet up and went to sleep - reliving my dream in a dream.

VII

I still spot business opportunities. For instance, there is a shopping mall in St. Augustine that cries out for a car wash. I've even got a name for it: 'Mr. Spoodles'. I'd have people out there with mops and buckets all smiling and dressed up in wacky costumes. The Americans would love that as much as the British would hate it. I've got a great name for a drive-through fast food bar too: the 'Chicken Shack'. I would serve the best wings you ever tasted. I would like to open or buy a rock venue, either in America or the UK, or even Malta.

It would be different from anything on offer elsewhere. The accent would be on listening in comfort, not purgatory, as so many are of the ones I've been to recently. There would be different types of music on each night, thus appealing to different audiences, but all over 21. Folks would come from miles just to be part of it. I expect these ideas will remain just that, though you never know!

Regrets? Of course there are a few, but I like to think that where I've done something wrong I've learnt from the experience and not gone there again, which includes marriage. I regret not seeing more of my grandson, Thomas, and I hope that will change as he grows older. I would love to take him skiing, motorcycling and go-carting whilst I'm still agile enough to do it. I would like to be able to have time with him to teach him about the importance of preserving things for his children and theirs. I would have liked Thomas to attend the local village school, but that's too late now. So, as long as he has happy school days, that's fine by me. This book is dedicated to him and I wish him a long, happy and adventurous life.

At the time of concluding this biography the motor industry is just coming through the biggest depression in its history. A couple of years ago, Toyota, the world's most successful motor company, posted a billion-pound loss. Everything looked bleak. Now there is a resurgence happening stateside with also American car manufacturing and sales on the up. In the UK, Range Rover are bouncing back with a passion under their new ownership. They are becoming the most sought after badge world wide. Likewise Jaguar too are coming good again, making giant strides in the thriving Asian markets. Why? Because they are upping their games and going the extra mile. Though sad, it doesn't matter that neither Jaguar or Range Rover are British owned anymore . What matters is they are once again creating lots of jobs domestically and globally, directly and indirectly.

I suppose it's easy for me to pontificate, being out of the loop, but let me leave you with a few thoughts. There is always opportunity, even in adversity. Yes, in the UK, people will put off buying cars till the economy improves, but that won't last forever, so make sure they have you as number one on their shopping list when the tide turns - as it surely will. In the meantime, the same old 'belt and braces' principles apply. Identify the scene and act accordingly; cut your costs without cutting your service. Work in the present and plan for the future. I developed my business by instinct; others equally and some more successful than me did it by academia. Both routes can take you to the same place. Be disciplined, be motivated and motivate others. Be kind, but don't ever let your kindness be mistaken for weakness.

Whether you are starting out in business or are already in it, I hope the challenges I have faced in my life and the routes I have taken to meet them will help you in yours. If you are thinking about going on your own then do your planning, your homework and prepare your blueprint; then put belt and braces on it before you open the shutters up for business. Above all else make it fun and remember what I said about moments in time. Recognise the opportunity and grasp the nettle when you sense the moment. Miss it, and that particular deal will be lost forever.

I'm sure I've said more than once in this book that one thing leads to another. Selling tyres led me to Uncle Jessie and Rednal Garage; Rednal took me from a tiny little creaking garage to a company with a sixty million turnover. My lasting epitaph today is, that although they are not mine (thank God!), Rednal is a Rolls Royce dealership, and Hagley an Aston Martin dealership. Isn't that something? I take pride that my spirit will walk there forever and I'm sure, that every so often, when the wind blows in the right direction, some salesman will hear the whisper of my voice telling them that there is a "Customer waiting!"

You may recall at the start of this book the part where I gave up my dream of a career in music? Well now I'm retired from business I'm having a ball reliving that dream, writing and recording my own material. Everywhere I go in the world I have a guitar, notepad and pocket recorder with me. In Malta I am working with a golden voiced singer called Daniela Delicata; we have released an album together entitled The Prickly Pair, prickly being Daniela's endearing term for me! In England I've put music to Euan's lyrics and visa versa and play gigs with the very accomplished guitarist and singer Mike Warley. Across the Atlantic in Saint Augustine I'm honoured to be jamming with some of America's finest country rock musicians. My life is fun, fruitful and full, You could say its gone full circle, from music to motors and finally back to music again. So one day you might walk into a club or bar somewhere in the world and spot me on the guitar. If you do please come and say hi!

Thank you for joining me on this voyage through the seas of my memory. I wish you well.

Douglas J. Clark.

Epilogue

The Last Word

The discovery that Doug Clark and I have the same dry, satirical sense of humour was a moment I shall treasure forever. To explain, Doug has a very subtle way of making you feel guilty about little things with comments such as: "It's a pity you did that really." Innocuous in content but deadly in context; it sets the mind racing to what you may have done. In my case, it referred to some notes I had accidently thrown away, which meant we had to go over certain details again. I have gathered that seemingly innocent phrase has made many an employee and business rival wonder what was coming next. Then you realise it's a serious message but all a bit tongue in cheek. One of my favourite chapters in this book is where Doug used to sit behind his desk at Rednal, surveying everything through his fish-eye lens view, saying the immortal words into his microphone: "Customer waiting, service please". I could envisage a scene ensuing like those depicted in many an old American movie where, as a car drove up, a team of four attendants, all in bow ties and striped waistcoats, would rush out and proceed to clean the windows, the lights, check the fuel, oil and water whilst singing the customer a song. I believe, if Doug Clark could have replicated that, he would have been in 'Garage Heaven'. As it was, he contented himself by observing a flurry of feet to meet, greet and service the said customer.

So, one day when we were working on his book and were interrupted for about the fifth time by one or other of his phones, I just said the magic words to him 'customer waiting' under my breath. Well, a good thir ty seconds passed before we both collapsed into helpless fits of laughter. In fact, I can't remember laughing so long and so hard over anything so unfunny since I was a carefree kid and you split your sides over the silliest things.

It has been over five years since my first meeting with Doug which I described in the prologue. We have met up many times since and I feel that I have got to know what drives him better than anyone. Underneath all the bravado, the quest for speed and power, there is this underlying need he has for recog nition. Whether that is by riding a motorbike into a duck pond to the delight of onlookers or creating an original way of doing something, it is a demand to be noticed. Like many great leaders he has always felt that he is not as good or as clever or as adept as he actually is and thus seeks reassurance which, from someone who has achieved so much, is an endearment not a fault. Apart from that give-away trait, Douglas Clark is a very difficult man to read; he is certainly a one-off original; he will tell you he is a simple soul, but believe me, it would take a team of psychoanalysts to fathom the complexity of that mind.

For a man who has made it to the very top of his chosen profession and, let's face it, one that is not exactly renowned for its selflessness, he radiates modesty and charisma in equal doses. I have found him to be a very generous man in many ways. He will tell you that charity begins at home. But, in his case, 'home' includes his neighbours, friends and extended families all over the world. He will give his time and labour freely when and where needed. In fact, for a man who has achieved so much, always leading and shooting from the hip, in a perverse way, he has actually lived his life in the service of others. Old habits die hard. A fitting epitaph would indeed be 'Customer Waiting'

Euan Rose.

Index